PART I

GREGG SHORTHAND FOR THE ELECTRONIC OFFICE

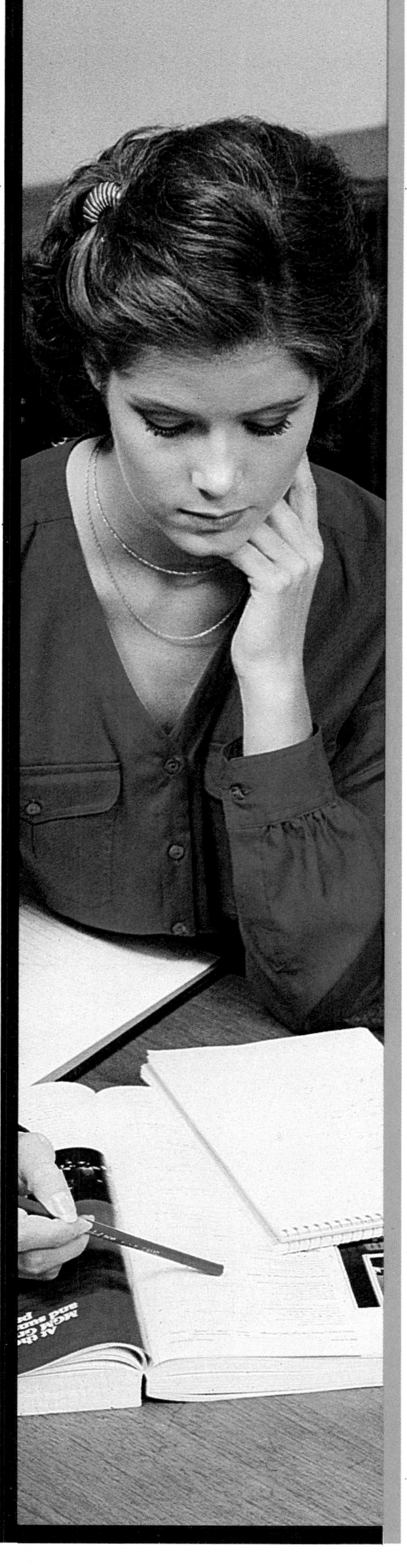

PART I

GREGG SHORTHAND FOR THE ELECTRONIC OFFICE

SHORT COURSE

SERIES 90

LOUIS A. LESLIE
CHARLES E. ZOUBEK
A. JAMES LEMASTER
GREGG A. CONDON

Shorthand written by **Jerome P. Edelman**

Gregg Division
McGraw-Hill Book Company

New York Atlanta Dallas St. Louis San Francisco Auckland
Bogotá Guatemala Hamburg Johannesburg Lisbon London
Madrid Mexico Montreal New Delhi Panama Paris San Juan
São Paulo Singapore Sydney Tokyo Toronto

Sponsoring Editor: Barbara Oakley
Shorthand Production Manager: Jerome P. Edelman
Shorthand Production Supervisor: Mary C. Buchanan
Shorthand Production Assistant: Louise Intorrella
Art & Design Supervisor/Interior Design: Karen Tureck
Photo Editor: Mary Ann Drury
Production Supervisor: Frank Bellantoni

Cover Design: Renee Kilbride and Karen Tureck
Cover Photographer: Karen Leeds
Cover Office Equipment:
Olivetti ET231 • Courtesy Docutel/Olivetti Corp.
Xerox Telecopier 455 • Courtesy Xerox Corp.
Saturn PABX • Courtesy Siemens Communication Systems, Inc.
Wang 01S115 • Courtesy Wang Laboratories Inc.

Section Photography:
Section 1: Courtesy Rosemount Office Systems, Inc.
Section 2: © Michal Heron 1983
Appendix Photography: Courtesy Haworth, Inc.
Interior Photography: © Michal Heron 1983
Interior Office Equipment:
Red Book Courtesy American Hotel Association Directory Corporation, Briefcase Courtesy Dextor Luggage, Magna III Word Processor Courtesy A.B. Dick Company, EXXON 215 Intelligent Typewriter Courtesy Exxon Office Systems Company, 3M Model 136 Microfiche Reader Courtesy 3M File Management Systems, Scanset XL Courtesy Tymshare, Inc.

Library of Congress Cataloging in Publication Data

Gregg shorthand for the electronic office, short course, part 1.

1. Shorthand—Gregg. I. Leslie, Louis A., date
II. Title.
Z56.2.G7L49 1983 653'.4270424 83-13584
ISBN 0-07-037914-9

Gregg Shorthand for the Electronic Office, Short Course, Part 1, Series 90

1 2 3 4 5 6 7 8 9 0 DOCDOC 8 9 0 9 8 7 6 5 4 3

To The Student

You are about to begin your study of Gregg Shorthand. It will prove to be one of the most valuable—and interesting—courses you will take, and for many reasons. One good reason is that, if you want to become a career secretary, you know that shorthand is an essential skill for a secretarial career. Employers are searching for workers who know shorthand, because these workers have the ability to increase productivity through the use of that skill. Employers also use shorthand as a screening tool—it is a fact that shorthand writers have strong language skills. Gregg Shorthand writers perform significantly better in tests of spelling, sentence structure, word division, and word usage. Secretaries with shorthand skills are able to communicate accurately, clearly, and effectively. These are skills that employers are seeking. In addition, employers believe that a person who has mastered shorthand has the discipline necessary for a successful secretarial career. And to top it off, employers are willing to pay more to a secretary who has shorthand. How much more? Between $1,000 and $2,000 a year.

Perhaps you are not interested in being a career secretary. Shorthand can be of value to you, too. Did you know that the study of shorthand was originally confined to the learned professions? It's true. However, as the vocational value of shorthand became clear, the administrative use was overshadowed. In the office, many executives find shorthand a useful skill. They can quickly jot down information discussed over the telephone or take notes in the many meetings they are required to attend. Drafting that long report required by a superior goes much faster if it is done in shorthand rather than longhand. You may ask, "Why do these executives know shorthand?" Some started out as secretaries and worked their way up into the executive ranks. Others knew just how valuable shorthand could be for noncareer purposes and took shorthand as a personal-use course.

Shorthand can also be of use to you in school—it is much easier taking notes in shorthand than in longhand, both in the classroom and in the library doing research. If you know shorthand and typing, it is easy to get part-time work both during the school year and during vacations. What's more, you have a much-needed skill to fall back on if your career plans change.

Shorthand plays many roles on the personal and on the professional scene. Don't let anyone tell you that the automated or electronic office has done away with the need for shorthand. It simply isn't true. Together, shorthand and office automation (word processing) greatly increase efficiency. No matter what role you play in the office of the future, you will discover that automation and shorthand are *partners in productivity.*

Features Of Gregg Shorthand For The Electronic Office

The two textbooks comprising *Gregg Shorthand for the Electronic Office, Short Course,* undoubtedly represent the most attractive and functional graphic arts techniques ever applied to shorthand textbooks.

Writing on Lines

For the first time in a Gregg Shorthand book, all copy is written on lines. While it is not necessary to write Gregg Shorthand on ruled paper, most people do use a steno pad that is ruled. This new design aspect, then, simply provides you with a point of reference and helps you judge proportions more easily.

Use of Color

With full-color printing, it is possible to reproduce the blue horizontal rules and red vertical rule of a typical steno pad page. Words within the shorthand plates are highlighted in color, while yet another color is used for marginal reminders. Attractive, full-color photographs portray the many-faceted role of shorthand in a technological society.

Large Page Size

The large page size simulates an actual page from a steno pad as well as providing ample room for the many marginal reminders that have been found to be extremely helpful to shorthand learners.

Top-Bound Format

Steno pads are bound at the top for ease in both writing and transcribing. Both parts of *Gregg Shorthand for the Electronic Office, Short Course,* are bound at the top, because you will be transcribing from them. With a typing easel, the books will stand up and make it easier for you to do the transcription exercises.

Nonshorthand Elements of Transcription

A very important part of learning shorthand is learning how to transcribe. Exercises in Part 1—called Building Transcription Skills—will help you develop your language skills, which are an important part of transcription. These exercises include the following:

Business Vocabulary Builders (begin in Lesson 11)

Spelling—Marginal Reminders (begin in Lesson 16)

Spelling—Families (begin in Lesson 38)

Similar-Words Drills (begin in Lesson 15)

Punctuation (begin in Lesson 26)

Common Prefixes (begin in Lesson 44)

Grammar Checkup (begin in Lesson 42)

Beginning with Lesson 41, each lesson contains a Transcription Quiz consisting of a letter in which you have to supply internal punctuation. This quiz gives you an opportunity to test yourself on how well you have mastered the punctuation rules presented in earlier lessons.

Shorthand Spelling Helps

When a new letter in the shorthand alphabet or a new theory principle is presented, the shorthand spelling is given.

Checklists

To keep you constantly reminded of the importance of good practice procedures, occasional checklists are provided. These checklists deal with writing shorthand, reading shorthand, doing homework, checking proportions, and so on.

Appendix

The appendix contains a number of study aids. These include:

1 A brief-form chart giving all brief forms in the order of their presentation in

Gregg Shorthand for the Electronic Office, Short Course.

2 A brief-form derivative chart that shows derivatives of brief forms other than those ending in -s or -ing.

3 A chart of frequently used phrases in Gregg Shorthand.

4 A list of the states, the shorthand outline for each state, and the two-letter state abbreviations.

5 A list of selected United States cities with shorthand outlines.

6 A list of other common geographical abbreviations.

7 A list of common metric expressions and their shorthand outlines.

8 The principles of joining—an explanation of how the shorthand outlines are formed.

Your Shorthand Practice Program

The speed with which you learn to read and write Gregg Shorthand will depend largely on two factors—the *time* you devote to practice and the *way* in which you practice. If you practice efficiently, you will be able to complete each lesson in the shortest possible time and derive the greatest possible benefit.

Here are some suggestions which will help you to get the maximum benefit from the time you invest in shorthand practice.

Before you begin, select a quiet place in which to practice. Do not try to practice while listening to music or watching television. Then follow the steps below.

Reading Word Lists

In each lesson there are a number of word lists that illustrate the principles introduced in the lesson. As part of your out-of-class practice, read these word lists in this way:

1 With the type key available, spell—aloud if possible—the shorthand characters in each outline in the list, thus: *"see, s-e; fee, f-e."* Reading aloud will help to impress the shorthand outlines firmly on your mind. Read all the shorthand words in the list in this way—with the type key exposed—until you feel you can read the shorthand outlines without referring to the key.

2 Cover the type key with a piece of paper and read aloud from the shorthand, thus: *"s-e, see; f-e, fee."*

3 If the spelling of a shorthand outline does not immediately give you the meaning, refer to the key and determine the meaning of any outline you cannot read. Do *not* spend more than a few seconds trying to decipher an outline.

4 After you have read all the words in the list, read them again if time permits.

Note: In reading brief forms for common words and phrases, which first occur in Lesson 3, do not spell the shorthand outlines.

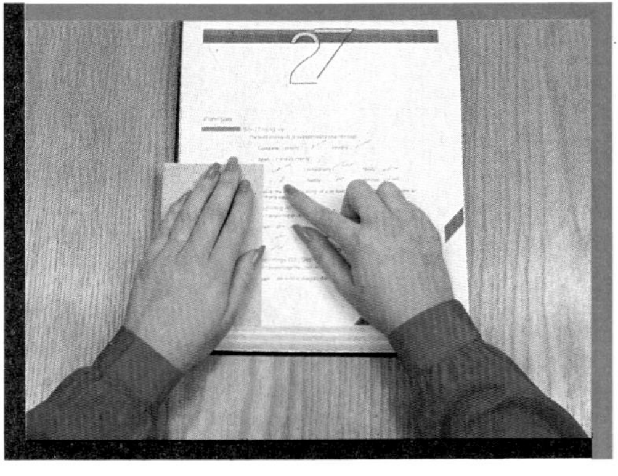

The student studies the word lists by placing a card over the type key and reading the shorthand words aloud.

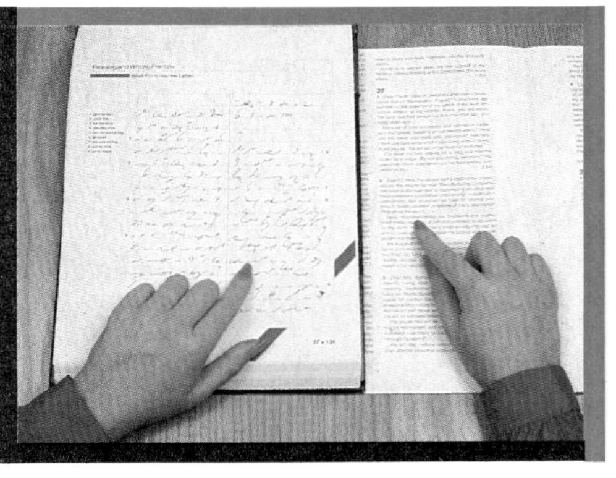

Refer to your Transcript whenever you cannot read an outline. Keep your left index finger anchored on the shorthand; the right index finger, on the corresponding place in the Transcript.

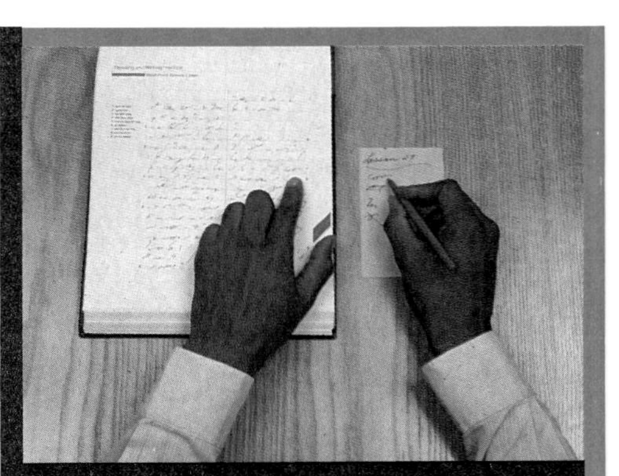

The student reads the Reading and Writing Practice, writing on the card any outlines that cannot be read after spelling them.

When copying, the student reads a convenient group of words aloud and then writes that group in the notebook. Notice how the student keeps the place in the shorthand.

Reading Sentences, Letters, and Articles

Each lesson contains a Reading Practice (Lessons 1-5) or a Reading and Writing Practice (Lessons 6-60) in which sentences, letters, or articles are written in shorthand. Proper practice on this material will help you develop your shorthand ability. First, *read* the material. Two procedures are suggested for reading shorthand—one with a Student's Transcript and one without a Student's Transcript.

Procedure With Student's Transcript If you have a Student's Transcript to the shorthand in this textbook, you should follow this procedure:

1. Place the Student's Transcript to the right of your textbook and open it to the key to the Reading Practice or the Reading and Writing Practice you are about to read.
2. Place your left index finger under the shorthand outline in the text that you are about to read and your right index finger under the corresponding word in the Student's Transcript.
3. Read the shorthand outlines aloud until you come to a word you cannot read. Spell the shorthand strokes in that outline. If this spelling does not *immediately* give you the meaning, anchor your left index finger on the outline and look at the transcript, where your right index finger is resting near the point at which you are reading.
4. Determine the meaning of the outline you cannot read and place your right index finger on it.
5. Return to the shorthand from which you are reading—your left index finger has kept your place for you—and continue reading in this manner until you have completed the material.
6. If time permits, read the material a second time.

By following this procedure, you will lose no time finding your place in the shorthand and in the transcript when you cannot read an outline.

Procedure Without Student's Transcript If you do not have a Student's Transcript, you should follow this procedure:

1. Before you start reading the shorthand, have a blank piece of paper or a blank card handy.
2. Read the shorthand aloud.
3. When you come to a shorthand outline that you cannot read, spell the shorthand strokes in the outline. If the spelling gives you the meaning, continue reading. If it does not, write the outline on your sheet of paper or card and continue reading. Do not spend more than a few seconds trying to decipher the outline.
4. After you have gone through the entire Reading and Writing Practice in this way, repeat this procedure if time permits. On this second reading you may be able to read some of the outlines that gave you trouble the first time. When that happens, cross those outlines off your sheet or card.

5 Finally—and very important—at the earliest opportunity ask your teacher or a classmate the meaning of the outlines that you could not read.

Remember, during the early stages your shorthand reading may not be very rapid. That is only natural as you are, in a sense, learning a new language. If you practice regularly, however, you will find your reading rate increasing almost daily.

Writing the Reading and Writing Practice

Before you do any writing of shorthand, you should give careful consideration to the tools of your trade—your notebook and your writing instrument.

Your Notebook The best notebook for shorthand writing is one that measures 6 x 9 inches and has a vertical rule down the center of each page. It should have a spiral binding so that the pages lie flat at all times. The paper should, of course, take ink well.

Your Writing Instrument A pen is a satisfactory instrument for writing Gregg Shorthand. A pencil is not recommended. Because writing with a pen requires little pressure, you can write for long periods of time without becoming fatigued. A pencil, however, requires considerable pressure. In addition, the pencil point quickly becomes blunt. The blunter it gets, the more effort you have to expend to write with it. Pen-written notes remain legible almost indefinitely; pencil notes become blurred and hard to read. In addition, pen-written notes are also easier to read under artificial light.

Having selected your writing tools, follow these steps in writing the Reading and Writing Practice:

1 Read the material you are going to copy. Always read the Reading and Writing Practice before copying it.

2 When you are ready to start writing, read a convenient group of words from the printed shorthand; then write the group, reading aloud as you write. Keep your place in the shorthand with your left index finger if you are right-handed or with your right index finger if you are left-handed.

In the early stages your writing may not be very rapid, nor will your notes be as well written as those in the book. With regular practice, however, your notes will rapidly improve.

Good luck with your study of Gregg Shorthand.

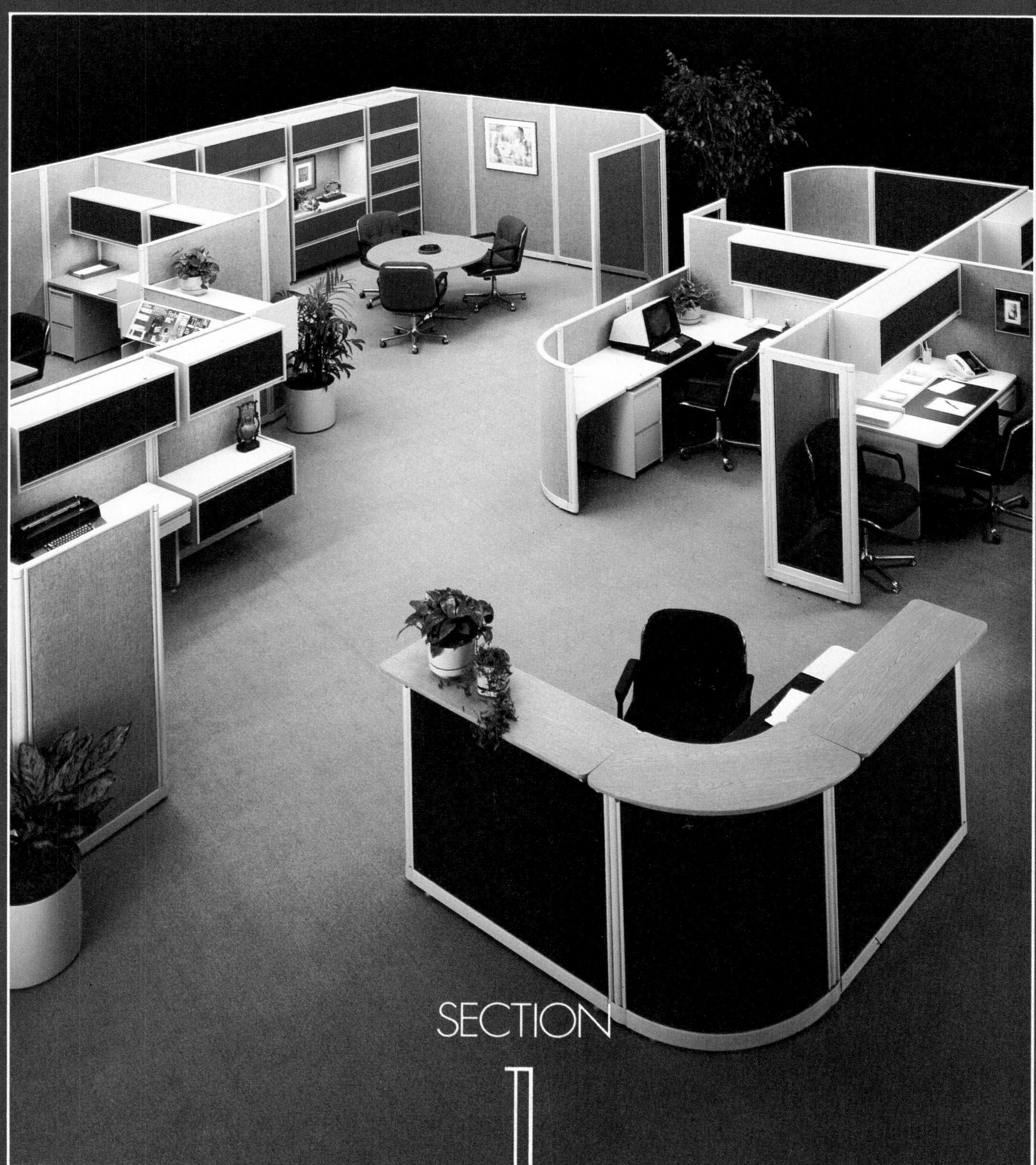

SECTION II

Gregg Shorthand Is Easy to Learn

When you decided to study shorthand, you probably asked yourself, "Can I really learn Gregg Shorthand?" Of course you can, just as millions of others have. If you learned to write longhand—and of course you did—you can learn to write Gregg Shorthand. The strokes you write in longhand—curves, hooks, circles, straight lines—are the same strokes you will write in Gregg Shorthand.

Actually, you will find that Gregg Shorthand is easier to learn than longhand. Skeptical? Well, the following illustration should convince you of its truth.

Do you know how many different ways you can write the longhand letter *f*? Here are six of them—and there are more!

In addition, in many words the sound of *f* is expressed by combinations of other letters of the English alphabet—*ph,* as in *phase; gh,* as in *rough.*

In Gregg Shorthand there is one way—and only one way—to express the sound of *f,* as you will learn later in this lesson.

With Gregg Shorthand you can reach any speed goal you set for yourself. All it takes is faithful, intelligent practice.

Principles

Group A

S-Z

Perhaps the most frequently used consonant in the English language is *s,* partly

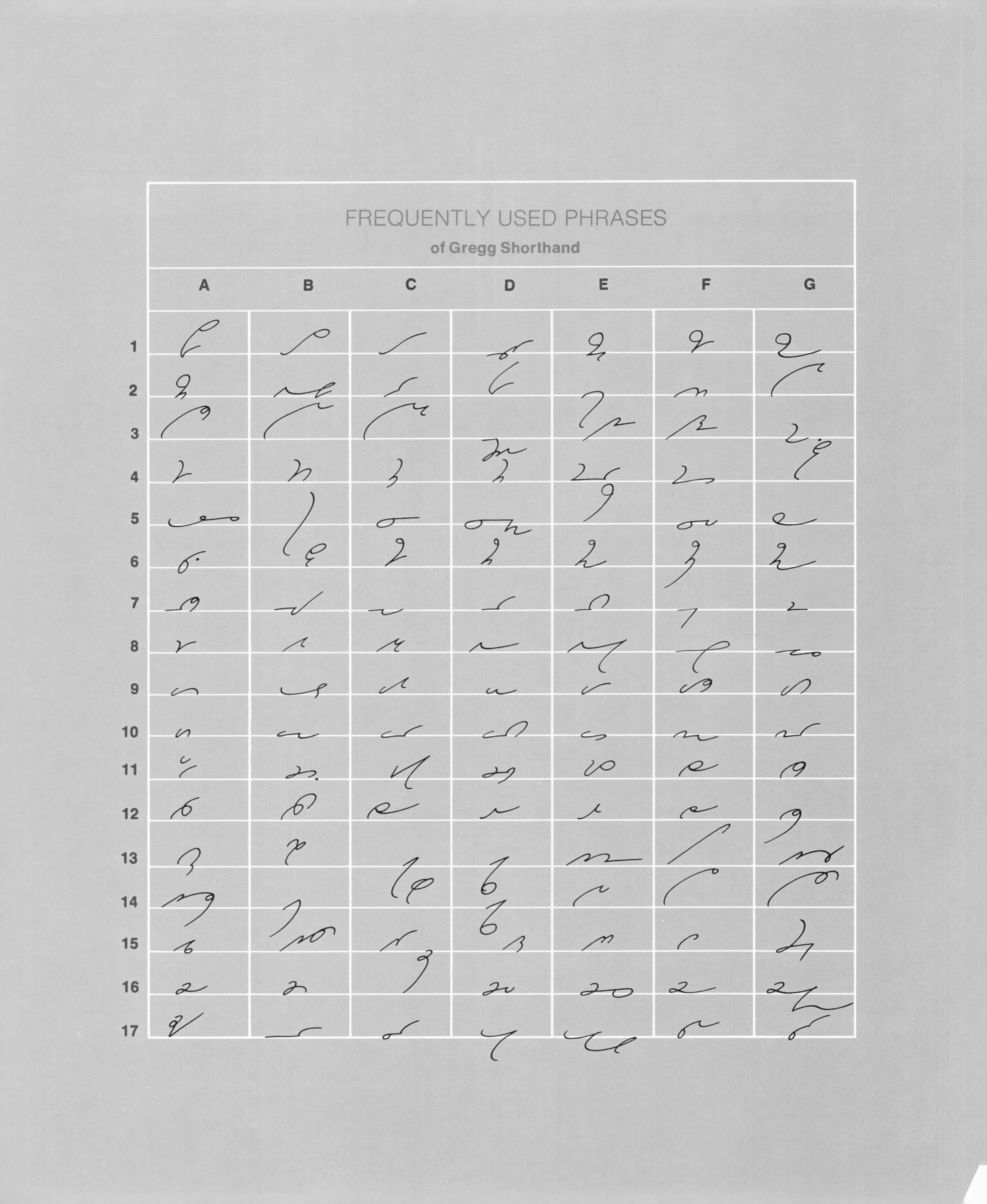

FREQUENTLY USED PHRASES

of Gregg Shorthand

	A	B	C	D	E	F	G
1							
2							
3							
4							
5							
6							
7							
8							
9							
10							
11							
12							
13							
14							
15							
16							
17							

because of the great many plurals that end with *s*. The shorthand *s* is a tiny downward curve that resembles the longhand comma in shape.

S ....

Because in the English language *s* often has the sound of *z*, as in *saves*, the same tiny stroke is used to express *z*.

A

A very important sound in the English language is *a*. In Gregg Shorthand, *a* is simply the longhand *a* with the final connecting stroke omitted.

A ....

The circle may be written in either direction.

Silent Letters

In English, there are many words containing letters that are not pronounced. In Gregg Shorthand, these silent letters are omitted; only the sounds that you actually hear are written. Example: the word *say* would be written *s-a;* the *y* would not be written because it is not pronounced. The word *face* would be represented by the shorthand characters *f-a-s;* the *e* would be omitted because it is not pronounced, and the *c* would be represented by the shorthand *s* because it is pronounced *s*. By omitting silent letters, we save a great deal of writing time.

In the following words what letters would not be written because they are not pronounced?

snow	dough	aid	save
main	day	right	knee

S-A Word

With the strokes for *s* and *a*, you can form the shorthand outline for the word *say*.

say, s-a ....

F, V

The next two shorthand strokes you will learn are *f* and *v*.

F The shorthand stroke for *f* is a downward curve the same shape as *s*, but it is somewhat longer—approximately half the height of the space between the lines of your shorthand notebook.

V The shorthand stroke for *v* is also a downward curve the same shape as

BRIEF-FORM DERIVATIVES

of Gregg Shorthand

	A	B	C	D	E	F	G
1							
2							
3							
4							
5							
6							
7							
8							
9							
10							
11							
12							
13							
14							
15							
16							
17							
18							
19							
20							

s and *f*, but it is very large—approximately the full height of the space between the lines of your shorthand notebook.

■ Observe the difference in the sizes of *s*, *f*, and *v*.

S .... **F** .... **V** ....

F

safe, s-a-f .... face, f-a-s .... safes, s-a-f-s ....

■ Observe that the *c* in *face* is represented by the shorthand *s* because it has the sound of *s*.

V

save, s-a-v .... vase, v-a-s .... saves, s-a-v-s ....

■ Observe that the final *s* in *saves* has the *z* sound, which is represented by the *s* stroke.

E

Another very important vowel in the English language is *e*. In shorthand, *e* is represented by a tiny circle. It is simply the longhand *e* with the two connecting strokes omitted. The circle may be written in either direction.

E ....

■ Observe the difference between the sizes of *a* and *e*.

A .... **E** ....

see, s-e .... sees, s-e-s .... ease, e-s ....

fee, f-e .... fees, f-e-s .... easy, e-s-e ....

■ Observe that the *y* in *easy* is pronounced *e*; therefore, it is represented by the *e* circle.

Suggestion: At this point you will find it helpful to read the procedures outlined for practicing lists of words on page xi. If you follow those procedures, you will derive the greatest benefit from the time you invest in practice.

Group B

N, M

The shorthand stroke for *n* is a very short forward straight line. The shorthand

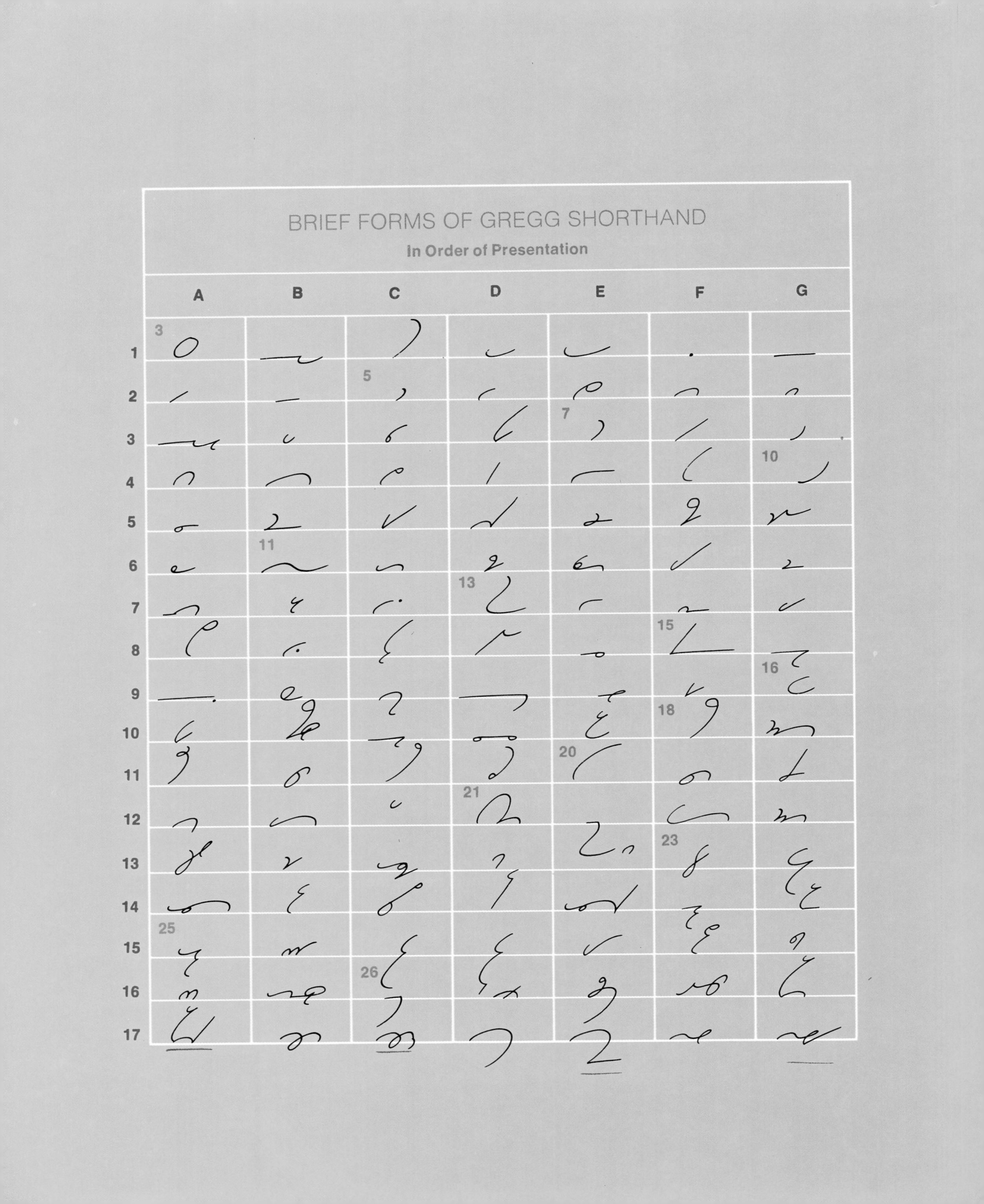

BRIEF FORMS OF GREGG SHORTHAND

In Order of Presentation

	A	B	C	D	E	F	G
1	3						
2			5				
3					7		
4							10
5							
6		11					
7				13			
8						15	
9							16
10						18	
11					20		
12				21			
13						23	
14							
15	25						
16			26				
17							

stroke for *m* is a longer forward straight line.

N .... **M** ....

N

see, s-e	say, s-a	vain, v-a-n
seen, s-e-n	sane, s-a-n	knee, n-e

■ Observe that the *k* and the final *e* in *knee* are not written because they are not pronounced.

M

may, m-a	mean, m-e-n	seem, s-e-m
main, m-a-n	aim, a-m	same, s-a-m

T, D

The shorthand stroke for *t* is a short upward straight line. The shorthand stroke for *d* is a longer upward straight line.

T .... **D** ....

T

eat, e-t	meet, m-e-t	stay, s-t-a
neat, n-e-t	tea, t-e	safety, s-a-f-t-e

D

aid, a-d	feed, f-e-d	stayed, s-t-a-d
made, m-a-d	day, d-a	deed, d-e-d
need, n-e-d	date, d-a-t	saved, s-a-v-d

Punctuation and Capitalization

period	paragraph	parentheses
question mark	dash	hyphen

The regular longhand forms are used for all other punctuation marks.

INDEX OF BUILDING TRANSCRIPTION SKILLS

The figure refers to the page on which the entry appears.

Capitalization is indicated by two upward dashes placed underneath the word to be capitalized.

Dave .... Fay .... Mae ....

Reading Practice

With the nine strokes you have studied in this lesson, you can already read shorthand sentences with the help of an occasional longhand word.

Read the following sentences in this way:

1 Spell each shorthand outline aloud as you read it, thus: *N-a-t, Nate; m-a, may; s-t-a, stay.*

2 If you cannot determine the meaning of a shorthand outline after you have spelled it, refer to the key that follows this reading practice.

3 Reread the entire reading practice if time permits.

Group A

① _____ on Labor _____ ② _____ a _____ with _____ ③ Mr. _____ for _____ ④ _____ will _____ at 5 on _____

⑥ _____ is _____; _____ is _____ ⑦ _____ ⑧ Mr. _____ on _____ St.

⑨ _____ a _____ for _____ ⑩ His _____ _____ ⑪ _____ can _____ on _____ 15; _____ can _____ the _____

Group B

Group C

WORD ENDINGS

INDEX OF BRIEF FORMS

The figure refers to the page on which the brief form is introduced.

Group D

[104]

GROUP A
1 Nate may see me on Labor Day. **2** Dave made a date with Fay. **3** Mr. Meade stayed for tea. **4** Amy will meet Mae at 5 on East Main.

GROUP B
5 Dave made me save the fee. **6** Mae is mean; Fay is vain. **7** Dave may eat meat. **8** Mr. East may meet Dave on Main Street.

GROUP C
9 Mamie saved a seat for me. **10** His fame made Dave vain. **11** Amy can see me on May 15; Amy can see Fay the same day.

GROUP D
12 Fay's room faced east. **13** Dean made the Navy team. Nate made the Navy team too. **14** I need aid. Will Mae aid me? **15** Dave's deed is in Fay's safe. **16** Amy heard Mamie say, "Save me."

Taking dictation and transcribing dictation are the secretary's main activities in the electronic office.

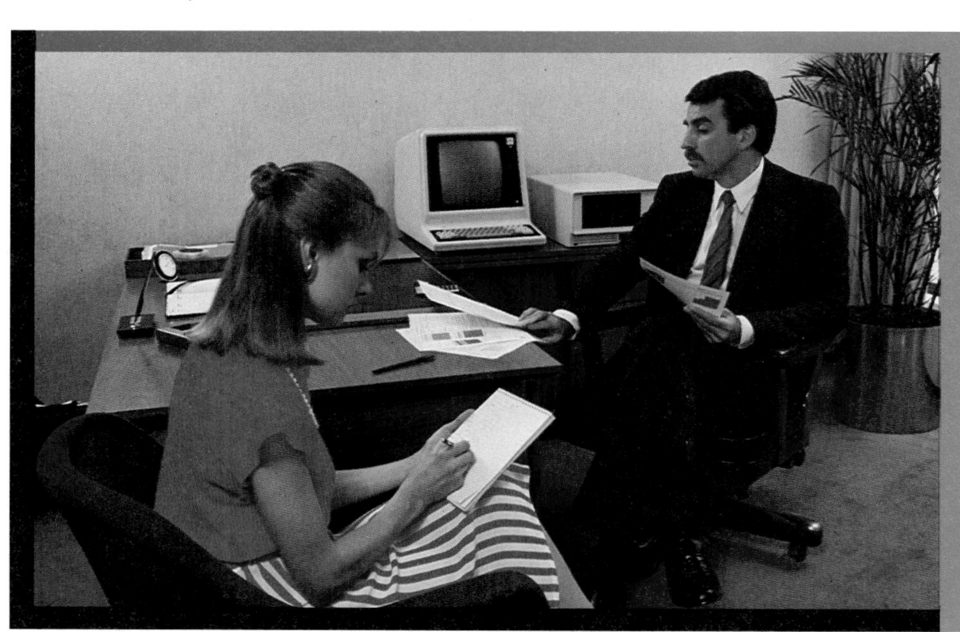

Index Of Gregg Shorthand

In order to facilitate finding, this Index has been divided into six main sections—Alphabetic Characters, Brief Forms, General, Phrasing, Word Beginnings, Word Endings.

The figure refers to the page on which the entry appears.

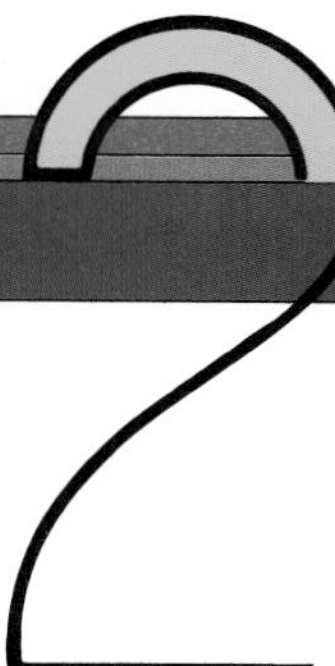

Principles

Alphabet Review

Here are the nine shorthand strokes you studied in Lesson 1. How rapidly can you read them?

O, R, L

In this paragraph you will study three extremely useful strokes—o, r, l.

O The shorthand stroke for *o* is a small deep hook.

R The shorthand stroke for *r* is a short forward curve.

L The shorthand stroke for *l* is a longer forward curve about three times as long as the stroke for *r*.

■ Observe how these three strokes are derived from their longhand forms.

O **R** **L**

O

no, n-o	so, s-o	own, o-n
tow, t-o	phone, f-o-n	stone, s-t-o-n
dough, d-o	vote, v-o-t	dome, d-o-m

■ Observe that in the words in the third column, the *o* is placed on its side before *n* and *m*. This enables us to obtain smoother, more easily written outlines than we would obtain if we wrote the *o* upright in these and similar words.

The metric system was devised by France and adopted there by law in 1799. Since that time its use has become almost universal except in Great Britain and the United States. It is rapidly coming into use in those two countries and, therefore, it is possible that you will need these special outlines. If the terms occur only infrequently in your dictation, it is better to write them in full.

The following abbreviations will be useful to those who must frequently take metric measurements in dictation.

		meter	liter	gram
kilo-	1,000			
hekto-	100			
deka-	10			
deci-	1/10			
centi-	1/100			
milli-	1/1,000			
micro-	1/1,000,000			
nano-	1/1,000,000,000			

Additional Metric Measurements

Celsius	kilowatt	microsecond
centigrade	kilowatt-hour	milliampere
cubic centimeter	megabit	millibar
kilobit	megahertz	millifarad
kilocalorie	megaton	millihenry
kilocycle	megawatt	millimicrosecond
kilohertz	megohm	millivolt
kiloton	micromicron	milliwatt
kilovolt	micron	nanosecond

R

ear, e-r .... raid, r-a-d .... fear, f-e-r ....

near, n-e-r .... trade, t-r-a-d .... fair, f-a-r ....

mere, m-e-r .... or, o-r .... radio, r-a-d-e-o ....

dear, d-e-r .... more, m-o-r .... freed, f-r-e-d ....

L

ail, a-l .... lay, l-a .... real, r-e-l ....

mail, m-a-l .... late, l-a-t .... leave, l-e-v ....

deal, d-e-l .... feel, f-e-l .... low, l-o ....

steal, s-t-e-l .... fail, f-a-l .... floor, f-l-o-r ....

■ Observe that *f-r,* as in *freed*, and *f-l*, as in *floor*, are written with one sweep of the pen, with no stop between the *f* and the *r* or *l.*

freed .... **floor** ....

H, -ing

The letter *h* is a dot placed above the following vowel. With few exceptions, *h* occurs at the beginning of a word.

Ing, which almost always occurs at the end of a word, is also represented by a dot.

H

he, h-e .... home, h-o-m .... whole, h-o-l ....

-ing

hearing, h-e-r-ing .... heating, h-e-t-ing .... mailing, m-a-l-ing ....

Long Ī

The shorthand stroke for the long sound of *i,* as in *my,* is a large broken circle.

I ....

my, m-ī .... sight, s-ī-t .... high, h-ī ....

Norfolk	Sacramento	Syracuse
Oakland	St. Louis	Tacoma
Oklahoma City	St. Paul	Tallahassee
Omaha	Salt Lake City	Tampa
Philadelphia	San Antonio	Toledo
Phoenix	San Diego	Trenton
Pittsburgh	San Francisco	Tucson
Portland	Seattle	Tulsa
Providence	Shreveport	Washington
Richmond	Spokane	Wichita
Rochester	Springfield	Wilmington

Common Geographical Abbreviations

America	England	Canada
American	English	Canadian
United States	Great Britain	Puerto Rico

The Metric System

If you take dictation in which there are many occurrences of metric measurements, you will have frequent use for the abbreviated forms given below. It is not wise to attempt to learn these forms until you know you will have use for them.

might, m-ī-t	side, s-ī-d	try, t-r-ī
sign, s-ī-n	line, l-ī-n	tire, t-ī-r

Omission of Minor Vowels

Many words in the English language contain vowels that are sounded only slightly or are slurred. For example, the word *even* is really pronounced *e-vn; meter* is pronounced *met-r.* (The dictionary calls these minor vowels "schwas.") These vowels are omitted in shorthand when their omission does not detract from facility of writing or from legibility.

evening, e-v-n-ing	writer, r-ī-t-r	season, s-e-s-n
meter, m-e-t-r	vital, v-ī-t-l	total, t-o-t-l
dealer, d-e-l-r	final, f-ī-n-l	heater, h-e-t-r

Reading Practice

With the aid of a few words in longhand, you can read the following sentences. Spell each shorthand word aloud as you read it; refer to the key when you cannot read a word.

Group A

Group B

Selected Cities of the United States

Akron	Cleveland	Jersey City
Albany	Columbia	Kansas City
Anchorage	Columbus	Knoxville
Atlanta	Dallas	Laramie
Baltimore	Dayton	Las Vegas
Baton Rouge	Denver	Lincoln
Birmingham	Des Moines	Little Rock
Boston	Detroit	Los Angeles
Bridgeport	El Paso	Louisville
Buffalo	Fairbanks	Memphis
Cambridge	Fargo	Miami
Camden	Fort Worth	Milwaukee
Charleston	Grand Rapids	Minneapolis
Charlotte	Hartford	Montpelier
Chattanooga	Honolulu	Nashville
Cheyenne	Houston	Newark
Chicago	Indianapolis	New Orleans
Cincinnati	Jacksonville	New York

Group C

Group D

Group E

[147]

GROUP A
1 He may drive me home at night. **2** Steve might stay here on May 15, or he might fly home. **3** My whole right side is sore. I may stay home. **4** I need a mail meter on my floor.

GROUP B
5 Who stole my nail file? **6** Steve may vote in May. **7** Ray drove me home in a driving storm. **8** Stephen Stone is feeling fine. He may drive to Maine for the Easter season.

GROUP C
9 Dale notified me that my heater was stolen. **10** Phone me at 8 at my retail store on East Main. **11** Ray wrote a fine story. He may write the story of my life. **12** Steve's train is late. He may get home late at night.

GROUP D
13 Mary might vote for Lee Mile this evening. **14** I might write Flo a note later. **15** May he rely on Lee Levy for aid?

GROUP E
16 Dave notified me that Lee stole my car radio. **17** My Maine flight is late. Amy will meet my flight.

States

The abbreviations in parentheses are those recommended by the Postal Service.

Alabama [AL]	Louisiana [LA]	Ohio [OH]
Alaska [AK]	Maine [ME]	Oklahoma [OK]
Arizona [AZ]	Maryland [MD]	Oregon [OR]
Arkansas [AR]	Massachusetts [MA]	Pennsylvania [PA]
California [CA]	Michigan [MI]	Rhode Island [RI]
Colorado [CO]	Minnesota [MN]	South Carolina [SC]
Connecticut [CT]	Mississippi [MS]	South Dakota [SD]
Delaware [DE]	Missouri [MO]	Tennessee [TN]
Florida [FL]	Montana [MT]	Texas [TX]
Georgia [GA]	Nebraska [NE]	Utah [UT]
Hawaii [HI]	Nevada [NV]	Vermont [VT]
Idaho [ID]	New Hampshire [NH]	Virginia [VA]
Illinois [IL]	New Jersey [NJ]	Washington [WA]
Indiana [IN]	New Mexico [NM]	West Virginia [WV]
Iowa [IA]	New York [NY]	Wisconsin [WI]
Kansas [KS]	North Carolina [NC]	Wyoming [WY]
Kentucky [KY]	North Dakota [ND]	

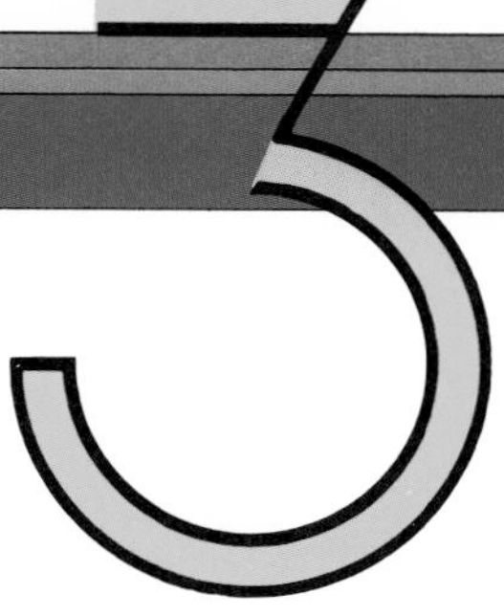

Principles

Alphabet Review

You have already studied 14 alphabet strokes. How fast can you identify them?

Brief Forms

There are some words in the English language that occur again and again when we speak or write. As an aid to rapid writing, special abbreviations, called brief forms, are provided for some of these common words.

This process of abbreviation is common in longhand. For example, we abbreviate *Street* to *St.; Mister* to *Mr.; Saturday* to *Sat.*

Because the words for which brief forms have been provided occur so frequently, be sure you learn them well.

I	have	it, at
am	will, well	in*, not
Mr.	a, an	are, our, hour

**In-* is also used as a word beginning in words like:

indeed, in-d-e-d   inside, in-s-ī-d   invite, in-v-ī-t

■ Did you observe that some shorthand outlines have two or more meanings, such as the shorthand forms for *are, our, hour; will, well?* You will have no problem selecting the correct meaning of a brief form when it appears in a sentence. The sense, or context, will give you the answer.

dealer .... chief .... space ....

At the beginning of a word and after *k, gay,* or a downstroke, the combination *oo-s* is written without an angle.

husky .... gust .... just ....

but

loose .... does .... rust ....

The word beginning *re-* is represented by *r* before a downstroke or a vowel.

research .... reference .... reopen ....

but

relate .... retake .... retreat ....

The word beginnings *de-, di-* are represented by *d* except before *k* or *gay.*

depressed .... deliver .... direction ....

but

declare .... decay .... degrade ....

As you have perhaps already noticed, the past tense of a verb is formed by adding the stroke for the sound that is heard in the past tense. In some words the past tense has the sound of *t,* as in *baked;* in others, it has the sound of *d,* as in *saved.* In some words, the past tense is incorporated in a blend, as in *planned, feared, mailed.*

baked .... saved .... feared ....

missed .... planned .... mailed ....

The word endings *-ure* and *-ual* are represented by *r* and *l* except when those endings are preceded by a downstroke.

nature .... procedure .... creature ....

annual .... gradual .... equal ....

but

pressure .... treasure .... ensure ....

casual .... visual .... visually ....

Phrasing

The use of brief forms for common words enables you to save time. Another device for saving writing time is called "phrasing," or the writing of two or more shorthand outlines together. Here are a number of phrases built with the brief forms you have studied.

I have	I will have	I am
I have not	he will	in our
I will	he will not	it will

Left S-Z

Earlier you learned one stroke for *s* and *z*. Another stroke for *s* and *z* is also used in order to provide an easy joining in any combination of strokes—a backward comma, which is also written downward. For convenience, it is called the "left s."

At this point you need not try to decide which *s* stroke to use in any given word; this will become clear to you as your study of Gregg Shorthand progresses.

S-Z

needs, n-e-d-s	least, l-e-s-t	series, s-e-r-e-s
names, n-a-m-s	writes, r-ī-t-s	seal, s-e-l
rise, r-ī-s	mails, m-a-l-s	sales, s-a-l-s
most, m-o-s-t	seems, s-e-m-s	homes, h-o-m-s

P, B

The shorthand stroke for *p* is a downward curve the same shape as the left *s* except that it is larger—approximately half the height of the space between the lines in your shorthand notebook.

The shorthand stroke for *b* is also a downward curve the same shape as the left *s* and *p* except that it is *much* larger—approximately the full height of the space between the lines in your shorthand notebook.

■ Observe the difference in the sizes of the *s, p,* and *b.*

S **P** **B**

P

hope, h-o-p	space, s-p-a-s	paper, p-a-p-r

The *oo* hook is written on its side after *n, m.*

news .... noon .... moved ....

The under *ith* is used when it is joined to *o, r, l*; in other cases, the over *ith* is used.

though .... through .... health ....

but

these .... thick .... then ....

The following principles deal with the joinings of the two forms of *s*.

At the beginning and end of words, the comma *s* is used before and after *f, v, k, gay;* the left *s*, before and after *p, b, r, l*.

saves .... sips .... series ....

seeks .... globes .... rags ....

The comma *s* is used before *t, d, n, m, o*; the left *s* is used after those strokes.

stones .... solos .... needs ....

The comma *s* is used before and after *ish, chay, j*.

sessions .... reaches .... stages ....

The comma *s* is used in words consisting of *s* and a circle vowel or *s* and *ith* and a circle vowel.

say .... these .... seethe ....

Gregg Shorthand is equally legible whether it is written on ruled or unruled paper; consequently, you need not worry about the exact placement of your outlines on the printed lines in your notebook. The main purpose of the printed lines in your notebook is to keep you from wandering uphill and downhill as you write.

However, so that all outlines may be uniformly placed in the shorthand books from which you study, this general rule has been followed:

The base of the first consonant of a word is placed on the line of writing. When *s* comes before a downstroke, however, the downstroke is placed on the line of writing.

name .... safe .... pace ....

open, o-p-n

pay, p-a

spare, s-p-a-r

please, p-l-e-s

place, p-l-a-s

price, p-r-ī-s

provide, p-r-o-v-ī-d

prepare, p-r-e-p-a-r

type, t-ī-p

B

bay, b-a

base, b-a-s

bare, b-a-r

boat, b-o-t

buy, b-ī

brief, b-r-e-f

bright, b-r-ī-t

blame, b-l-a-m

able, a-b-l

labor, l-a-b-r

neighbor, n-a-b-r

label, l-a-b-l

■ Observe that the combinations *p-r,* as in *price; p-l,* as in *please; b-r,* as in *bright*; and *b-l* as in *blame,* are written with one sweep of the pen without a pause between the *p* or *b* and the *r* or *l.*

price please bright blame

Reading Practice

You can already read sentences written entirely in shorthand.

Suggestion: Before you start your work on this Reading Practice, take a few minutes to read the practice procedures for reading shorthand on page xiii.

Group A

(1) 75 (2) 75 (3) (4)

Principles of Joining

The following is a summary of the principles that govern the various joinings of Gregg Shorthand. They are presented as a matter of interest.

Circles are written inside curves and outside angles.

appeal ... late ... same ...
give ... relief ... needless ...

Circles are written clockwise (in this direction) on a straight stroke or between two straight strokes in the same direction.

may ... date ... aim ...
man ... stayed ... name ...

Between two curves written in opposite directions, the circle is written on the back of the first curve.

care ... gear ... vapor ...
rack ... lake ... pave ...

The *o* hook is written on its side before *n*, *m* unless a downward stroke comes before the hook.

own ... stone ... loan ...

but

phone ... bone ... zone ...

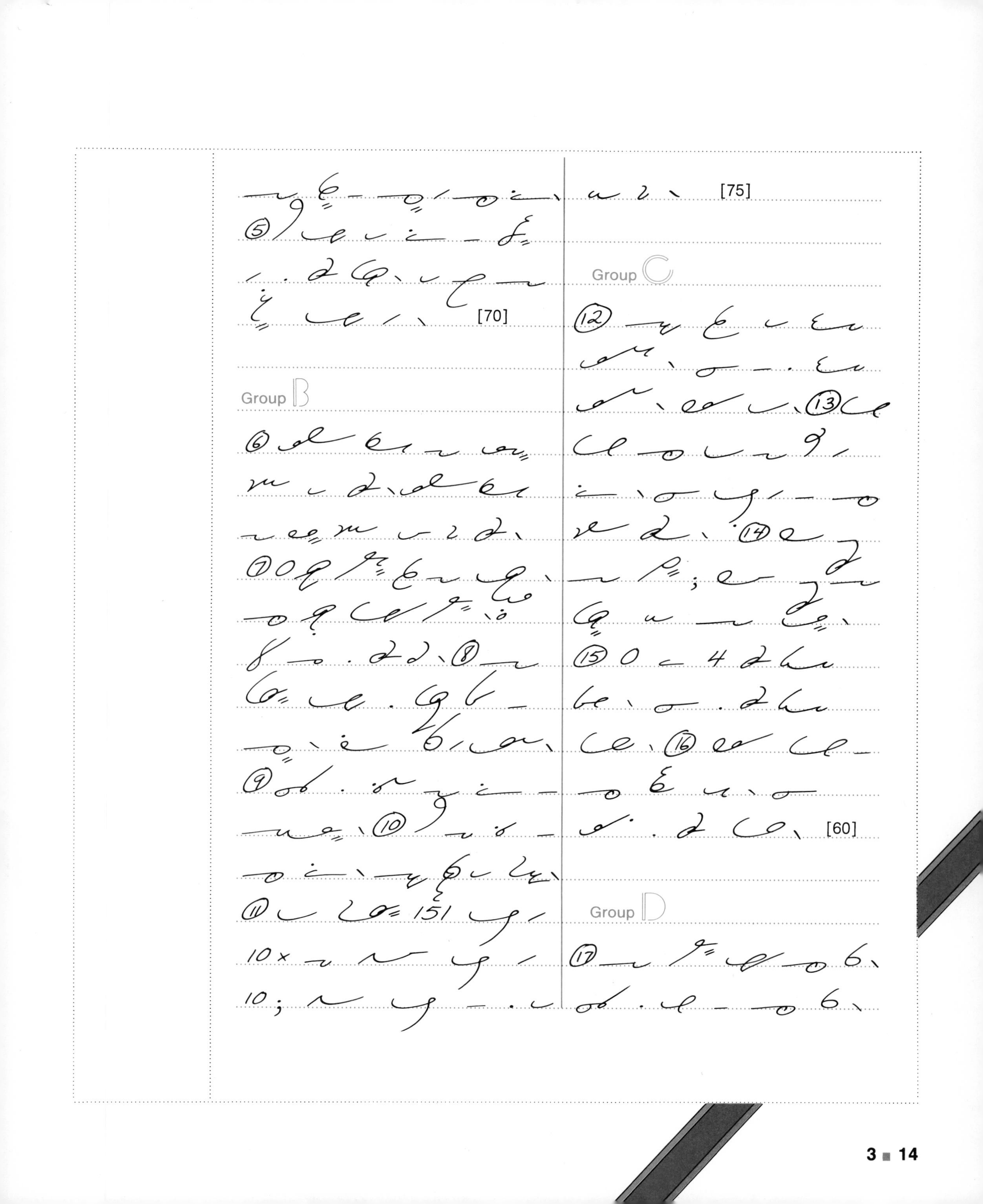

[70]

Group B

[75]

Group C

[60]

Group D

APPENDIX

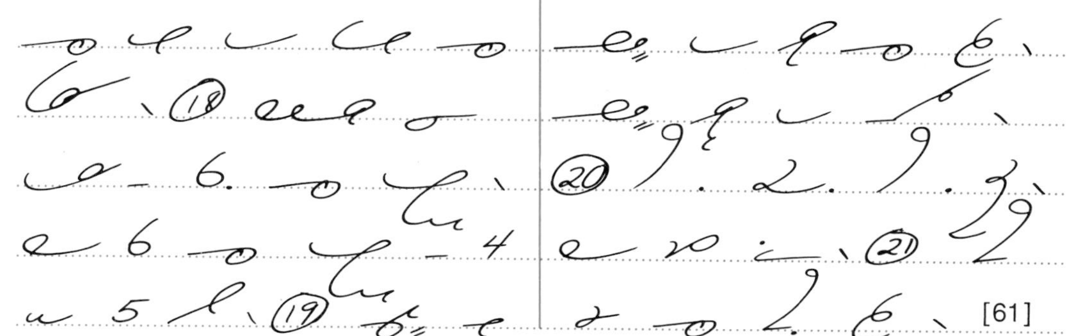

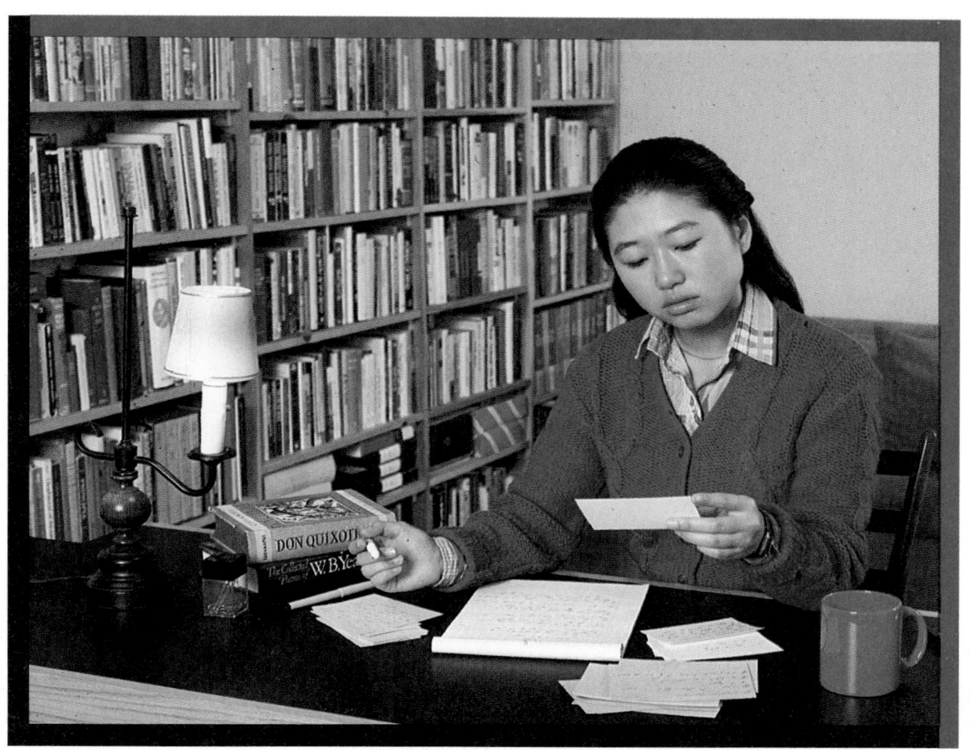

As a student, you can use your shorthand skill while drafting a report for a class assignment.

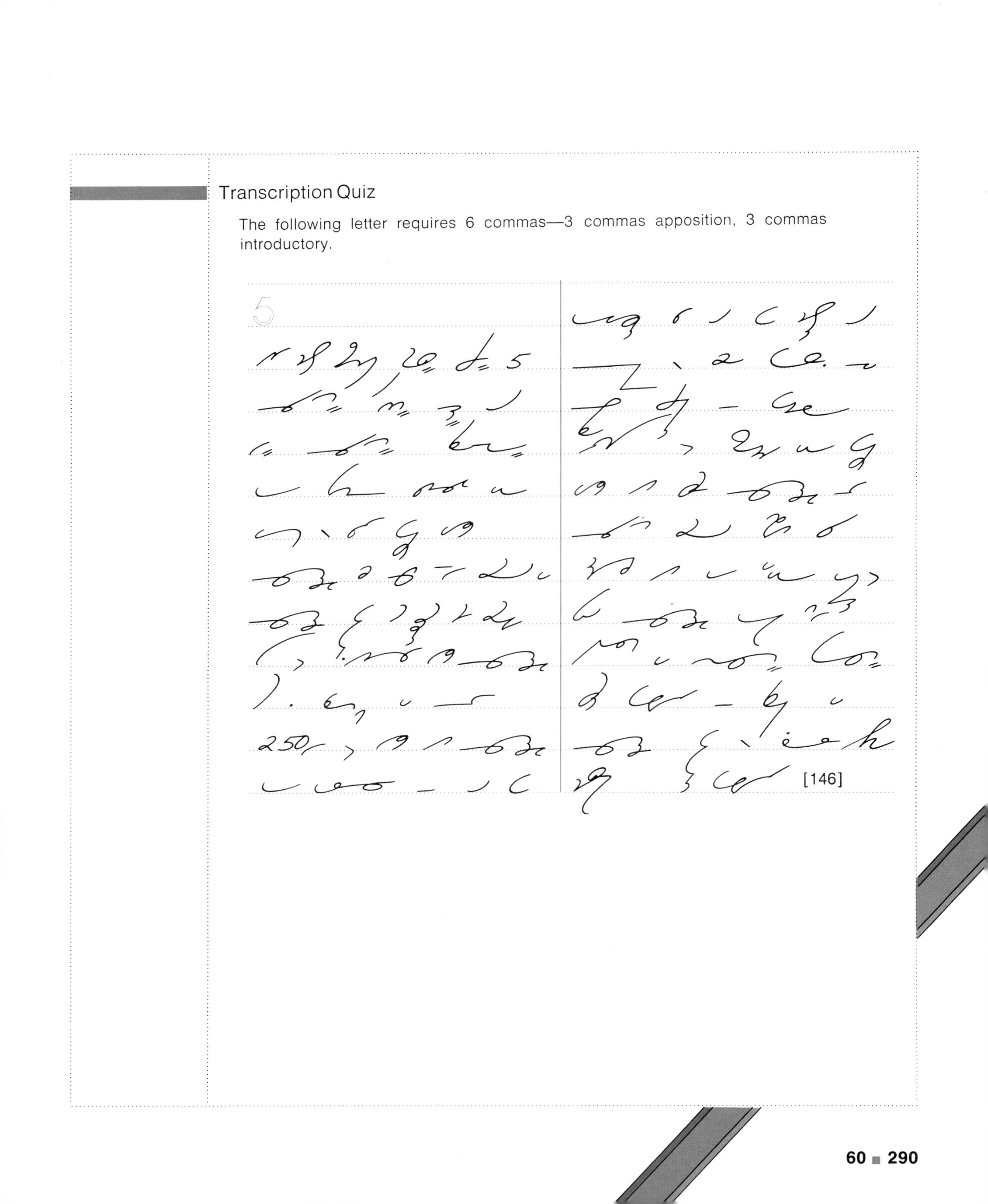

Transcription Quiz

The following letter requires 6 commas—3 commas apposition, 3 commas introductory.

5

[146]

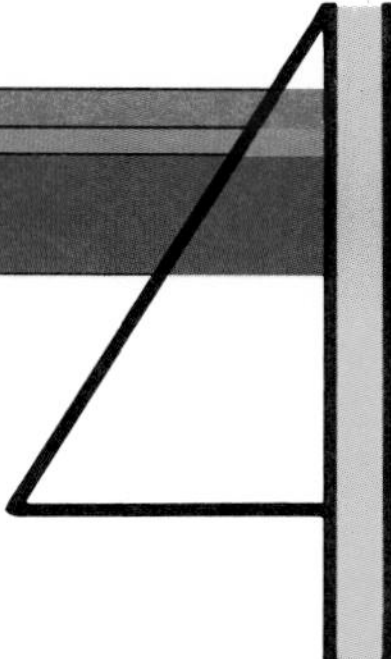

Principles

Alphabet Review

You have already studied 17 strokes in the Gregg Shorthand alphabet. How fast can you read them?

OO

The shorthand stroke for the sound of *oo*, as in *to*, is a tiny upward hook.

oo

to (two, too), t-oo	suit, s-oo-t	produce, p-r-o-d-oo-s
do (due), d-oo	room, r-oo-m	new (knew), n-oo
who, h-oo	poor, p-oo-r	noon, n-oo-n
food, f-oo-d	true, t-r-oo	move, m-oo-v

■ Observe that the *oo* is placed on its side when it follows *n* or *m*, as in *new, noon, move.* By placing the hook on its side in these combinations rather than writing it upright, we obtain smooth joinings.

W, Sw

At the beginning of words *w*, as in *we*, is represented by the *oo* hook; *sw*, as in *sweet*, by *s-oo*.

enough

yours

par

intro

[134]

4

wor·ried

over·weight

as

known

phy·si·cians

when

intro

lec·ture

rel·e·vant

if

intro

ser

intro

and o

[178]

we, oo-e	wade, oo-a-d	sweet, s-oo-e-t
way, oo-a	wear, oo-a-r	sway, s-oo-a
wait, oo-a-t	wife, oo-ī-f	swear, s-oo-a-r

Wh

Wh, as in *why* and *while,* is also represented by the *oo* hook.

why, oo-ī	white, oo-ī-t	whale, oo-a-l
while, oo-ī-l	wheel, oo-e-l	wheat, oo-e-t

Useful Phrases

Here are a number of useful phrases that use the *oo* hook.

we are	we may	who will not
we will	who are	I do
we have	who will	I do not

K, G

The shorthand stroke for *k* is a short forward curve.

The shorthand stroke for the hard sound of *g,* as in *game,* is a much longer forward curve. It is called *gay.*

■ Observe the difference in the size and shape of *oo, k,* and *gay.*

OO **K** **Gay**

K

take, t-a-k	week (weak) oo-e-k	clear, k-l-e-r
cake, k-a-k	cool, k-oo-l	increase, in-k-r-e-s
make, m-a-k	case, k-a-s	claim, k-l-a-m
came, k-a-m	scale, s-k-a-l	clean, k-l-e-n

Gay

gain, gay-a-n	go, gay-o	gale, gay-a-l
game, gay-a-m	goal, gay-o-l	glue, gay-l-oo

due

conj

ser

canceled

par

intro

requirements

par

[153]

3

au·to·mat·i·cal·ly

op·er·a·tor

if

gate, gay-a-t
gave, gay-a-v
great, gay-r-a-t
grade, gay-r-a-d
legal, l-e-gay-l
gleam, gay-l-e-m

■ Observe that *k-r,* as in *increase,* and *gay-l,* as in *legal,* are written with a smooth wavelike motion.

increase **legal**

But *k-l,* as in *claim,* and *gay-r,* as in *great,* are written with a hump between the *k* and the *l* and the *gay* and the *r.*

claim **great**

Reading Practice

The sentences that follow contain many illustrations of the new shorthand strokes you studied in this lesson. They also contain many illustrations of the strokes, brief forms, and phrases you studied in Lessons 1 through 3.

Read the sentences aloud, spelling each shorthand outline you cannot immediately read.

Group A

[66]

Business Vocabulary Builder

nutritional Pertaining to the processes of nourishing or being nourished.

relevant Having a bearing on the matter being considered.

expenditures Amounts paid out.

Reading and Writing Practice

1

due

conj

intro

re·ceived

intro

el·i·gi·ble

par

re·in·state

par

do

ser

at·tach

50

and o

self-ad·dressed

par

ac·cept

[136]

2

neigh·bor·hood

ser

Group B

[50]

Group C

[35]

Group D

[38]

Group E

[30]

Lesson 60 contains a review of the disjoined word beginnings and endings of Gregg Shorthand.

Building Transcription Skills

Similar Words ■ do, due

do To carry out; to perform.

Can you *do* this work for me?

due Owing; payable.

Your payment was *due* two weeks ago.

Principles

Alphabet Review

In Lessons 1 through 4 you studied 20 shorthand strokes. See how fast you can read them.

A, Ä

The large circle that represents the long sound of *a,* as in *main,* also represents the vowel sounds heard in *as* and *arm.*

A

as, a-s
man, m-a-n
past, p-a-s-t
has, h-a-s
back, b-a-k
plan, p-l-a-n
act, a-k-t
matter, m-a-t-r
swam, s-oo-a-m

Ä

arm, a-r-m
car, k-a-r
start, s-t-a-r-t
art, a-r-t
far, f-a-r
dark, d-a-r-k
heart, h-a-r-t
farm, f-a-r-m
park, p-a-r-k

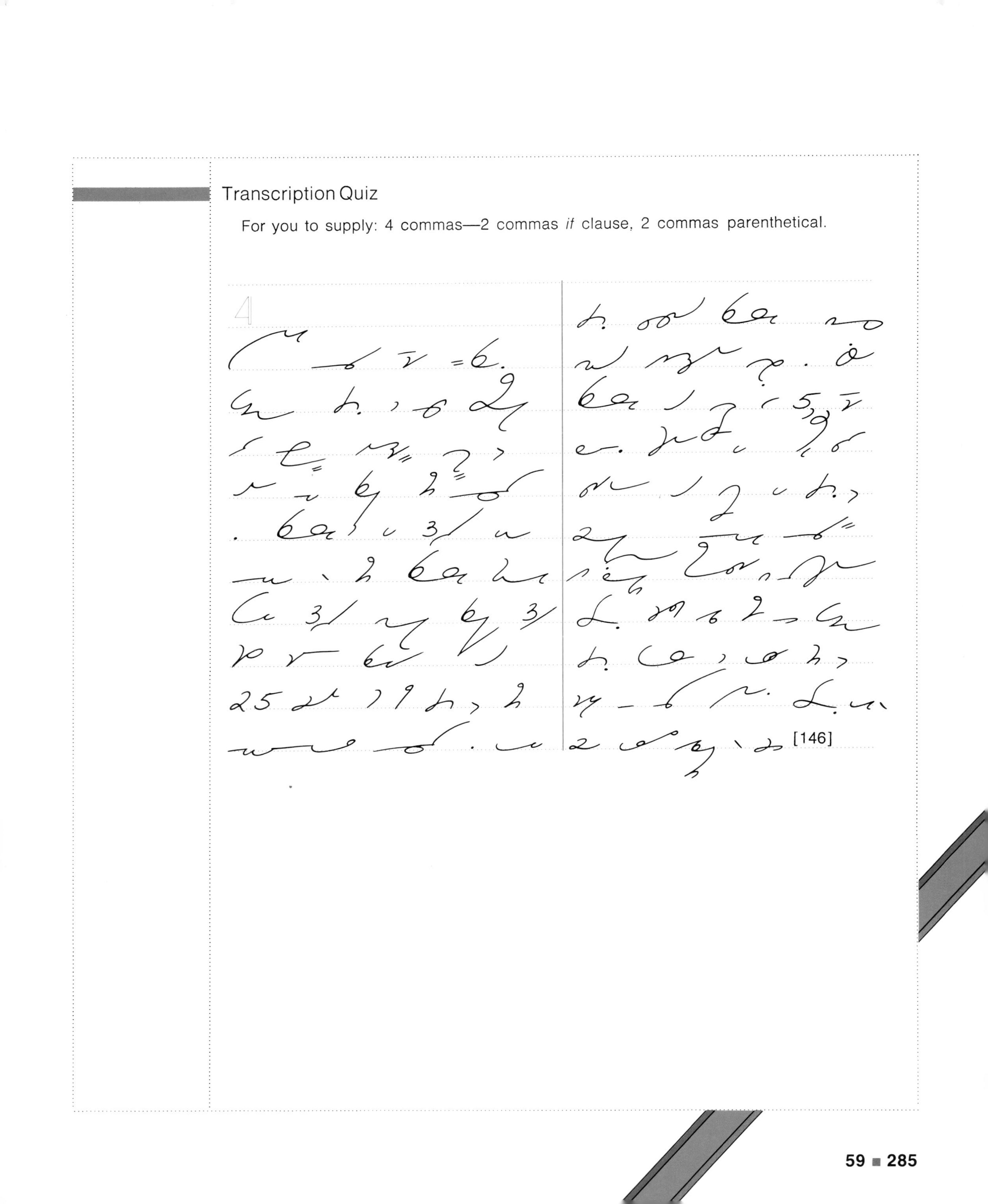

Transcription Quiz

For you to supply: 4 commas—2 commas *if* clause, 2 commas parenthetical.

4

[146]

E, I, Obscure Vowel

The tiny circle that represents the sound of *e,* as in *heat,* also represents the vowel sounds heard in *let, him,* and the obscure vowel sound (called "schwa" in some dictionaries) in *her, hurt.*

E

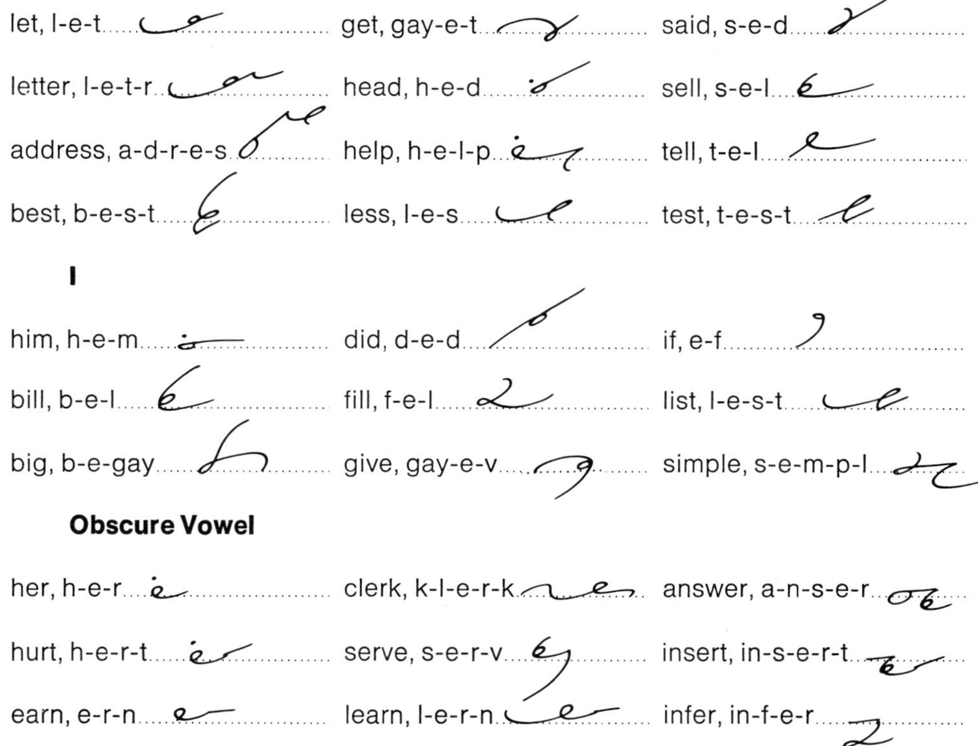

let, l-e-t
get, gay-e-t
said, s-e-d
letter, l-e-t-r
head, h-e-d
sell, s-e-l
address, a-d-r-e-s
help, h-e-l-p
tell, t-e-l
best, b-e-s-t
less, l-e-s
test, t-e-s-t
I
him, h-e-m
did, d-e-d
if, e-f
bill, b-e-l
fill, f-e-l
list, l-e-s-t
big, b-e-gay
give, gay-e-v
simple, s-e-m-p-l
Obscure Vowel
her, h-e-r
clerk, k-l-e-r-k
answer, a-n-s-e-r
hurt, h-e-r-t
serve, s-e-r-v
insert, in-s-e-r-t
earn, e-r-n
learn, l-e-r-n
infer, in-f-e-r

Th

Two tiny curves, written upward, are provided for the sounds of *th.* These curves are called "ith."

At this time you need not try to decide which *th* stroke to use in a word; this will become clear to you as your study of Gregg Shorthand progresses.

Over Ith .... **Under Ith** ....

Over Ith

these, ith-e-s .... theater, ith-e-t-r .... teeth, t-e-ith ....

then, ith-e-n .... thick, ith-e-k .... faith, f-a-ith ....

theme, ith-e-m .... thief, ith-e-f .... truth, t-r-oo-ith ....

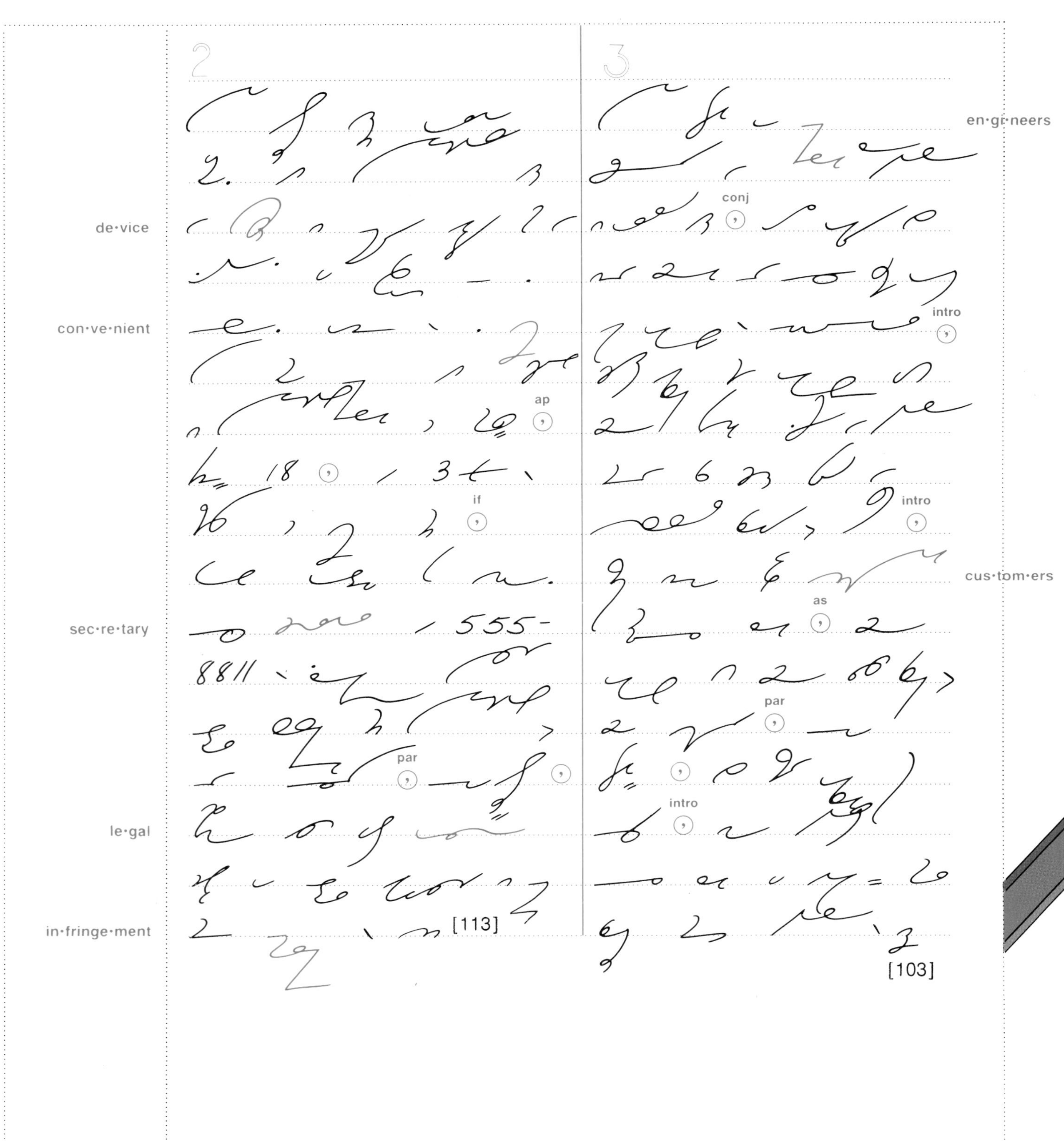
2
3
en·gi·neers
de·vice
con·ve·nient
cus·tom·ers
sec·re·tary
le·gal
in·fringe·ment
conj
intro
ap
if
as
par
[113]
[103]

Under Ith

though, ith-o	both, b-o-ith	health, h-e-l-ith
those, ith-o-s	birth, b-r-ith	thorough, ith-e-r-o
three, ith-r-e	earth, e-r-ith	through, ith-r-oo

Brief Forms

Here is another group of brief forms for frequently used words. You will be wise to learn them well.

the	you, your	is, his
that	can	Mrs.
with	of	but

Common Phrases

Here are some useful phrases employing these brief forms.

in the	with you	it is
in that	I can	in his
you are	I cannot	with his

■ Observe that in the phrases in the third column, the left *s* is used for *is* and *his.*

Reading Practice

You have made such rapid progress that you can already read business letters written entirely in shorthand.

Brief-Form Letter

The following letter contains one or more illustrations of the brief forms in this lesson and in Lesson 3.

Reading and Writing Practice

women
seg·ments
com·mer·cial
fore·front

par par conj intro as

80's 70

rec·og·nize
growth
tech·niques
sem·i·nars

ser as if intro

80's

555-
1181 [227]

1555-1818

[69]

2

[76]

3

[67]

4

Lesson 59 gives you one more opportunity to sharpen your phrasing skills. The letters in the Reading and Writing Practice contain illustrations of all the phrasing principles of Gregg Shorthand.

Building Transcription Skills

Spelling Families ■ -cial, -tial

Words Ending in -cial

ben-e-fi-cial es-pe-cial ra-cial
com-mer-cial fi-nan-cial so-cial
cru-cial of-fi-cial spe-cial

Words Ending in -tial

cir-cum-stan-tial im-par-tial par-tial
cre-den-tial in-flu-en-tial po-ten-tial
es-sen-tial ini-tial sub-stan-tial

Business Vocabulary Builder

segments Separate parts of something.

seminar An advanced course featuring informality and discussion.

malicious Desiring to see another suffer.

forefront The head of.

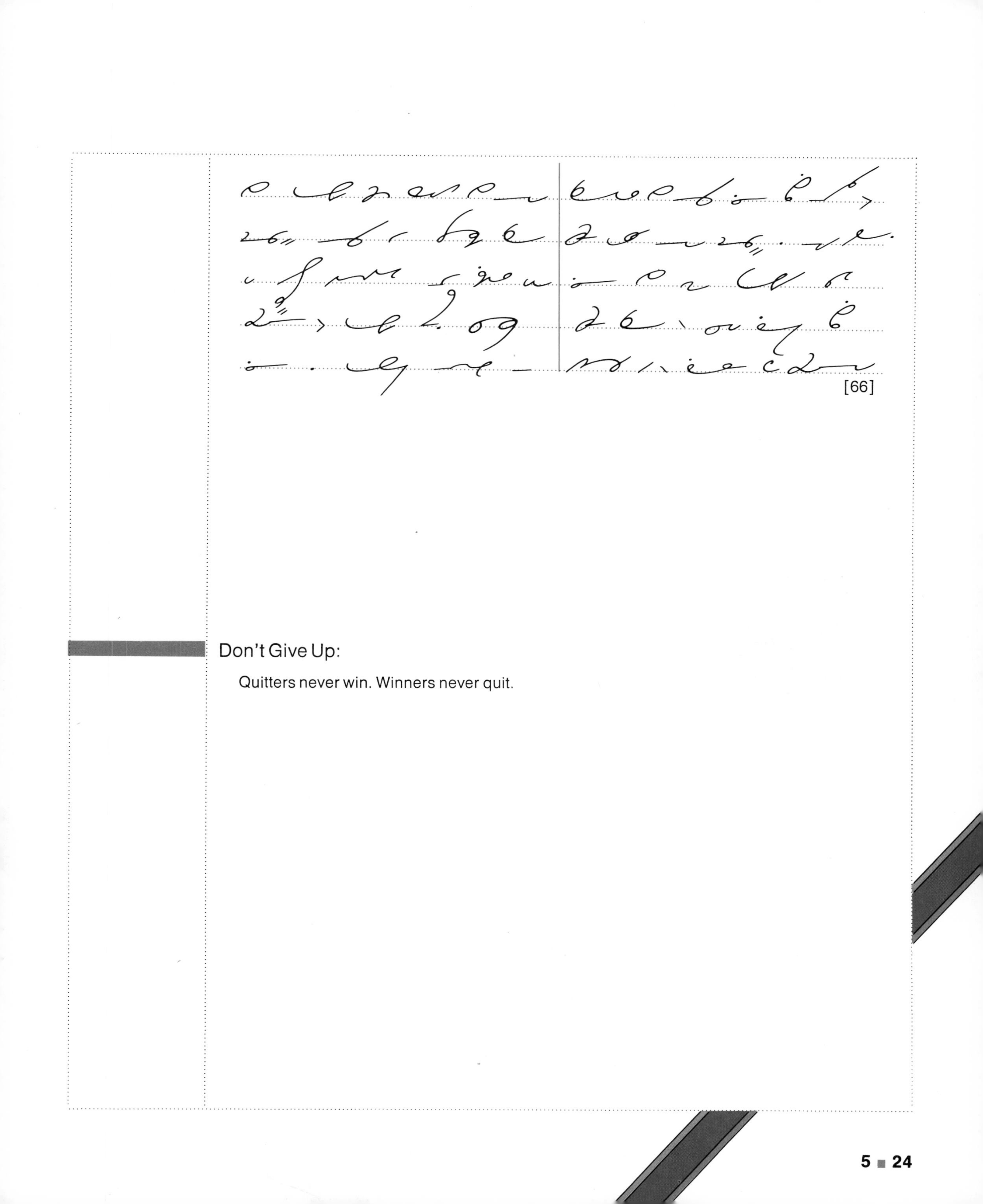

[66]

Don't Give Up:

Quitters never win. Winners never quit.

[133]

Transcription Quiz

The correct punctuation to the following letter calls for 6 commas—4 commas series, 2 commas parenthetical.

As you copy the Transcription Quiz in your notebook, be sure to insert the necessary commas at the proper points and to indicate the reason for the punctuation.

6

[114]

Principles

Sh, Ch, J

These three sounds are represented by downward straight lines.

Sh The shorthand stroke for *sh* (called "ish") is a very short downward straight stroke.

Ch The shorthand stroke for *ch* (called "chay") is a somewhat longer straight downward stroke approximately one-half the height of the space between the lines in your shorthand notebook.

J The shorthand stroke for the sound of *j*, as in *age* and *jury,* is a long downward straight stroke almost the full height of the space between the lines in your shorthand notebook.

■ Observe carefully the difference in the sizes of these strokes.

Ish .... **Chay** .... **J** ....

Ish

she, ish-e .... share, ish-a-r .... ship, ish-e-p ....

shown, ish-o-n .... issue, e-ish-oo .... insure, in-ish-oo-r ....

Chay

check, chay-e-k .... chair, chay-a-r .... search, s-e-r-chay ....

choose, chay-oo-s .... teach, t-e-chay .... church, chay-e-r-chay ....

hand·some

in·stalled

break

en·gi·neer

[136]

5

draw·ers

im·me·di·ate·ly

ar·ea

J

age, a-j | change, chay-a-n-j | jury, j-oo-r-e

wages, oo-a-j-s | large, l-a-r-j | jewels, j-oo-l-s

O, Aw

The small deep hook that represents the sound of *o,* as in *no,* also represents the vowel sounds heard in *hot* and *all.*

O

hot, h-o-t | office, o-f-e-s | sorry, s-o-r-e

copy, k-o-p-e | policy, p-o-l-s-e | stop, s-t-o-p

job, j-o-b | stock, s-t-o-k | watch, oo-o-chay

Aw

all, o-l | bought, b-o-t | author, o-ith-r

small, s-m-o-l | thought, ith-o-t | install, in-s-t-o-l

cause, k-o-s | daughter, d-o-t-r | wall, oo-o-l

Common Business Letter Salutations and Closings

Dear Sir | Yours truly | Yours very truly

Dear Madam | Sincerely yours | Very truly yours

Note: Although the expressions *Dear Sir, Dear Madam,* and *Yours truly* are considered too impersonal by letter-writing experts, they are still used by many dictators. Therefore, special abbreviations have been provided for them.

Reading and Writing Practice

Suggestion: Before you begin your work on the letters that follow, turn to page xiii and read the procedures outlined there for reading and writing shorthand. To make the most rapid progress, follow those procedures carefully.

conj

debt

and o

conj

too

con·sump·tion

[116]

3

when

de·sir·able

ap

[170]

4

coun·try's

Brief-Form Review Letter

This letter reviews the brief forms you have studied thus far.

1

[86]

2

[74]

3

Reading and Writing Practice

ours

breaks

ac·cess

equip·ment

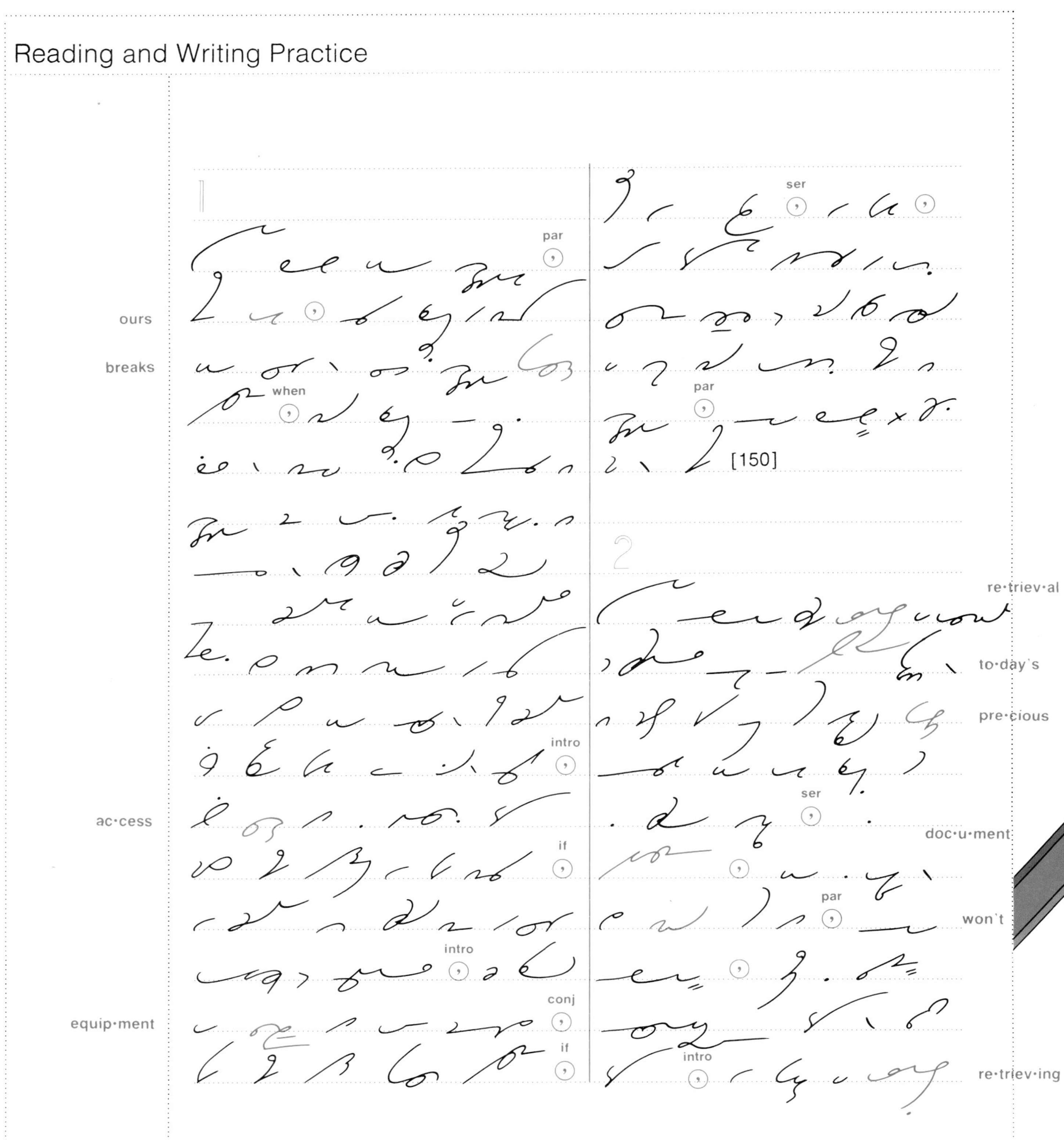

re·triev·al

to·day's

pre·cious

doc·u·ment

won't

re·triev·ing

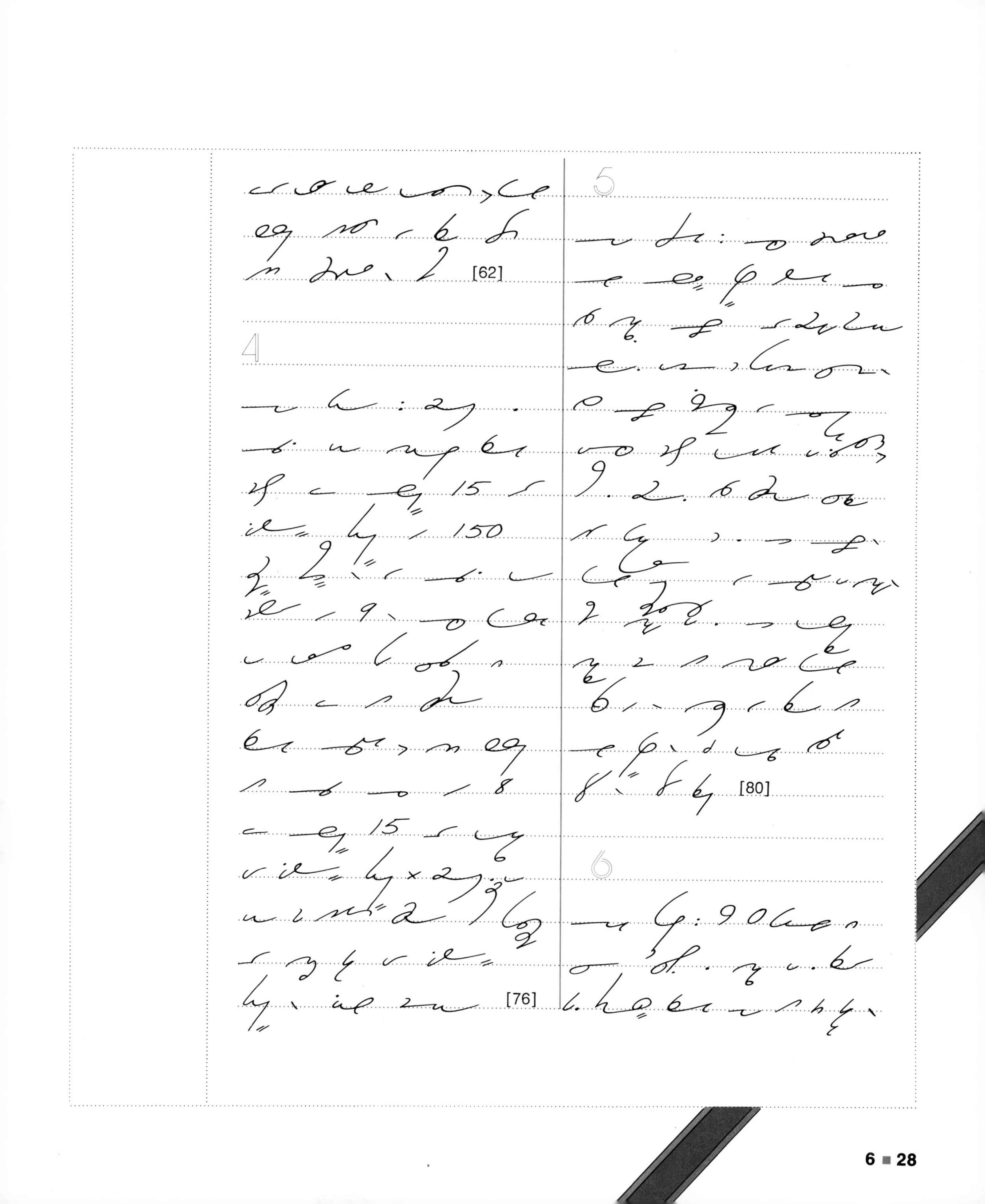

[62]

4

[76]

5

[80]

6

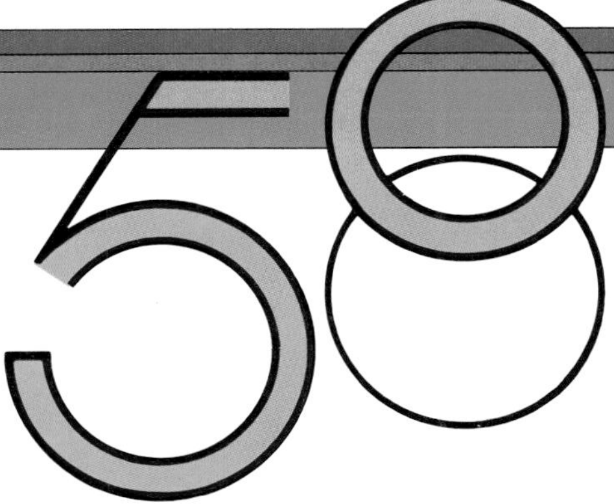

In Lesson 58 you will review all the joined word endings of Gregg Shorthand. The letters in the Reading and Writing Practice contain many illustrations of joined word endings.

Building Transcription Skills

Common Prefixes ■ re-

re- again

review To examine again.
retrieve To get back (as information) from storage again.
repeat To say again.
replenish To fill or supply again.
reconsider To take up again.

Business Vocabulary Builder

complex Hard to analyze and solve.

access The ability to enter.

compilation Collection.

[65]

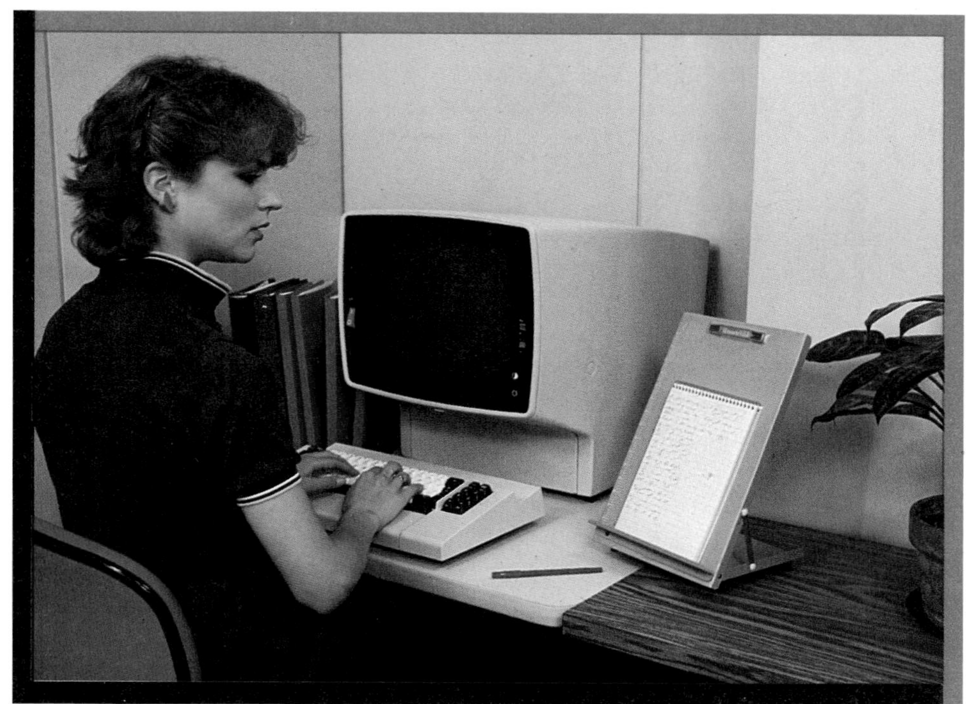

Shorthand skill and word processing equipment are partners in productivity—both helping to increase office efficiency.

par

ap

conj

daugh·ter

[124]

6

un·til

[35]

Transcription Quiz

For you to supply 6 commas—2 commas apposition, 1 comma *as* clause, 2 commas parenthetical, 1 comma *if* clause.

7

[121]

7

Principles

Brief Forms

Here is another group of nine brief forms for very common words. Learn them well!

would	this	them
for	good	which
there (their)	they	be,* by

**Be* is also used as a word beginning in words such as *believe* and *because.*

Spell: be-l-e-v, believe

believe	because	begin

Word Ending -ly

The common word ending *-ly* is represented by the *e* circle.

Spell: l-a-t-lē, lately

lately	mainly	mostly
nearly	plainly	only
badly	briefly	highly
costly	namely	daily

■ Observe that in *highly* the small circle for *-ly* is written inside the large circle; that in *daily* it is added to the other side of the *d* after the *a* has been written.

[121]

5

lo·cal

ev·ery·one

re·al·ize

of·ten

up·date

fu·el

emis·sion

to·day's

than

Amer·i·ca's

rev·e·nue

strength

intro

as

as

conj

intro

when

ser

Amounts and Quantities

When you take dictation in the business office, you will frequently have occasion to write amounts and quantities. Here are some devices that will enable you to write them rapidly.

600	$12	$3.40
8,000	$3,000	8 percent
800,000	$700,000	7 o'clock

■ Observe that the *n* for *hundred* and the *ith* for *thousand* are placed underneath the figure.

Reading and Writing Practice

Brief-Form Letter

The following letter contains one or more illustrations of the brief forms in this lesson.

[111]

bud·get

Wil·son's

ef·fect

ap

intro

as

or·di·nance

ex·pan·sion

par

[150]

[131]

3

par

4

com·plain·ing

when

neigh·bor

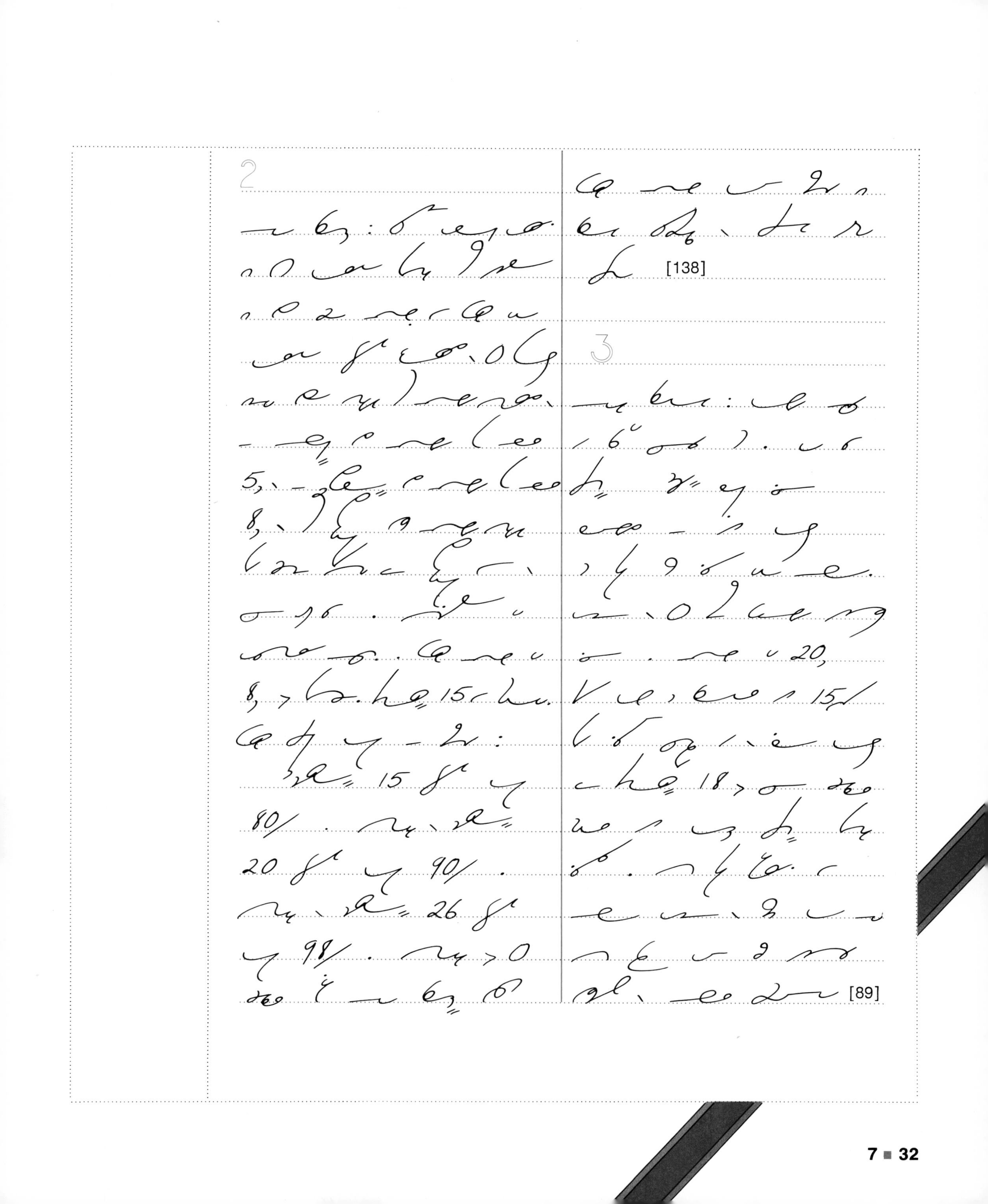

2

[138]

3

[89]

Business Vocabulary Builder

emission Substance discharged into the air as by an automobile engine.

utilize To turn to profitable use; to make use of.

marketing The field of business concerned with distributing and selling goods and services.

complimentary Expressing approval or admiration; favorable.

Reading and Writing Practice

1

sum·ma·ry

ca·reer

ter·ri·to·ry

ser

va·can·cy

if par

touch

par

mean·while

[115]

2

ap

15

intro

sec·re·tary

40

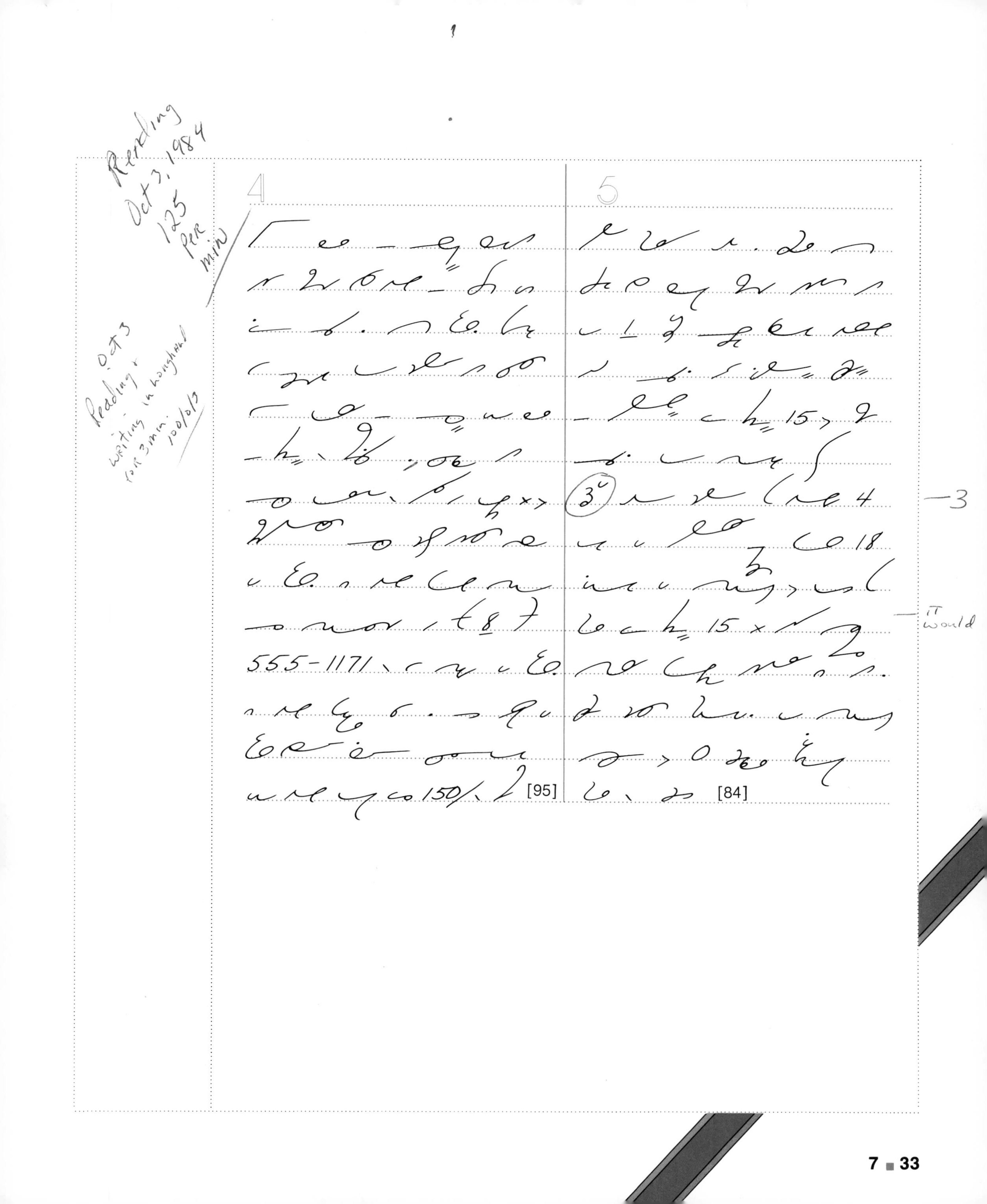

4

[95]

5

[84]

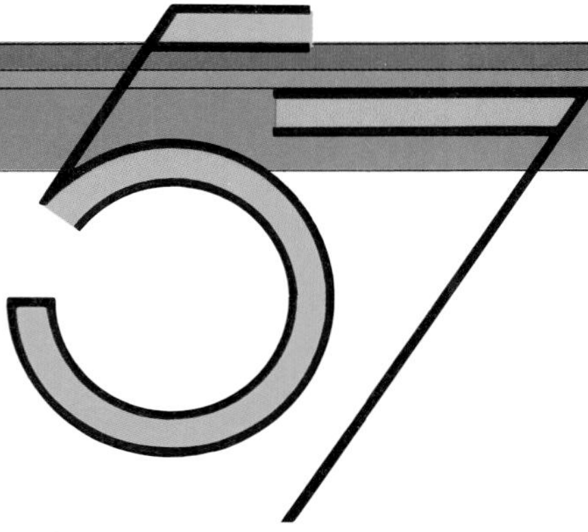

As you read in the early stages of your Gregg Shorthand, vowels may be omitted in some words to help gain fluency of writing. In this assignment you will find many illustrations of words from which vowels are omitted.

Building Transcription Skills

Spelling Families ■ -ery, -ary, -ory

Words Ending in -ery

bind-ery	ma-chin-ery	re-cov-ery
de-liv-ery	mas-tery	re-fin-ery
dis-cov-ery	mys-tery	scen-ery
gro-cery	que-ry	sta-tio-nery

Words Ending in -ary

an-ni-ver-sa-ry	el-e-men-ta-ry	pri-ma-ry
com-pli-men-ta-ry	glos-sa-ry	sec-ond-ary
con-trary	itin-er-ary	sec-re-tary
cus-tom-ary	li-brary	tem-po-rary
dic-tio-nary	nec-es-sary	vo-cab-u-lary

Words Ending in -ory

de-pos-i-tory	fac-to-ry	man-da-to-ry
di-rec-to-ry	his-to-ry	sat-is-fac-to-ry
ex-ec-u-to-ry	in-tro-duc-to-ry	ter-ri-to-ry
ex-plan-a-to-ry	in-ven-to-ry	vic-to-ry

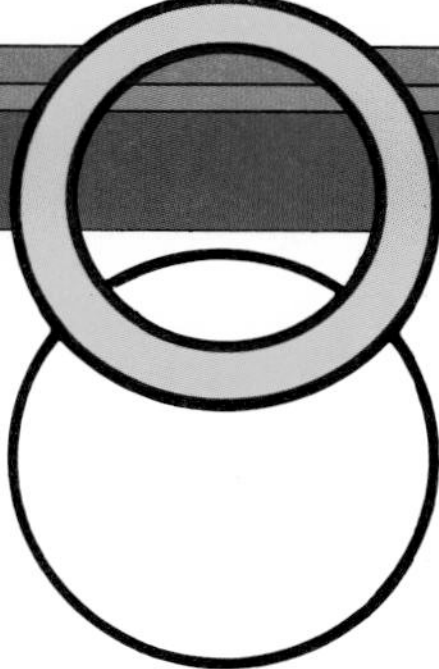

Principles

Word Ending -tion

The word ending *-tion* (sometimes spelled *-sion, -cian,* or *-shion)* is represented by *ish.*

Spell: a-k-shun, action

action .... operation .... national ....
occasion .... physician .... nationally ....
election .... fashion .... cautioned ....
position .... nations .... inflation ....

Word Endings -cient, -ciency

The word ending *-cient* (or *-tient*) is represented by *ish-t*; *-ciency*, by *ish-s-e.*

Spell: p-a-shun-t, patient

e-f-e-shun-s-e, efficiency

patient .... ancient .... efficiency ....
patiently .... efficient .... proficiency ....

T for To in Phrases

In phrases, *to* is represented by *t* when it is followed by a downstroke.

to have .... to check .... to sell ....

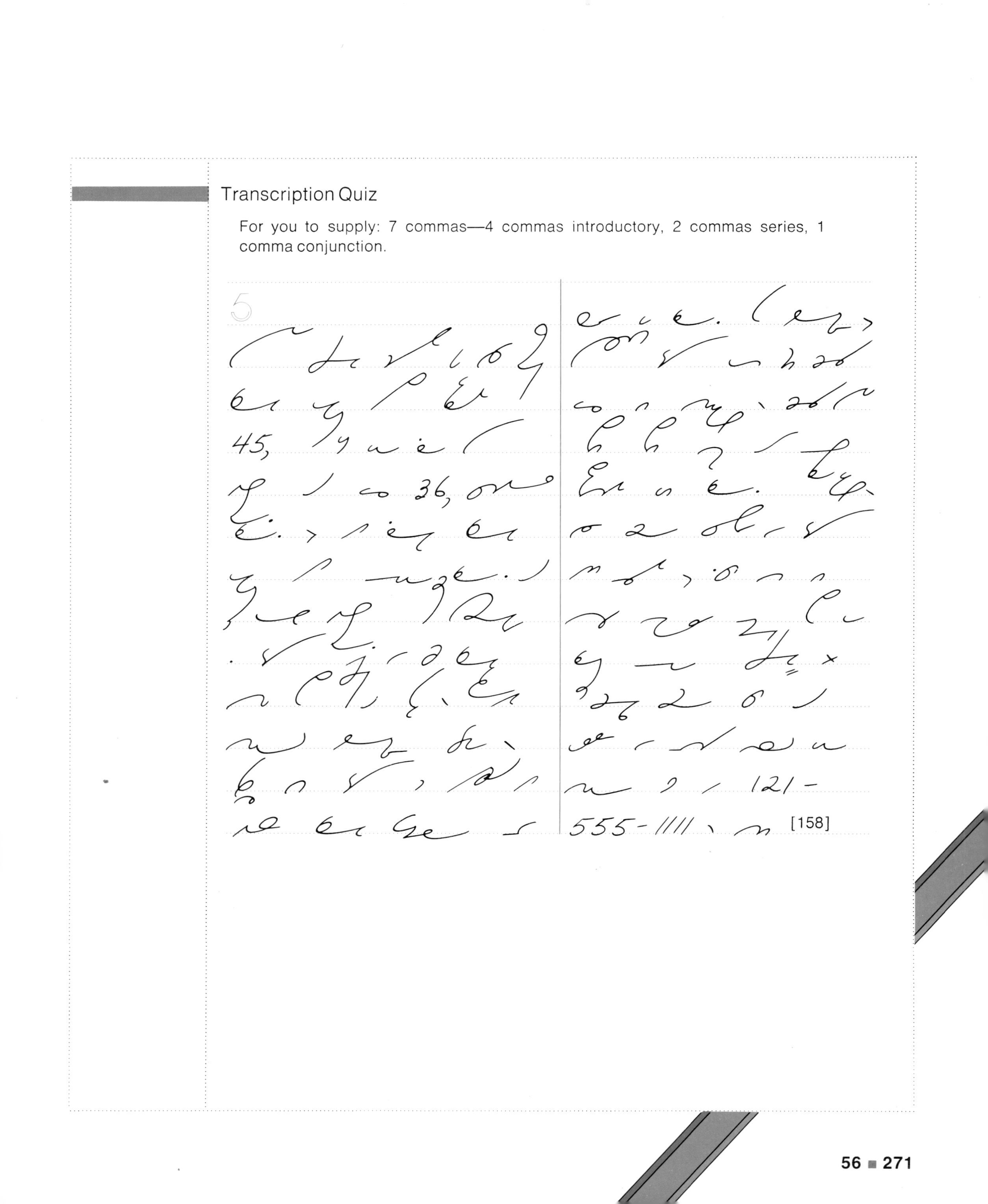

Transcription Quiz

For you to supply: 7 commas—4 commas introductory, 2 commas series, 1 comma conjunction.

5

[158]

to be	to buy	to serve
to say	to plan	to charge
to see	to place	to change

Reading and Writing Practice

Brief-Form Review Letter

The following letter reviews the brief forms you studied in Lesson 8.

1

[138]

2

if

ar·ea

ap

con·ve·nient

[181]

4

adopt

and o

intro

de·pen·dents

re·im·bursed

intro

if

touch

per·son·nel

[137]

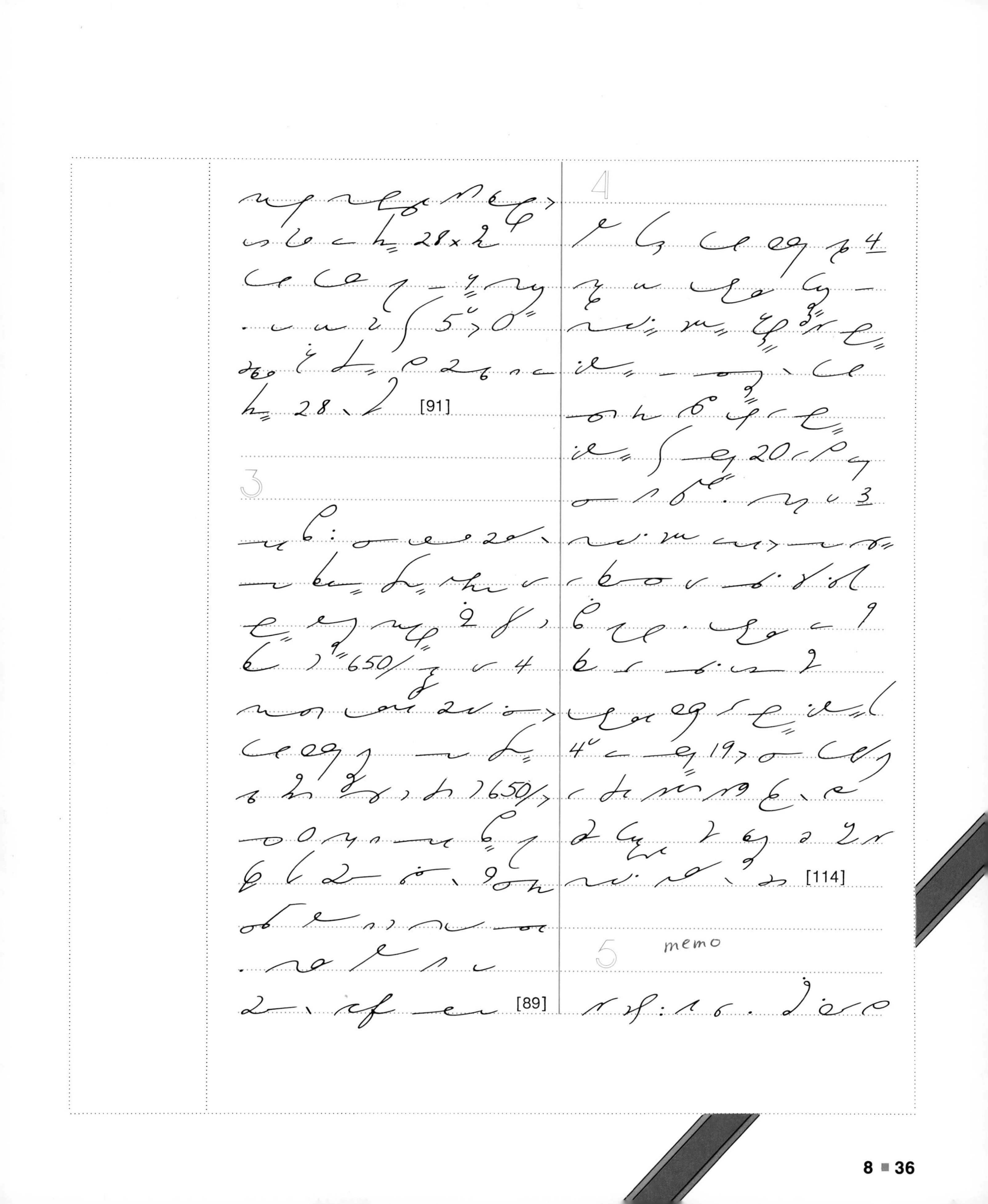

[91]

3

[89]

4

[114]

5

memo

[147]

cour·te·ous

and o

or·ga·ni·za·tion

intro

intro

pro·mot·ing

as

agen·cy

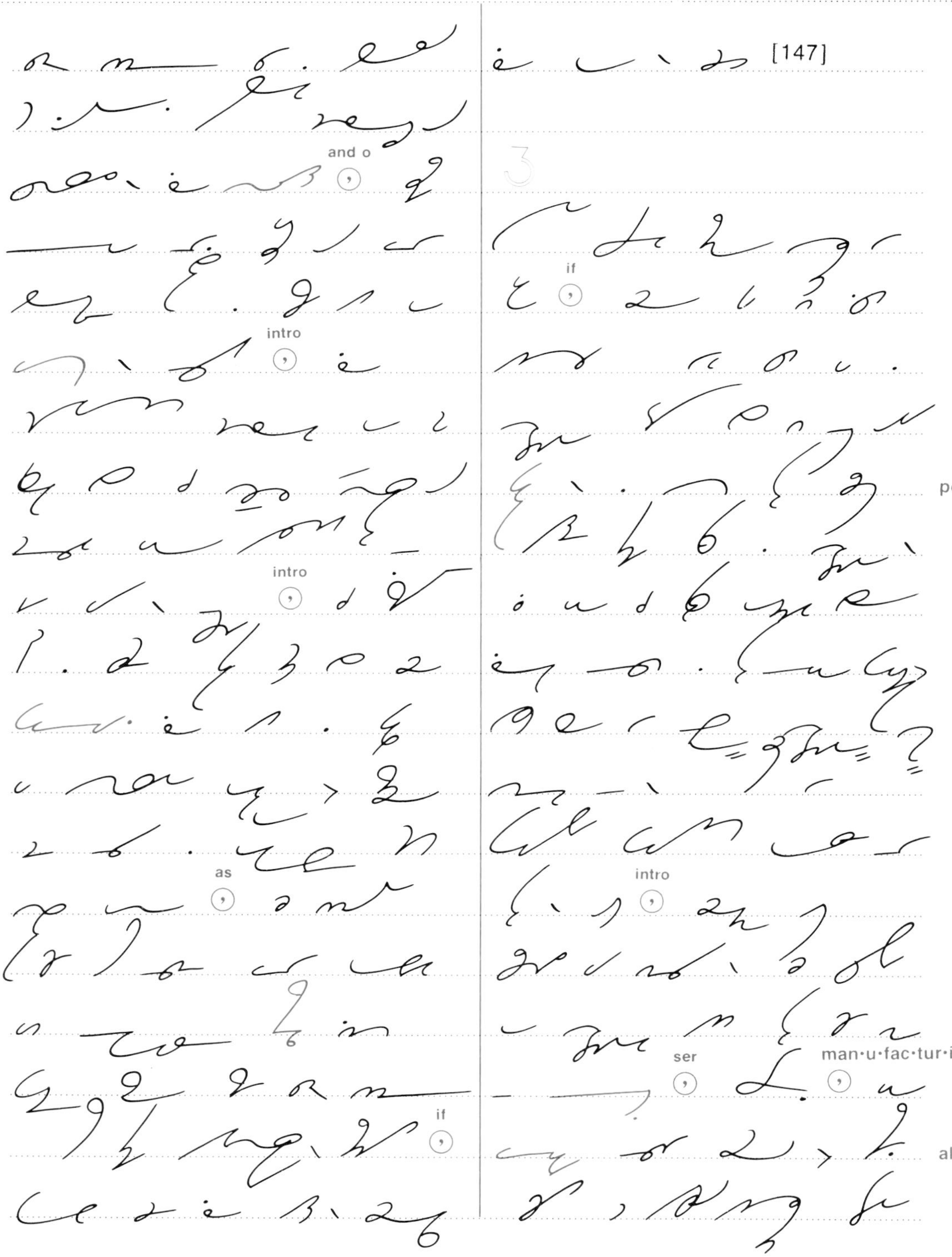

if

3

if

pos·si·ble

intro

ser

man·u·fac·tur·ing

al·most

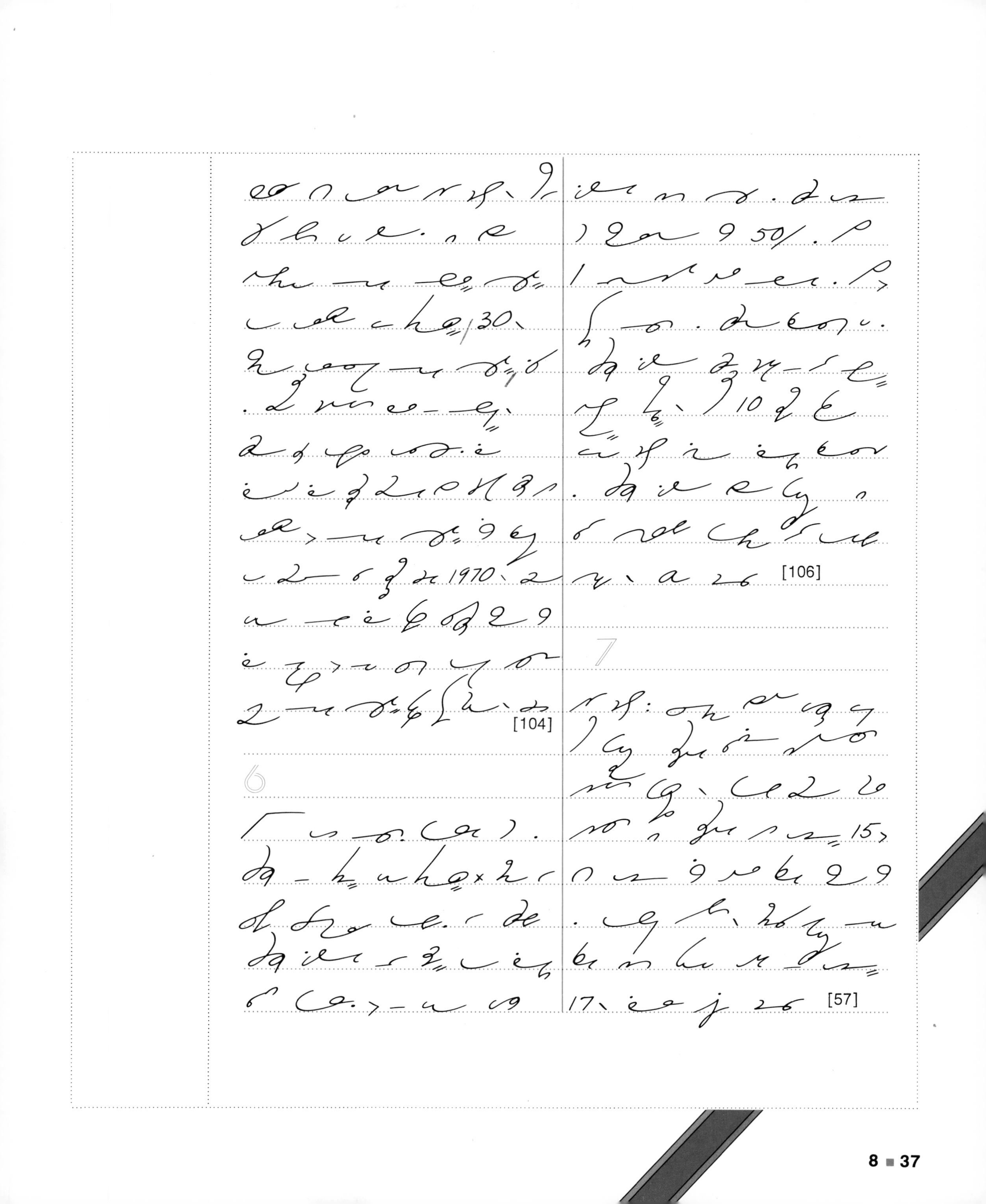

[104]

6

[106]

7

[57]

Business Vocabulary Builder

adhere To stick by.

personable Pleasing, attractive.

reimbursed Repaid.

Reading and Writing Practice

1

over·weight

if

par

lose

if

when

ad·here

ser

sen·si·ble

hearty

conj

[122]

2

per·son·able

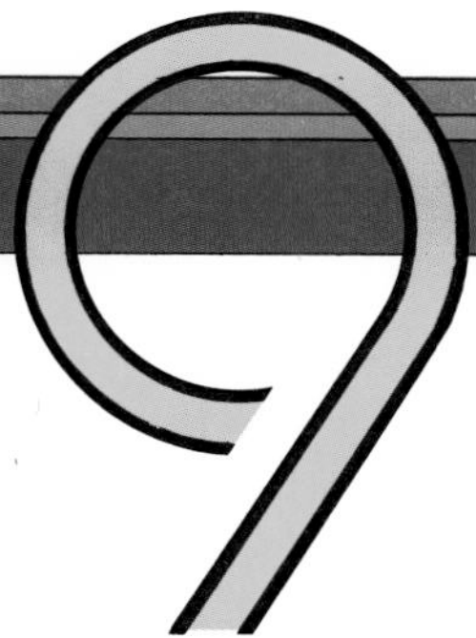

Principles

Nd

The shorthand strokes for *n-d* are joined without an angle to form the *nd* blend, as in *signed.*

Nd

Compare: sign signed

Spell: s-ī-end, signed; end-o-r-s, endorse

land friend kind

planned spend mind

trained happened bind

errand brand endorse

Nt

The stroke that represents *nd* also represents *nt,* as in *sent.*

Spell: s-e-ent, sent; ent-oo, into

sent printed agent

rent painted vacant

prevent planted into

current parents entire

Lesson 56 also contains a general review of the major principles of Gregg Shorthand.

Building Transcription Skills

Similar-Words Drill ■ adapt, adopt, adept

adapt To adjust to a situation.

We will adapt our computer to the needs of your business.

adopt To take as one's own.

If you adopt this plan, you will be delighted with it.

adept Skillful, proficient.

He is adept at solving financial problems.

Ses

The sound of *ses,* as in *senses,* is represented by joining the two forms of *s.*

Compare: sense .... senses ....

face .... faces ....

Spell: s-e-n-sez, senses

places	causes	reduces ....
prices	chances	produces ....
addresses	increases	cases ....
glasses	necessary	services ....

Sis, Sus

The similar sounds of *sis,* as in *sister,* and *sus,* as in *versus,* are also represented by joining the two forms of *s.*

Spell: sez-t-r, sister; v-e-r-sez, versus

sister	assist	analysis ....
basis	insist	versus ....

Reading and Writing Practice

Brief-Form Review Letter

This letter reviews the brief forms you studied in Lesson 7 as well as many of those in previous lessons.

equipped

conj

,

[134]

Transcription Quiz

For you to supply: 5 commas—1 comma *and* omitted, 1 comma apposition, 1 comma *if* clause, 1 comma parenthetical, 1 comma introductory.

6

[133]

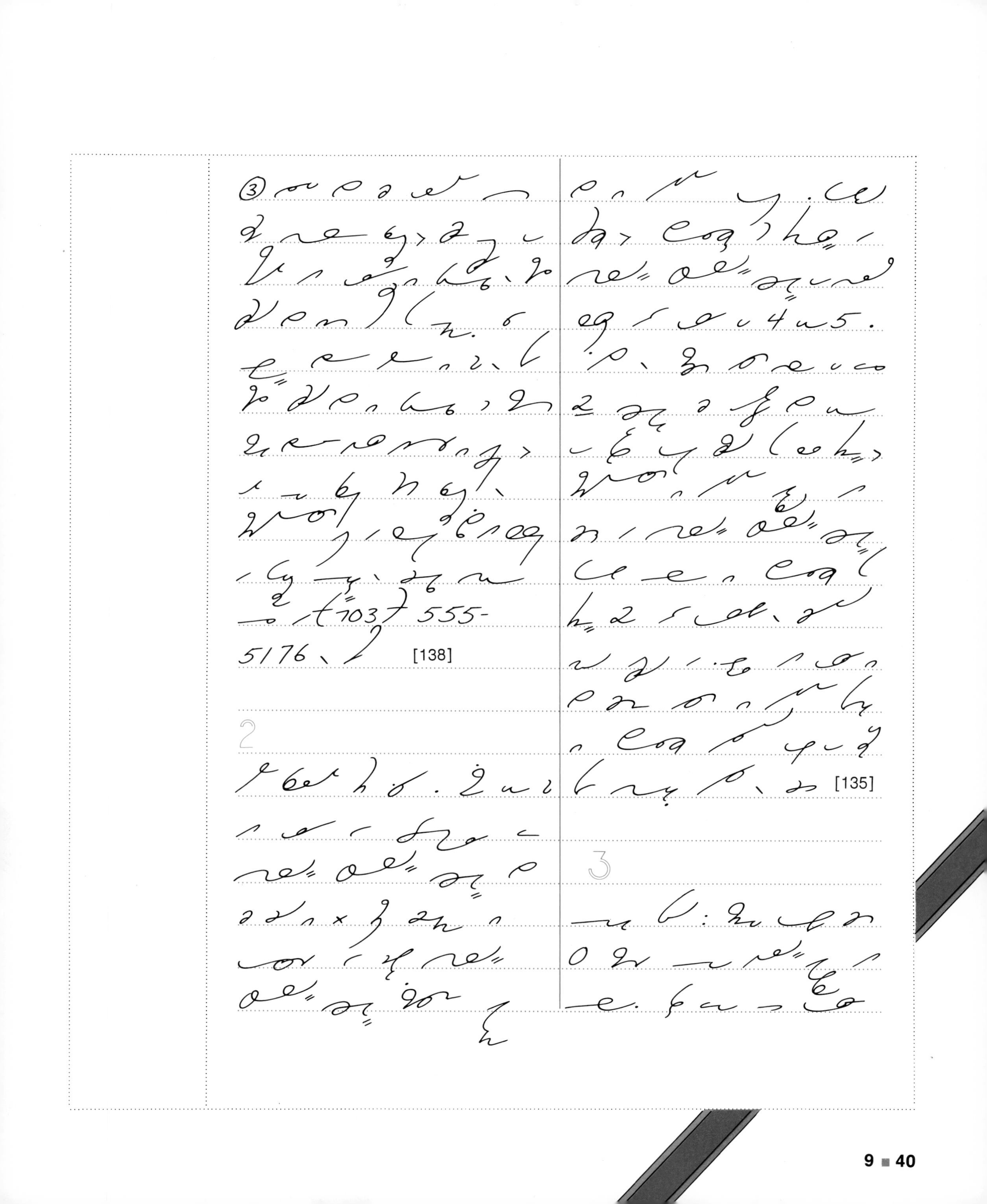

(103) 555-5176 [138]

2

[135]

3

[136]

[114]

4

5

prompt·ly

intro

later

conj

here·to·fore

intro

when

hand·some·ly

conj

intro

en·trance

vol·ume

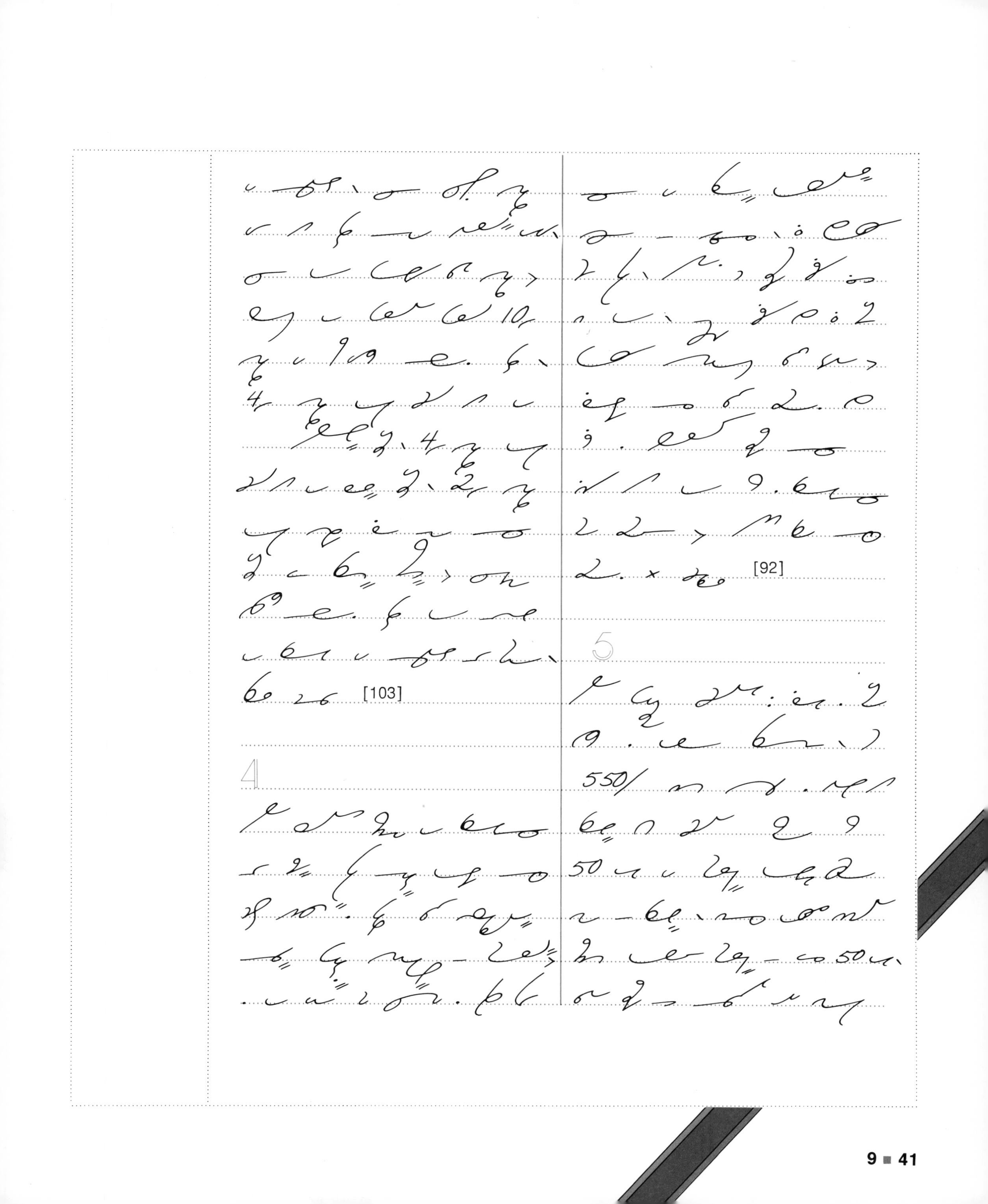

[103]

4

[92]

5

han·dle

their

Chi·ca·go

par ser intro

[133]

3

an·a·lyze

ex·ces·sive

af·fects

deci·bels

lev·els

when

rec·om·mend

if

sur·vey

[103]

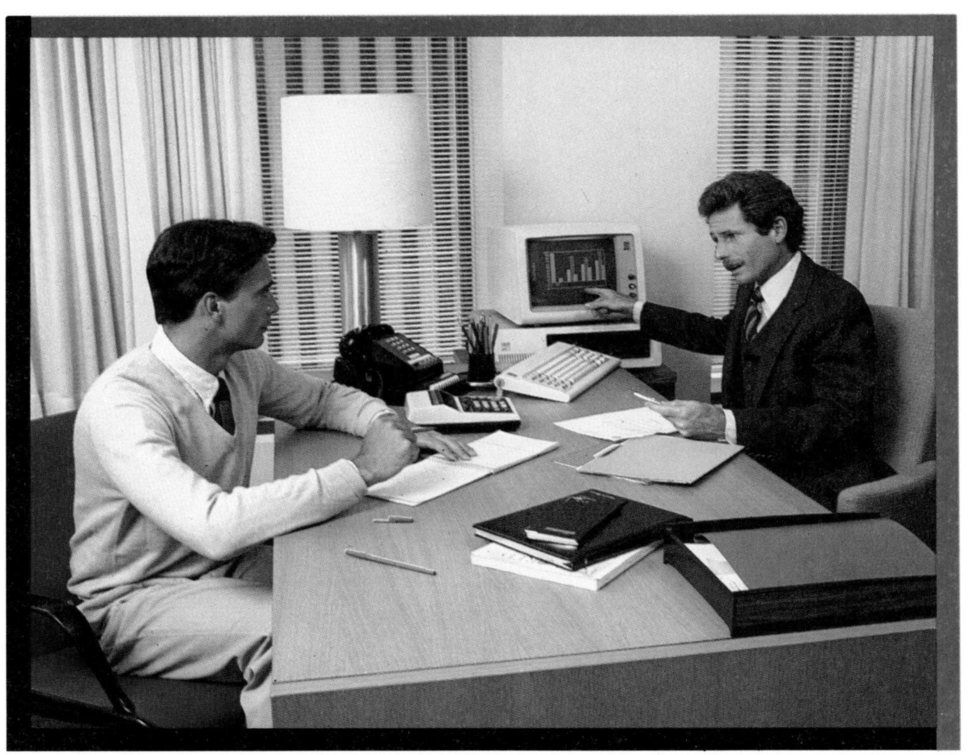

Secretaries and their managers often work as a team in the development of documents, such as reports.

Reading and Writing Practice

1

ap

its

known

when

1935

manufacturers

intro

appropriate

descriptive

ser

copiers

intro

accurately

intro

investor

[158]

2

unique

if

intro

foliage

10

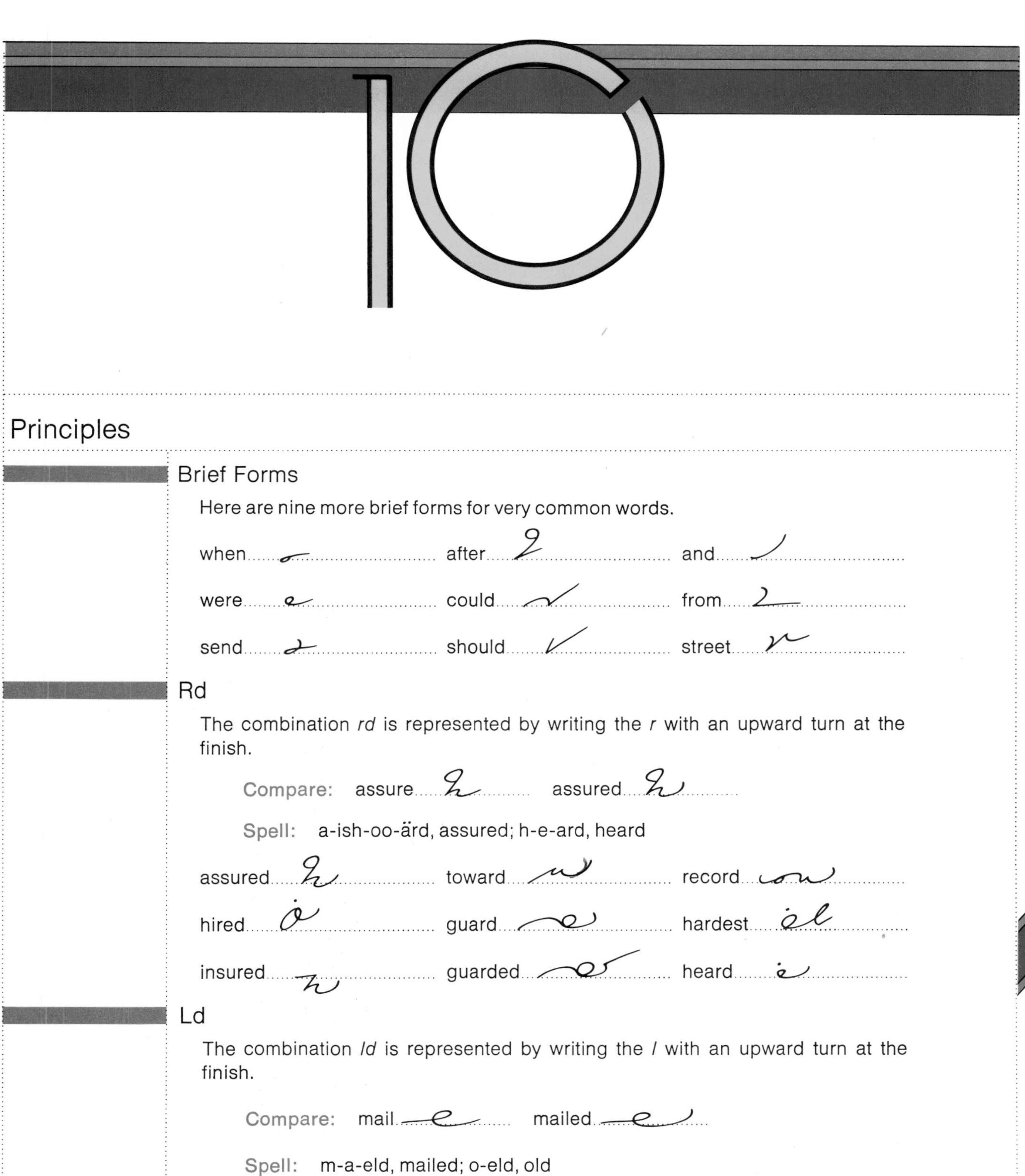

Principles

Brief Forms

Here are nine more brief forms for very common words.

when	after	and
were	could	from
send	should	street

Rd

The combination *rd* is represented by writing the *r* with an upward turn at the finish.

Compare: assure ... assured

Spell: a-ish-oo-ärd, assured; h-e-ard, heard

assured	toward	record
hired	guard	hardest
insured	guarded	heard

Ld

The combination *ld* is represented by writing the *l* with an upward turn at the finish.

Compare: mail ... mailed

Spell: m-a-eld, mailed; o-eld, old

This lesson contains a general review of the major principles of Gregg Shorthand.

Building Transcription Skills

Common Suffixes ■ -er, -or

-er, -or One who.
gardener One who cultivates fruits, flowers, herbs, vegetables, etc.
customer One who buys.
manufacturer One who makes products for use.
supplier One who provides materials that fill needs.
investor One who commits money in order to earn a financial return.

Business Vocabulary Builder

excessive Too much.

decades Periods of ten years.

foliage A cluster of leaves, flowers, and branches.

decibel A unit for measuring the intensity of sound.

mailed	failed	build
old	filled	builder
sold	told	folded

Tighten curb

Been in Phrases

The word *been* is represented by *b* after *have, has, had.*

have been	had been	I could have been
I have been	I have not been	I should have been
you have been	it has been	had not been

Able in Phrases

The word *able* is represented by *a* after *be* or *been.*

I have been able	I should be able
I have not been able	you will be able
you have been able	you should be able
you have not been able	I may be able

Reading and Writing Practice

Brief-Form Letter

The following letter contains one or more illustrations of the brief forms presented in this lesson.

150

uten·sils

intro

set·tlers 1623

site

intro

1650

conj

opened

era

1860

[317]

Be sure to take a steno notepad with you when you go on a job interview because you may be asked to take a dictation and transcription test.

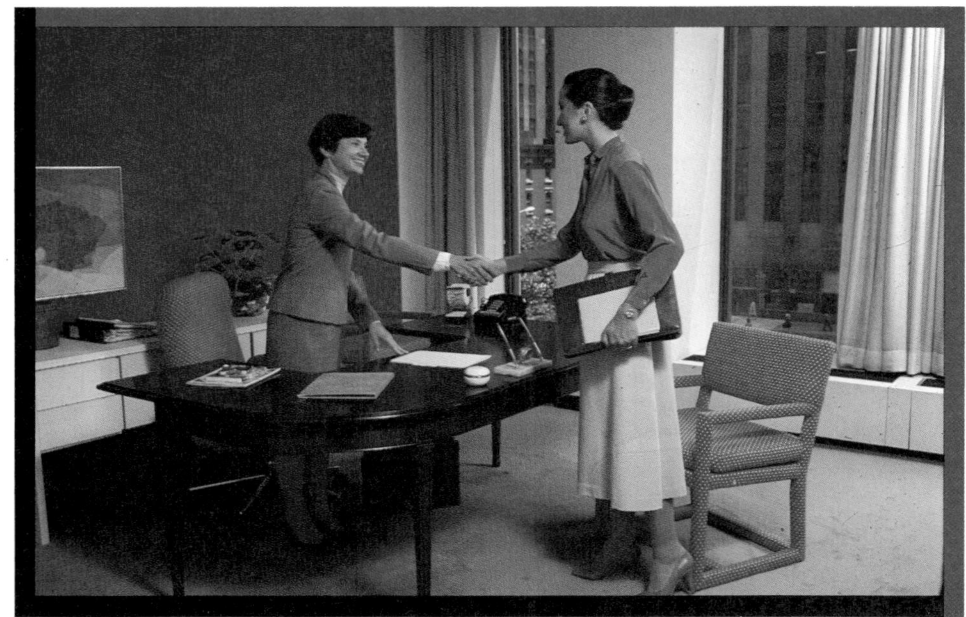

[167]

2

[89]

3

Reading and Writing Practice

The Retail Store

in·sti·tu·tion

fa·mil·iar

di·rect·ly

chan·nel

gram·mar

al·ways

aware

Retailing Is Important.

for·est

ocean

fac·to·ry

re·tail·er

co·lors

com·pet·i·tive

Early Trading.

trad·ing

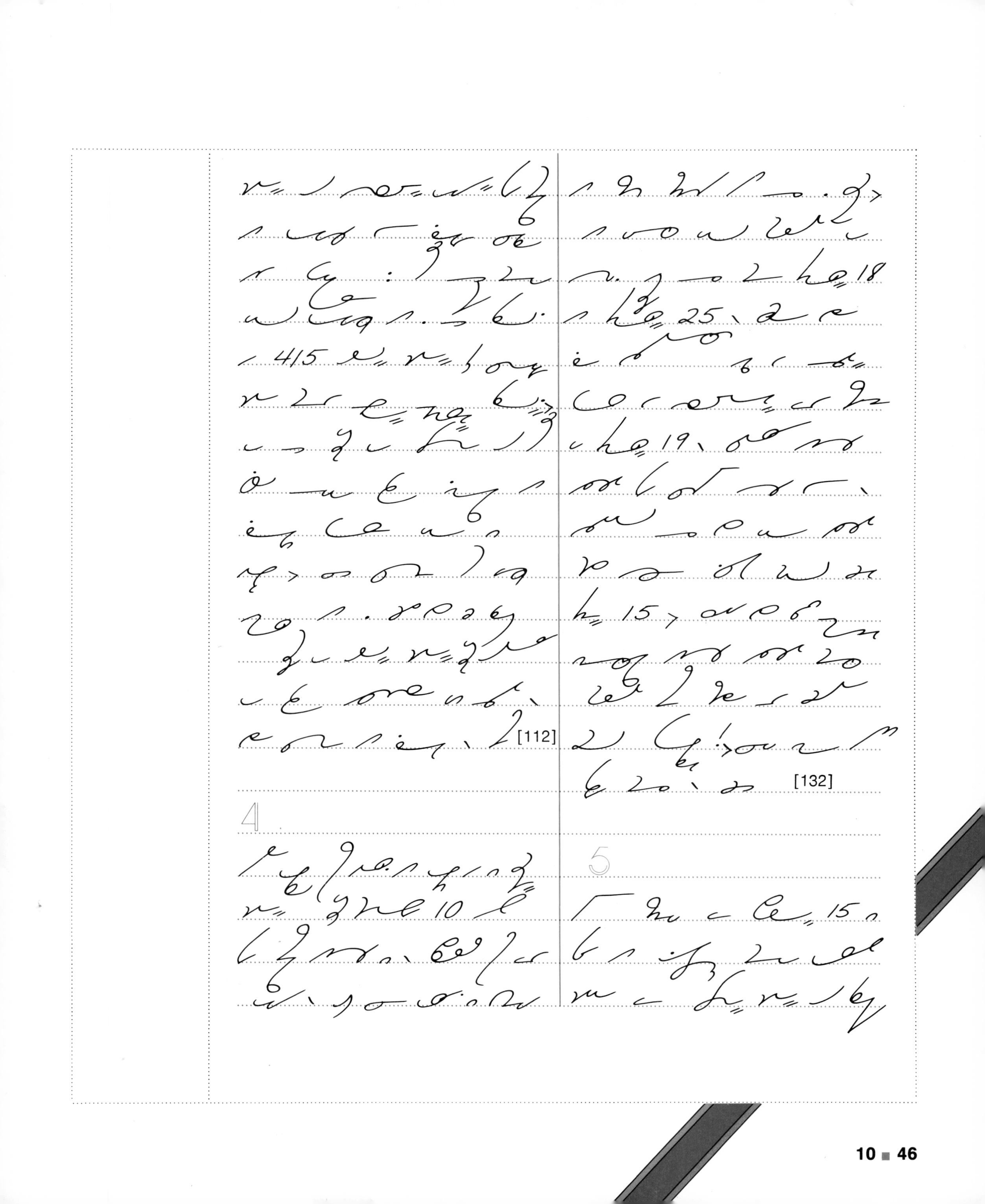

[112]

[132]

4

5

You will find the article in Lesson 54 interesting and enlightening.

Building Transcription Skills

Spelling Families ■ -er, -or, -ar

Be very careful when transcribing words ending in the sound of *er*; the ending may be spelled *-er*, *-or*, or *-ar*. When in doubt, look the word up!

Words Ending in -er

con-sum-er	of-fer	set-tler
cus-tom-er	read-er	sweat-er
man-ag-er	re-tail-er	sub-scrib-er

Words Ending in -or

col-or	gov-er-nor	pro-fes-sor
dic-ta-tor	hu-mor	sen-a-tor
fac-tor	ma-jor	su-per-vi-sor

Words Ending in -ar

cel-lar	gram-mar	reg-u-lar
col-lar	par-tic-u-lar	sug-ar

Business Vocabulary Builder

basically Fundamentally.

site The place, scene, or point of something.

era The period of existence of something.

[82]

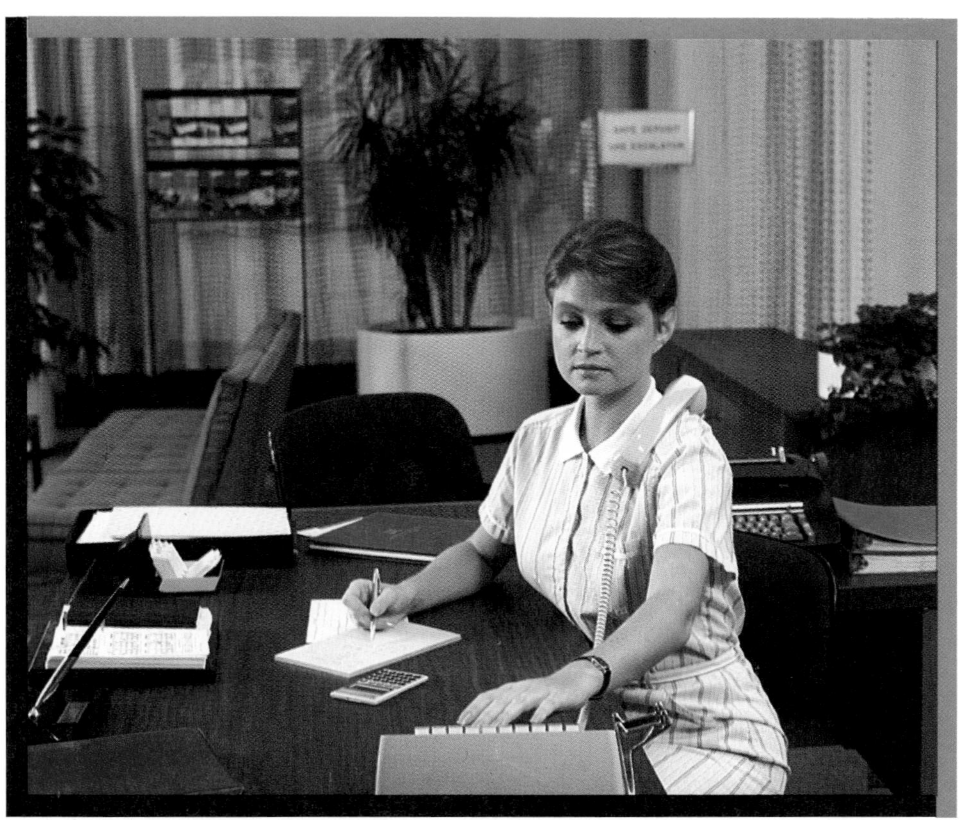

Shorthand is a door opener to many careers. For example, secretaries to bank executives have the opportunity to become customer service representatives.

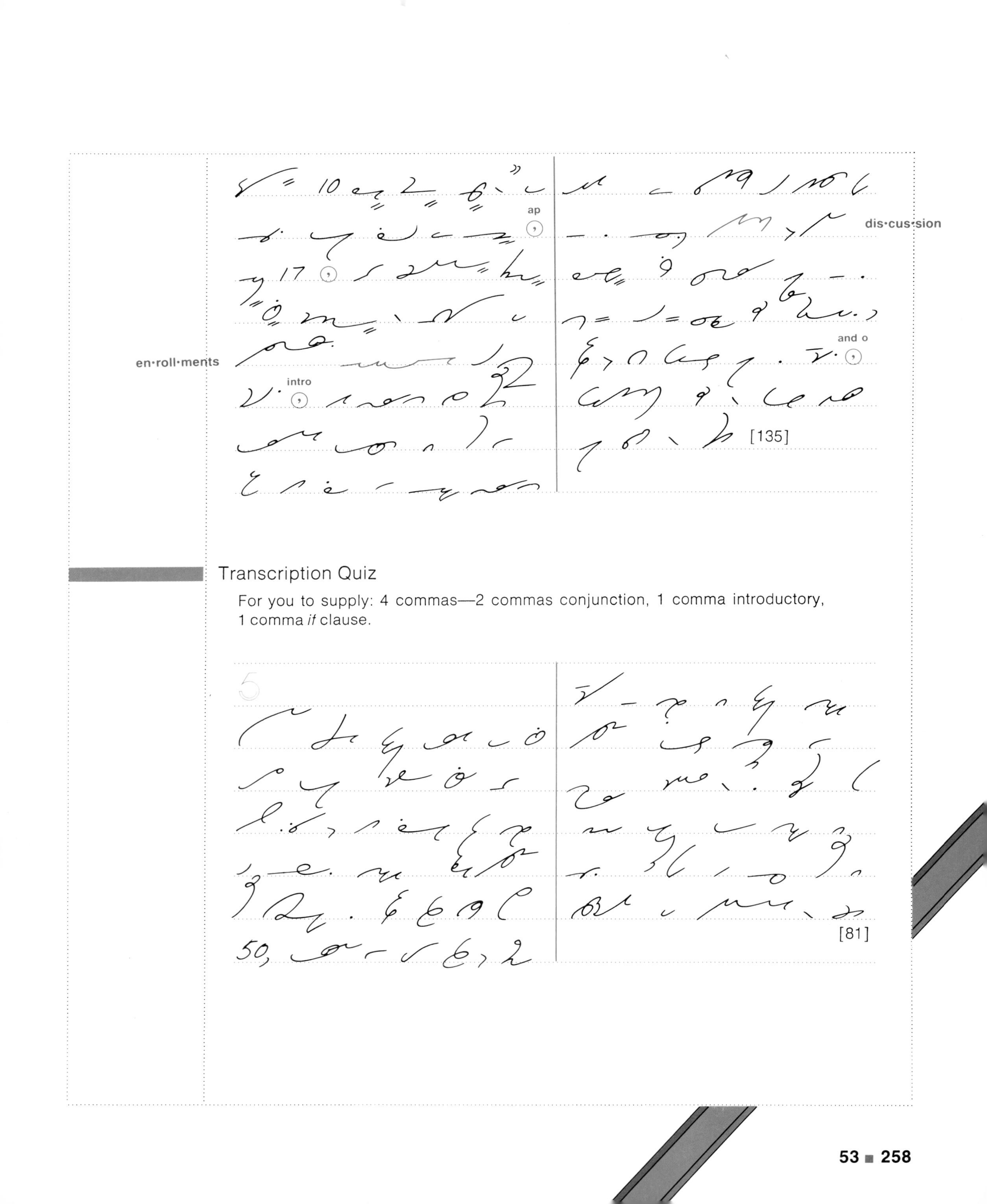

ap

en·roll·ments

intro

dis·cus·sion

and o

[135]

Transcription Quiz

For you to supply: 4 commas—2 commas conjunction, 1 comma introductory, 1 comma *if* clause.

5

[81]

Principles

Brief Forms

work .... circular .... enclose ....

yesterday .... order .... was ....

glad .... soon .... thank ....

Brief-Form Derivatives and Phrases

thanks .... gladly .... thank you ....

worked .... ordered .... thank you for ....

■ **Observe:** **1** *Thanks* is written with a disjoined left *s* in the dot position.

2 The *d* representing the past tense of *order* is joined with a jog.

3 The dot in *thank* is omitted in phrases.

U, OO

The hook that represents the sound of *oo,* as in *to,* also represents the vowel sounds in *does* and *book.*

U

Spell: d-oo-s, does

does .... none .... us ....

res·er·va·tions

and o

ef·fi·cient

linked

[124]

3

aware

conj

as·sist

de·par·ture

ef·fort·less

if

as

intro

check·out

if

store·room

[142]

4

ap

drug ..... number ..... just .....

up ..... enough ..... adjust .....

product ..... must ..... precious .....

■ **Observe:** 1 The hook in the words in the second column is turned on its side.

2 The *oo-s* in the words in the third column is joined without an angle.

oo

Spell: b-oo-k, book

book ..... put ..... pull .....

cook ..... push ..... stood .....

look ..... foot ..... sugar .....

took ..... full ..... wood .....

Building Transcription Skills

Business Vocabulary Builder

As a stenographer or secretary, you will constantly be dealing with words. Consequently, the larger the vocabulary you have at your command, the easier your task will be when taking dictation and transcribing.

To help you build your vocabulary at the same time that you are learning shorthand, a Business Vocabulary Builder is provided in Lesson 11 and in many of the lessons that follow. The Business Vocabulary Builder consists of brief definitions of business words and expressions, selected from the Reading and Writing Practice of the lesson, that may be unfamiliar to you.

Be sure to read each Business Vocabulary Builder before you begin your work on the Reading and Writing Practice that follows it.

Business Vocabulary Builder

nursing home An establishment where care is provided for the aged or sick who are unable to take care of themselves properly.

utmost The most possible; the greatest amount.

Reading and Writing Practice

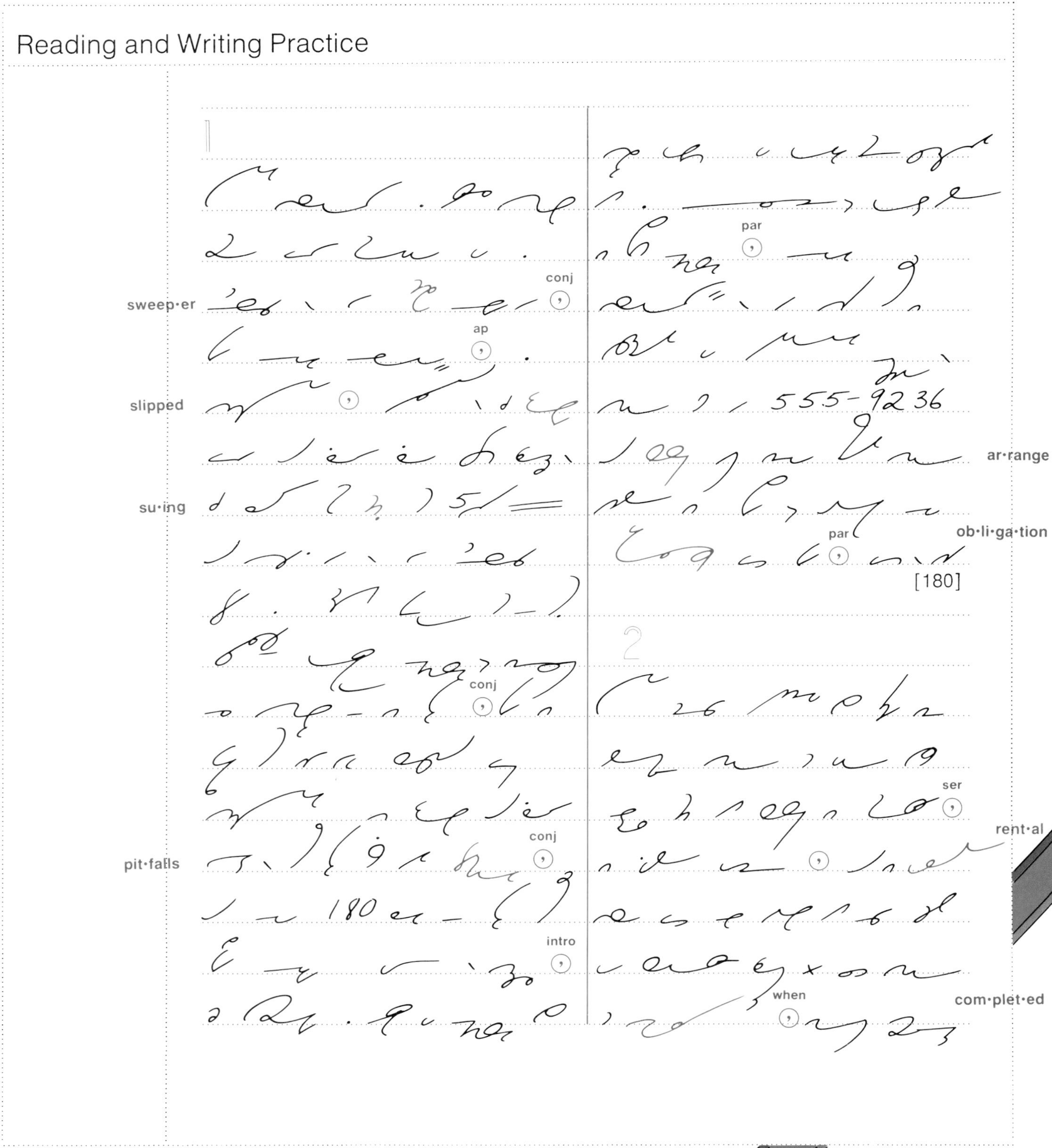

Reading and Writing Practice

Brief-Form Letter

1

[119]

2

Lesson 53, like Lesson 52, contains a general review of the major principles of Gregg Shorthand.

Building Transcription Skills

Common Prefixes ■ trans-

trans- across; over; from one place to another

transcontinental Across a continent.
transfer Convey from one person or place to another.
transport Carry from one place to another.
transmit Hand over from one person to another.

Business Vocabulary Builder

pitfalls Hidden or not easily recognized dangers or difficulties.

confirmations New assurances of the validity of something.

linked Joined to.

555-9274 [144]

3

[99]

4

3

1,450

[102]

when

if

re·trac·tion

suit

de·lin·quent

intro

intro

pre·pay·ment

[214]

Transcription Quiz

For you to supply: 7 commas—3 commas introductory, 2 commas parenthetical, 2 commas series.

5

[115]

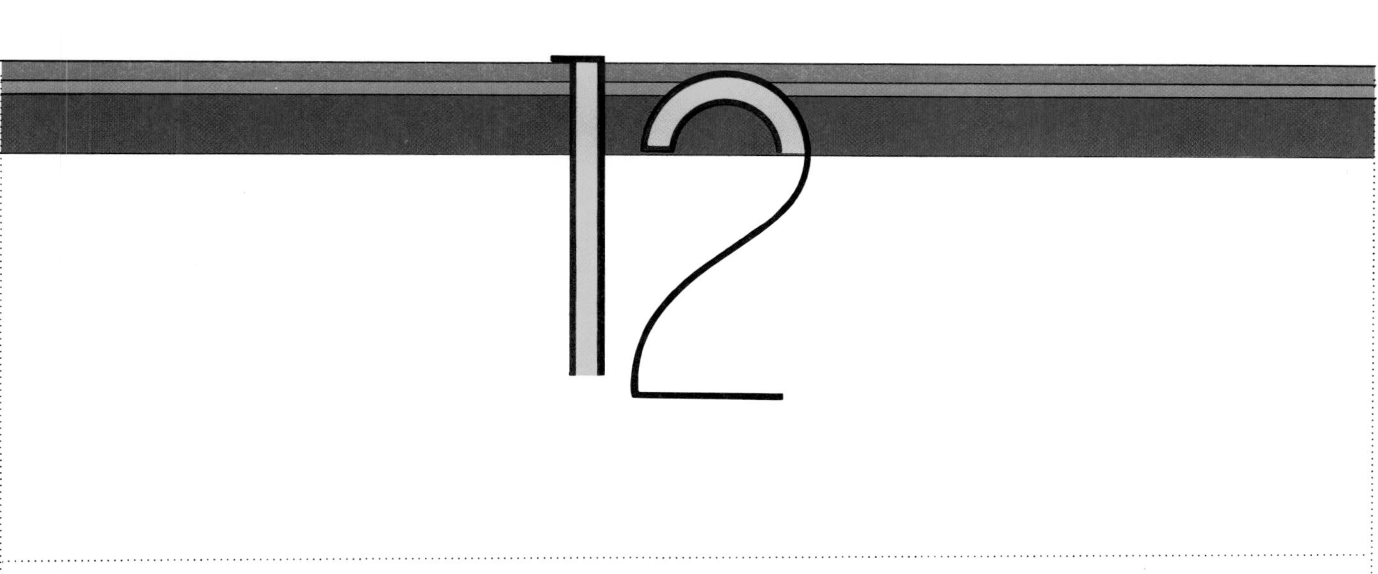

Principles

W in the Body of a Word

When the sound of *w* occurs in the body of a word, as in *quick,* it is represented by a short dash underneath the vowel following the *w* sound. The dash is inserted after the rest of the outline has been written.

Spell: k-oo-e-k, quick

quick, between, qualify, quote, square, hardware, quit, twice, roadway, equip, twine, always

Ted

The combination *ted* is represented by joining *t* and *d* into one long upward stroke.

Ted

Compare: heat, heed, heated

Spell: h-e-ted, heated

listed, accepted, adopted, acted, rested, located

fu·els

loose-leaf

sub·ur·ban

[159]

3

re·ferred

agree·able

[108]

4

ac·cused

fore·closed

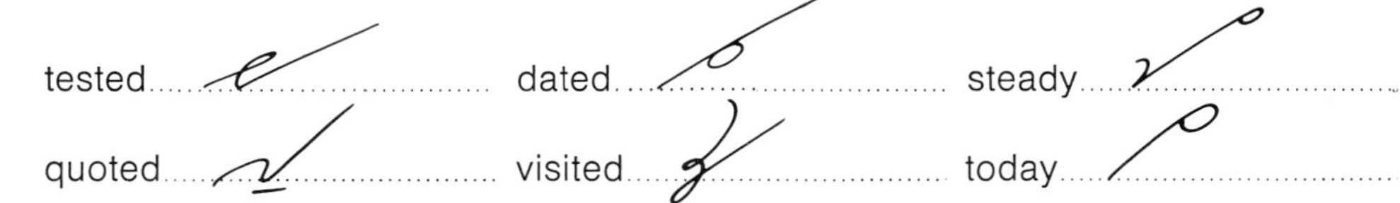
tested
dated
steady
quoted
visited
today

Ded, Dit, Det

The long stroke that represents *ted* also represents *ded* and the similar sounds of *dit* and *det.*

Spell: gay-ī-ded, guided; det-a-l, detail

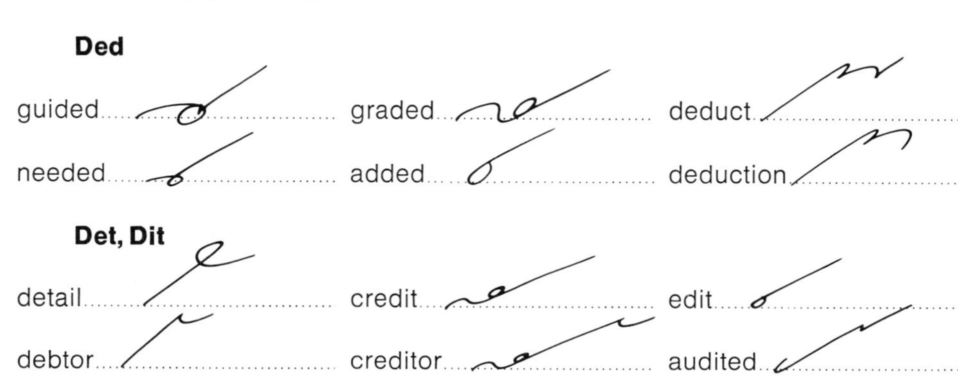
Ded
guided
graded
deduct
needed
added
deduction
Det, Dit
detail
credit
edit
debtor
creditor
audited

■ Observe that the *d* representing the past tense in *audited* is joined to *dit* with a jog.

Building Transcription Skills

Business Vocabulary Builder

Twin Cities Minneapolis and St. Paul, Minnesota.

premises A tract of land with a building or buildings on it.

toll A great price.

queries Questions.

Business Vocabulary Builder

versatile Having many uses or applications.

delinquent (noun) One who is behind in payments.

retraction An act of taking back.

pharmacists Druggists.

Reading and Writing Practice

1

if

au·to·mat·i·cal·ly

loss

theft

ser

ex·ceed·ing·ly

world's

and o

suc·cess·ful

if

lose

[120]

2

conj

ver·sa·tile

mys·te·ri·ous

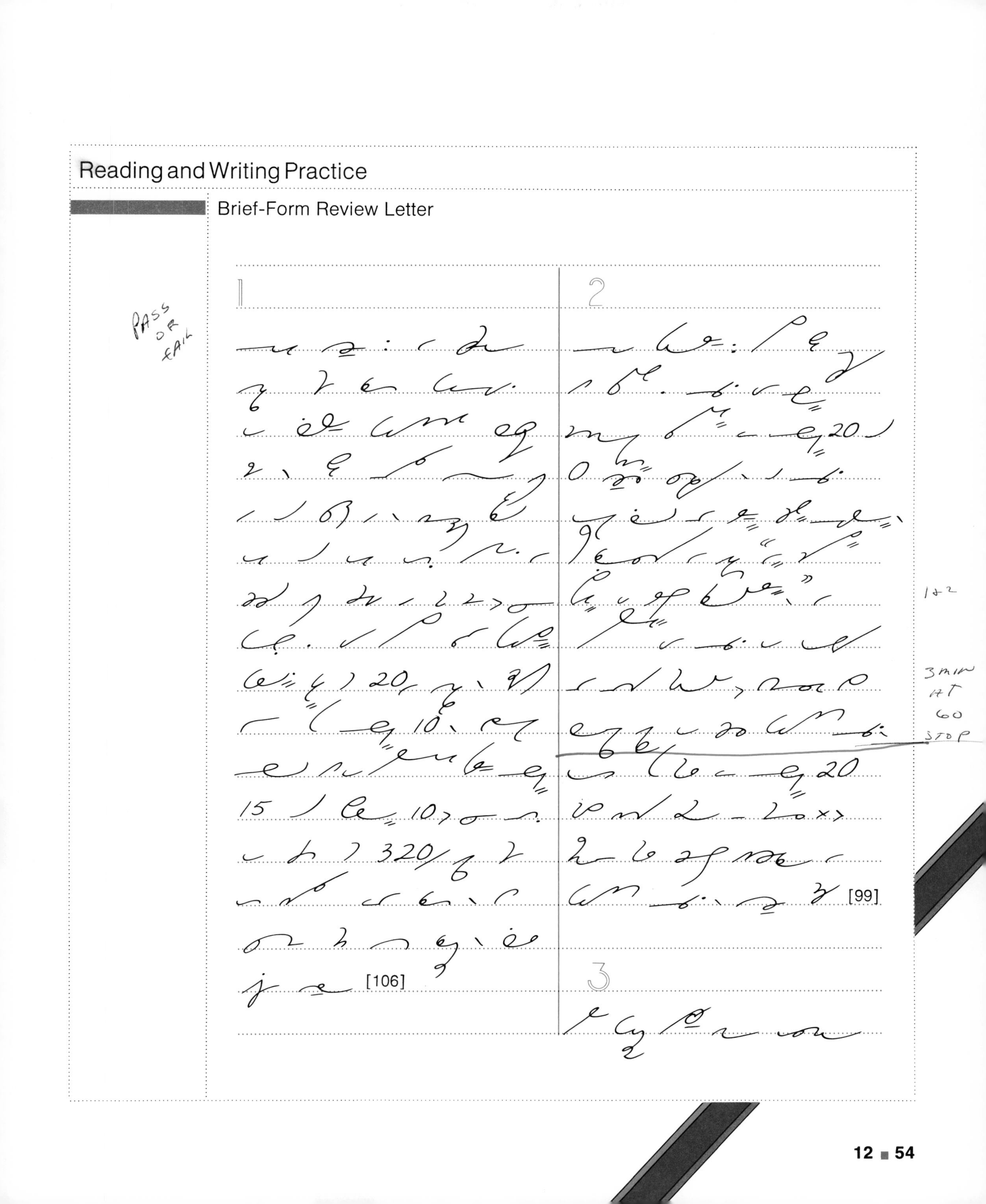

Reading and Writing Practice

Brief-Form Review Letter

1

[106]

2

[99]

3

Lesson 52 contains a general review of the major principles of Gregg Shorthand.

Building Transcription Skills

Similar-Words Drill ■ loss, lose, loose

loss (noun) That which one is deprived of.

We suffered a major financial *loss.*

lose (verb) To be deprived of.

Did you *lose* the contract?

loose Unattached; not fastened.

The screw in the table is *loose.*

[122]

[116]

5

[33]

4

[93]

Transcription Quiz

For you to supply: 6 commas—3 commas *if* clause, 1 comma introductory, 1 comma *when* clause, 1 comma parenthetical.

6

90 50

[127]

Spelling and Punctuation Checklist

Be careful to punctuate and spell correctly when you:

1 Write your compositions in English.
2 Prepare papers for other classes.
3 Correspond with friends.

Principles

Brief Forms

business	what	value
doctor	about	than
any	thing, think	one (won)

Brief-Form Derivatives

things, thinks	anything	businesses
thinking	once	businessman

■ **Observe:** **1** A disjoined left *s* is used to express *things, thinks.*

2 The plural of *business* is formed by adding another left *s.*

Word Ending -ble

The word ending *-ble* is represented by *b.*

Spell: p-o-s-bul, possible

possible	terrible	double
available	valuable	table
reliable	favorable	tabled

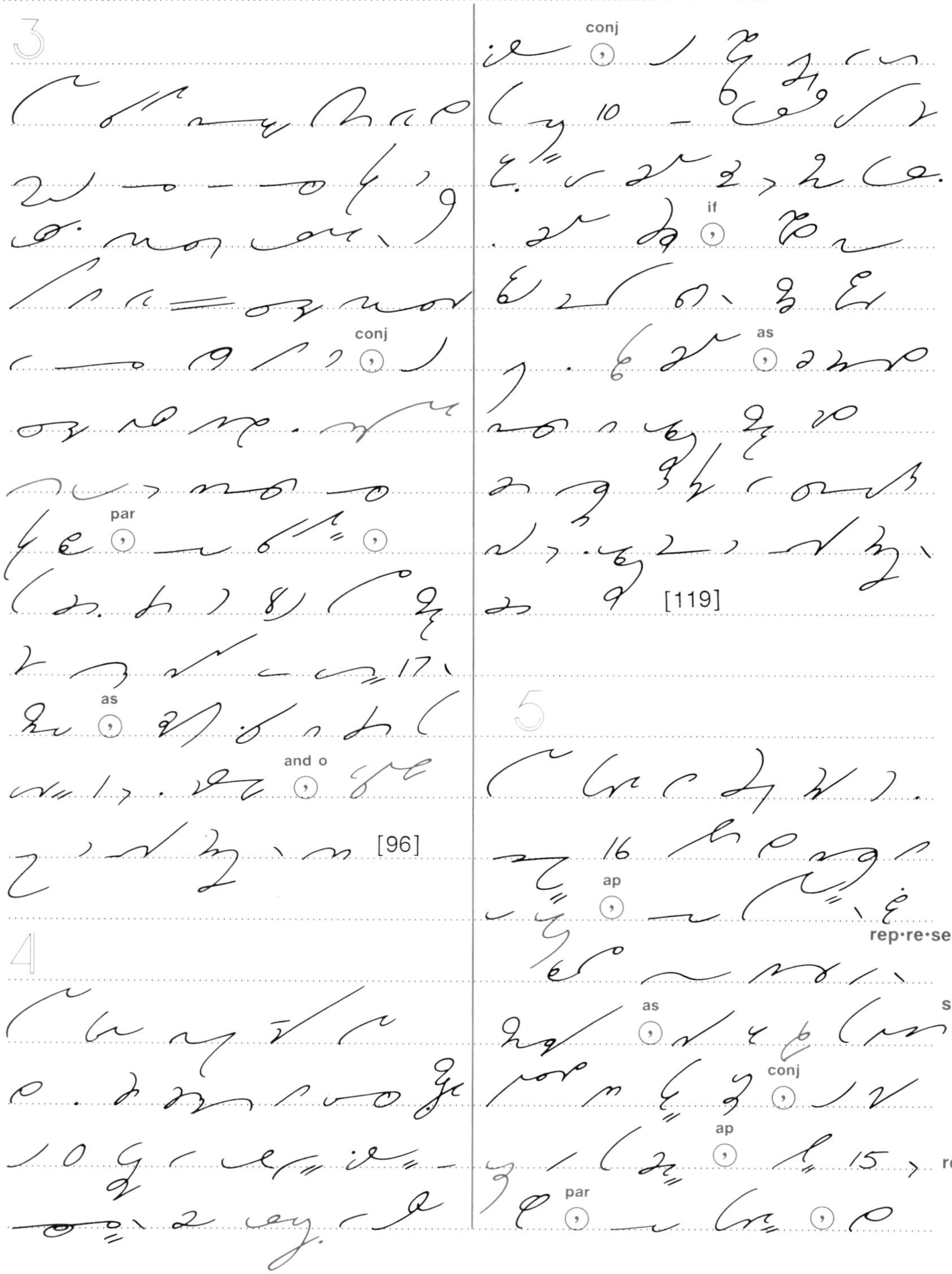

3

conj

cus·tom·er's

good·will

par

as

self-ad·dressed

and o

[96]

4

ren·o·vat·ing

conj

if

as

busy

[119]

5

ap

rep·re·sen·ta·tive

as

shipped

conj

ap

re·ceive

par

capable sensible cables

Word Beginning Re-

The word beginning *re-* is represented by *r*.

Spell: re-s-e-v, receive

receive revise reasonable

reply repair reappear

research reception rearrange

replace receipt reopen

Building Transcription Skills

Business Vocabulary Builder

sizable Very large.

jeopardize Place in great peril.

resolve Find an answer to.

Reading and Writing Practice

Brief-Form Letter

50

Reading and Writing Practice

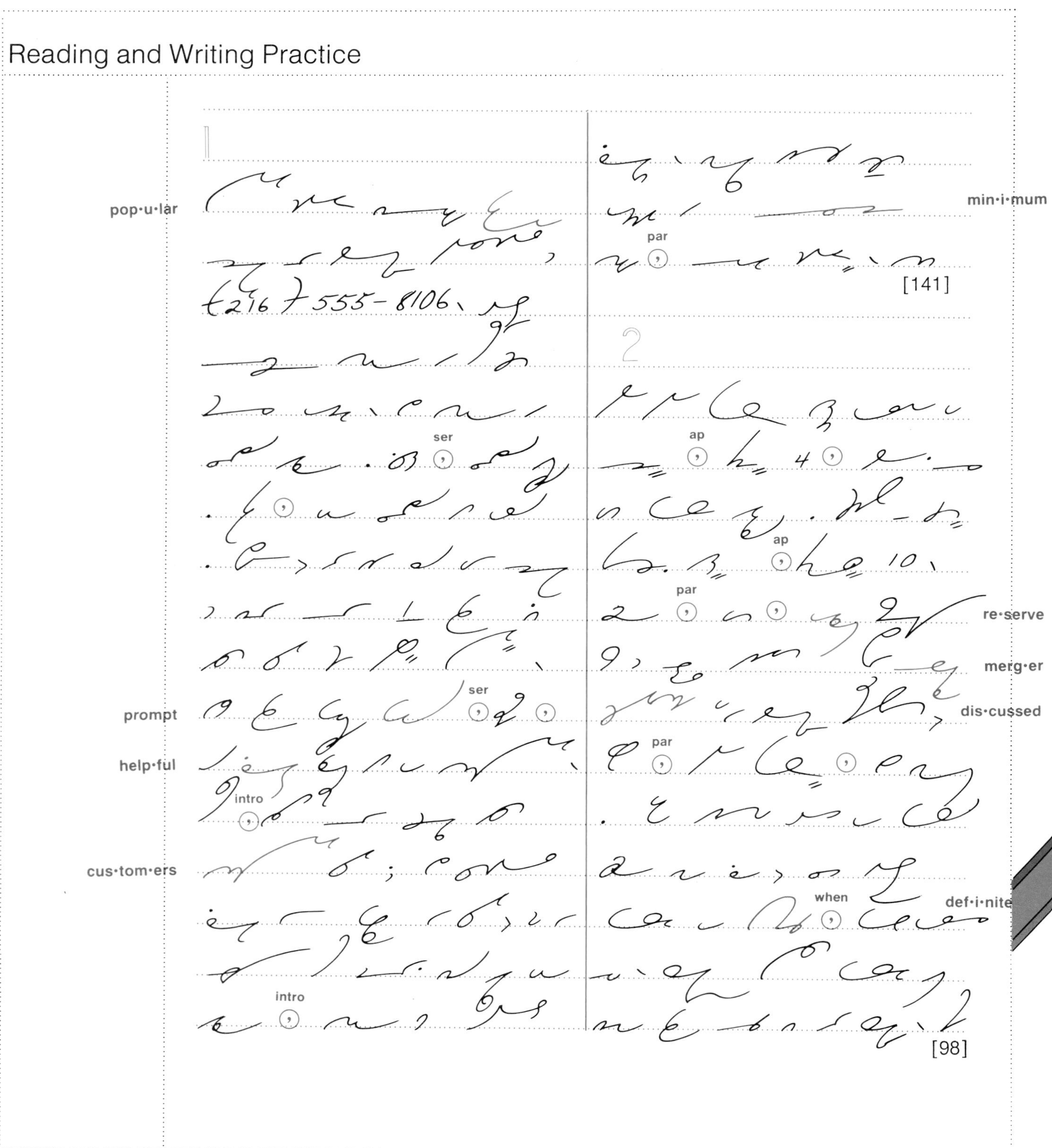

[158]

2

[110]

3

You have another opportunity in Lesson 51 to develop your phrasing skill. The letters in the Reading and Writing Practice contain a number of illustrations of the phrasing principles of Gregg Shorthand.

Building Transcription Skills

Grammar Checkup ■ verbs—with "one of"

1 In most cases, the expression *one of* takes a singular verb, which agrees with the subject *one.*

One of the workers on the staff is out of the office.
One of our computers is out of order.

2 When *one of* is part of an expression such as *one of those who* or *one of the things that*, the verb following is usually plural, to agree with the plural object of the preposition *of.*

Mark is one of those who drive to work.
We solved one of the problems that have been causing us difficulty.

Business Vocabulary Builder

merger A joining; a union.

confront To face.

renovating Improving by cleaning, repairing, or rebuilding.

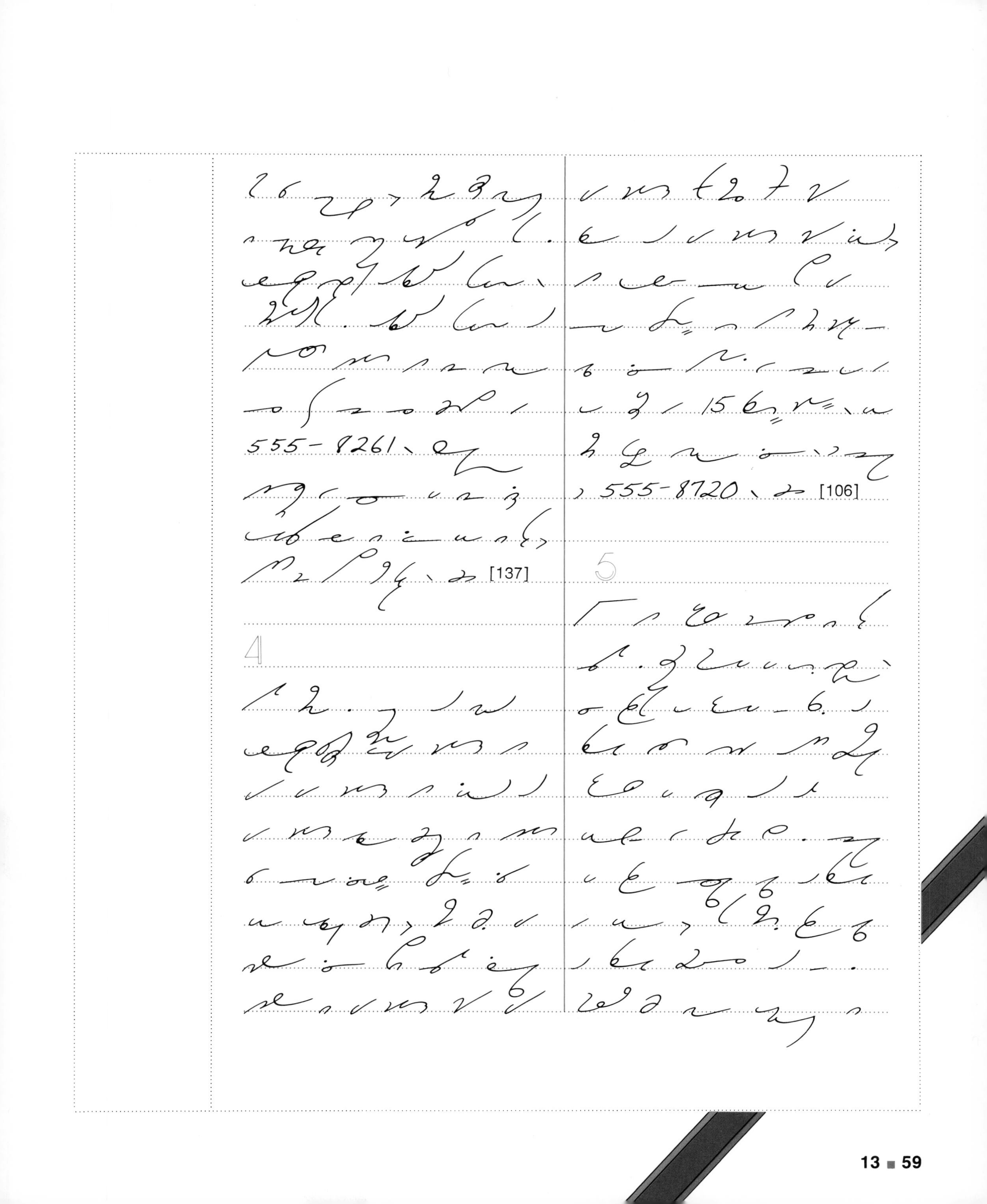

555-8261 [137]

4

156

555-8720 [106]

5

[138]

Transcription Quiz

For you to supply: 4 commas—1 comma introductory, 1 comma conjunction, 2 commas parenthetical.

Dictation Checklist

When you take dictation, be sure to:

1 Make every effort to keep up with the dictator.
2 Refer to your textbook whenever you are in doubt about any outline.
3 Insert periods and question marks in your shorthand notes.
4 Make a real effort to observe good proportion as you write.
5 Write down the first column of your notebook and then down the second column.

[112]

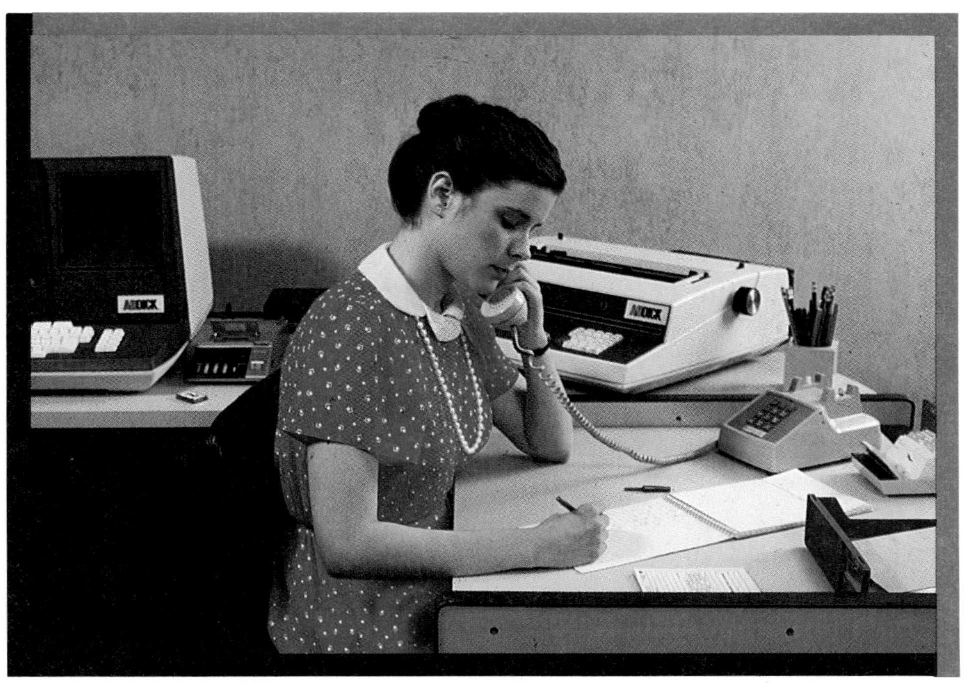

When away on a business trip, the manager may mail in recorded dictation or may call and dictate to the secretary over the telephone.

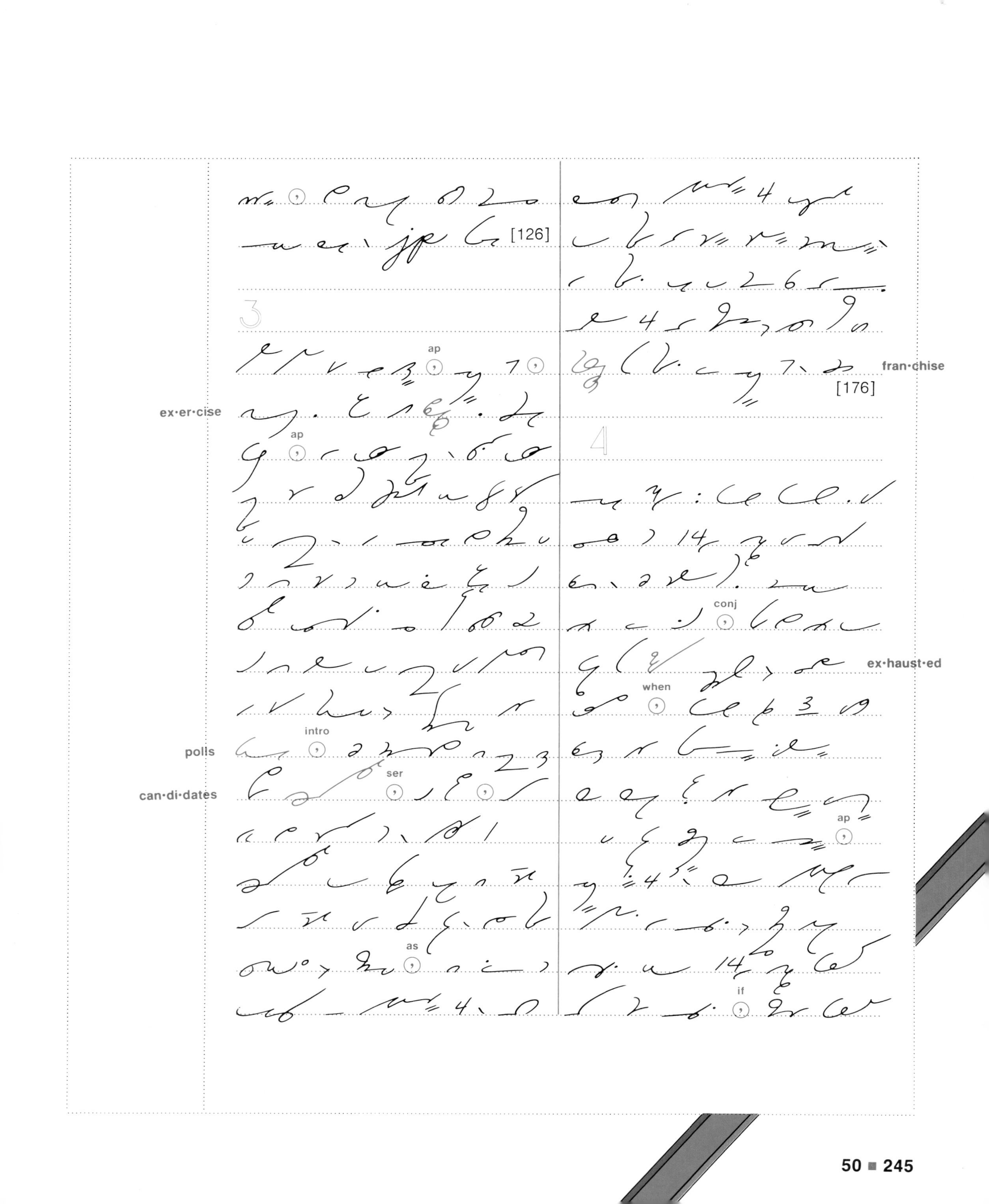

[126]

3

ap

ex·er·cise

ap

intro

polls

ser

can·di·dates

as

fran·chise

[176]

4

conj

ex·haust·ed

when

ap

if

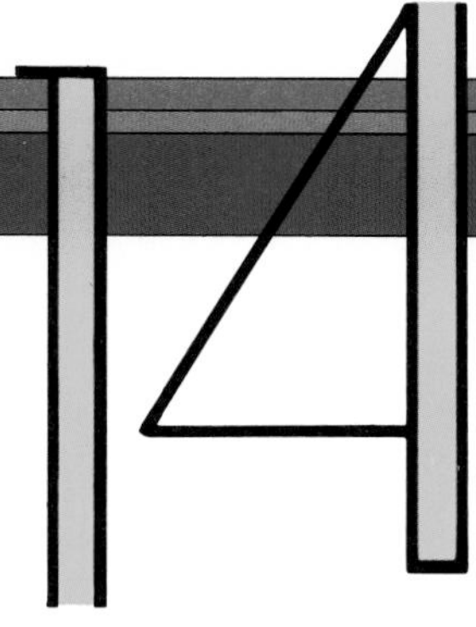

Principles

Oi

The sound of *oi,* as in *toy,* is represented by [shorthand outline].

Spell: b-oi, boy

boy .... oil .... annoy ....
toy .... spoil .... point ....
join .... boil .... appoint ....

Men

The sound of *men* is represented by joining *m* and *n* into one long forward stroke.

Men ....

Compare: knee .... me .... many ....

Spell: men-e, many

men .... mentioned .... businessmen ....
meant .... women .... mended ....
mental .... salesmen .... immense ....

Reading and Writing Practice

if

[169]

2

intro

suc·cess·ful·ly

launched

un·dis·put·ed

cel·e·brate

ser

cor·re·spon·dents

intro

and o

conj

ex·traor·di·nary

un·doubt·ed·ly

great

ser

re·spon·si·bly

Com·pa·ny's

to·ken

par

Min, Mon, Man

The similar sounding combinations *min, mon,* and *man* are also represented by the long forward stroke that represents *men.*

Spell: men-e-t, minute; men-r, manner

minute .... month .... manner ....

minimum .... money .... manage ....

Ye, Ya

Ye, as in *year,* is represented by the *e* circle; *ya,* as in *yard,* by the *a* circle.

Spell: e-r, year; a-ȧ̈rd, yard

Ye

year .... yellow .... yield ....

yet .... yes .... yielded ....

Ya

yard .... yarn .... Yale ....

Building Transcription Skills

Business Vocabulary Builder

solicit Try to obtain; ask for.

pledges (noun) Binding promises or agreements.

eligible Qualified to be chosen.

hazard A source of danger.

This lesson provides another opportunity for you to test your knowledge of the brief forms of Gregg Shorthand. The Reading and Writing Practice contains the brief forms or brief-form derivatives of Gregg Shorthand.

Building Transcription Skills

Common Prefixes ■ un-

un- not

undisputed Not disputed; accepted without argument.
unsatisfactory Not satisfactory; not acceptable.
uncommon Not common; rare.
uncertain Not sure; indefinite.
unsolicited Not asked for; voluntary.

Business Vocabulary Builder

franchise The right to vote.

exhausted Used up; entirely consumed.

mystified Perplexed; bewildered.

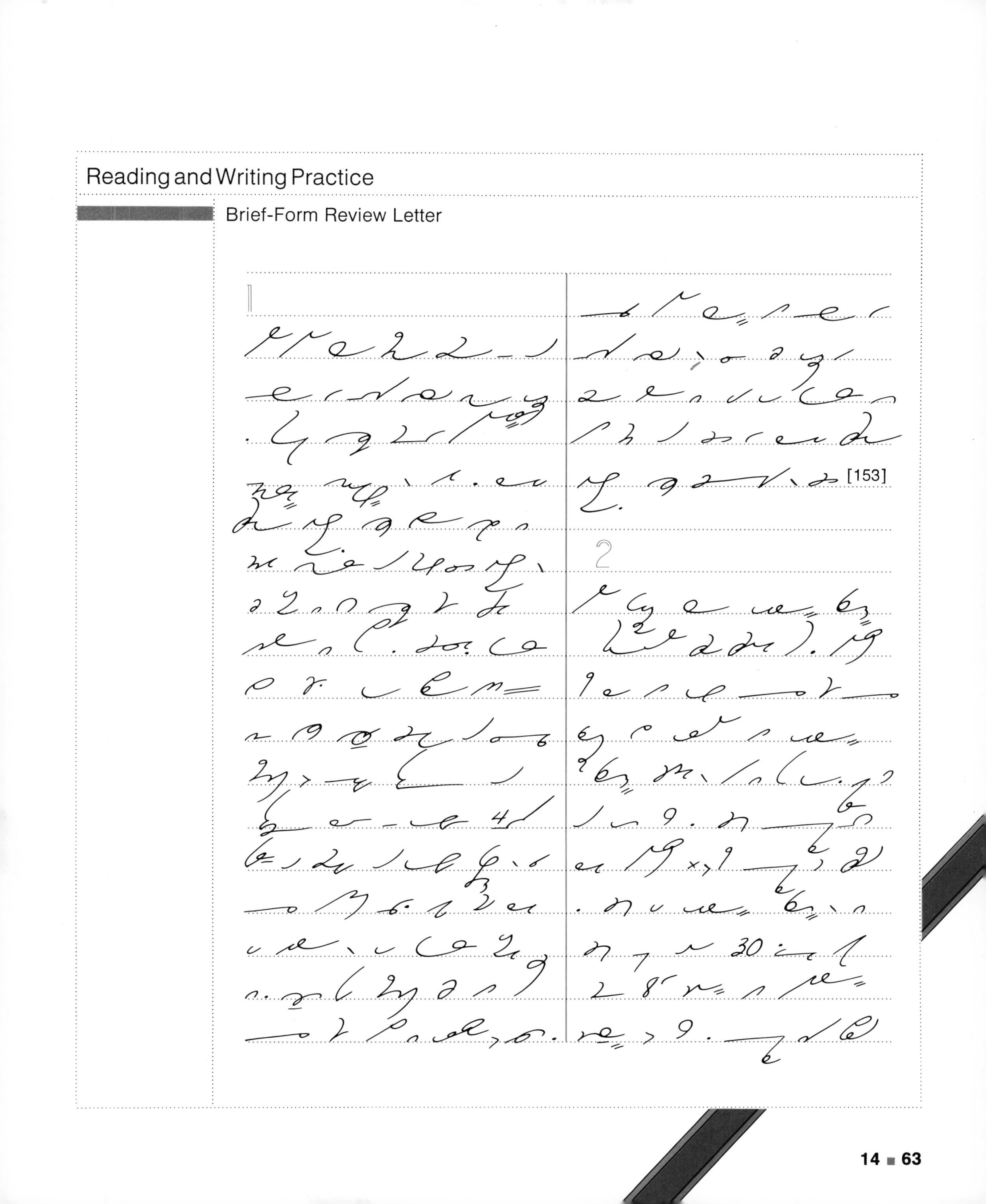

Reading and Writing Practice

Brief-Form Review Letter

1

[153]

2

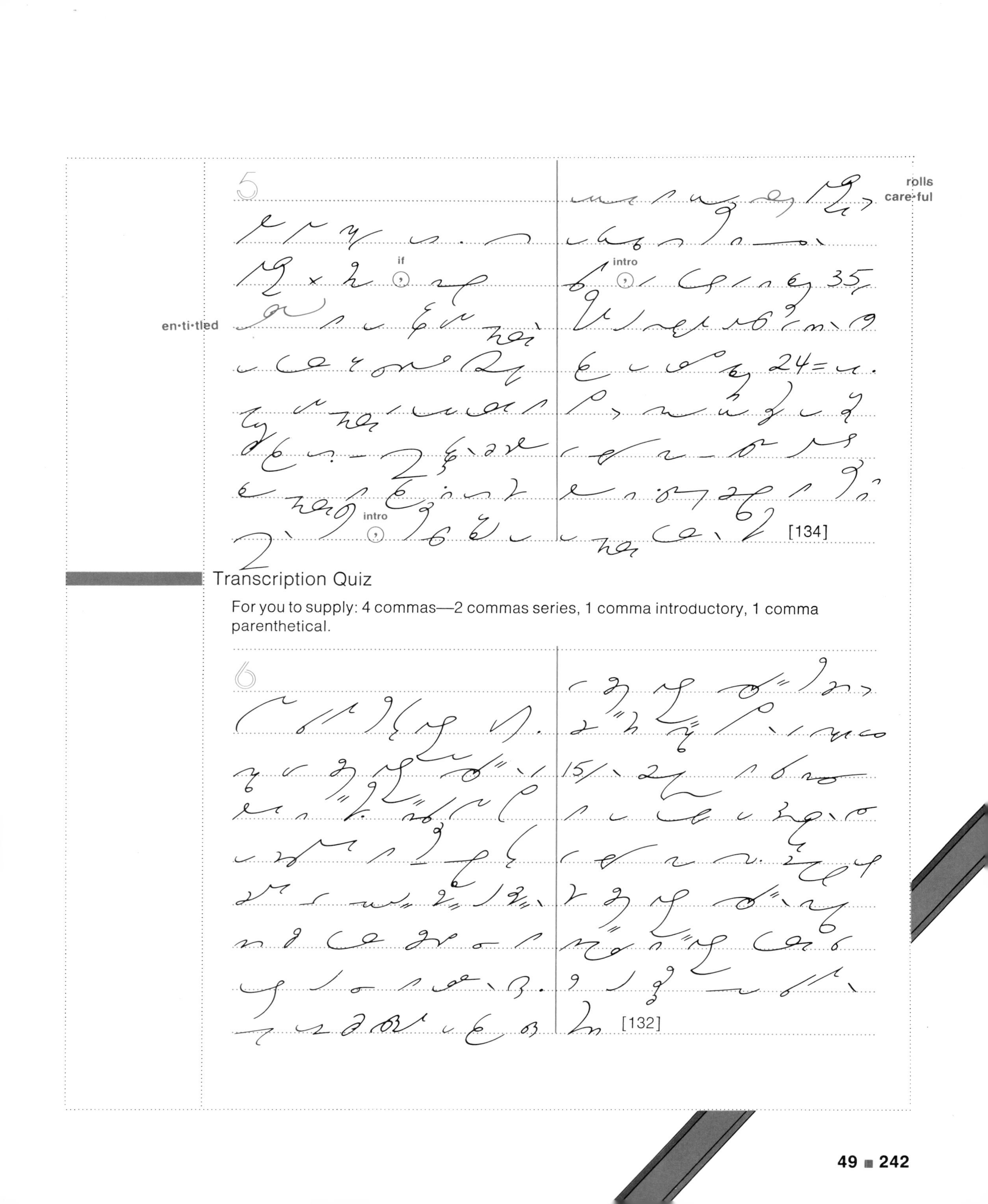

5

rolls

care·ful

if

intro

en·ti·tled

intro

[134]

Transcription Quiz

For you to supply: 4 commas—2 commas series, 1 comma introductory, 1 comma parenthetical.

6

[132]

[141]

3

[80]

4

15

[92]

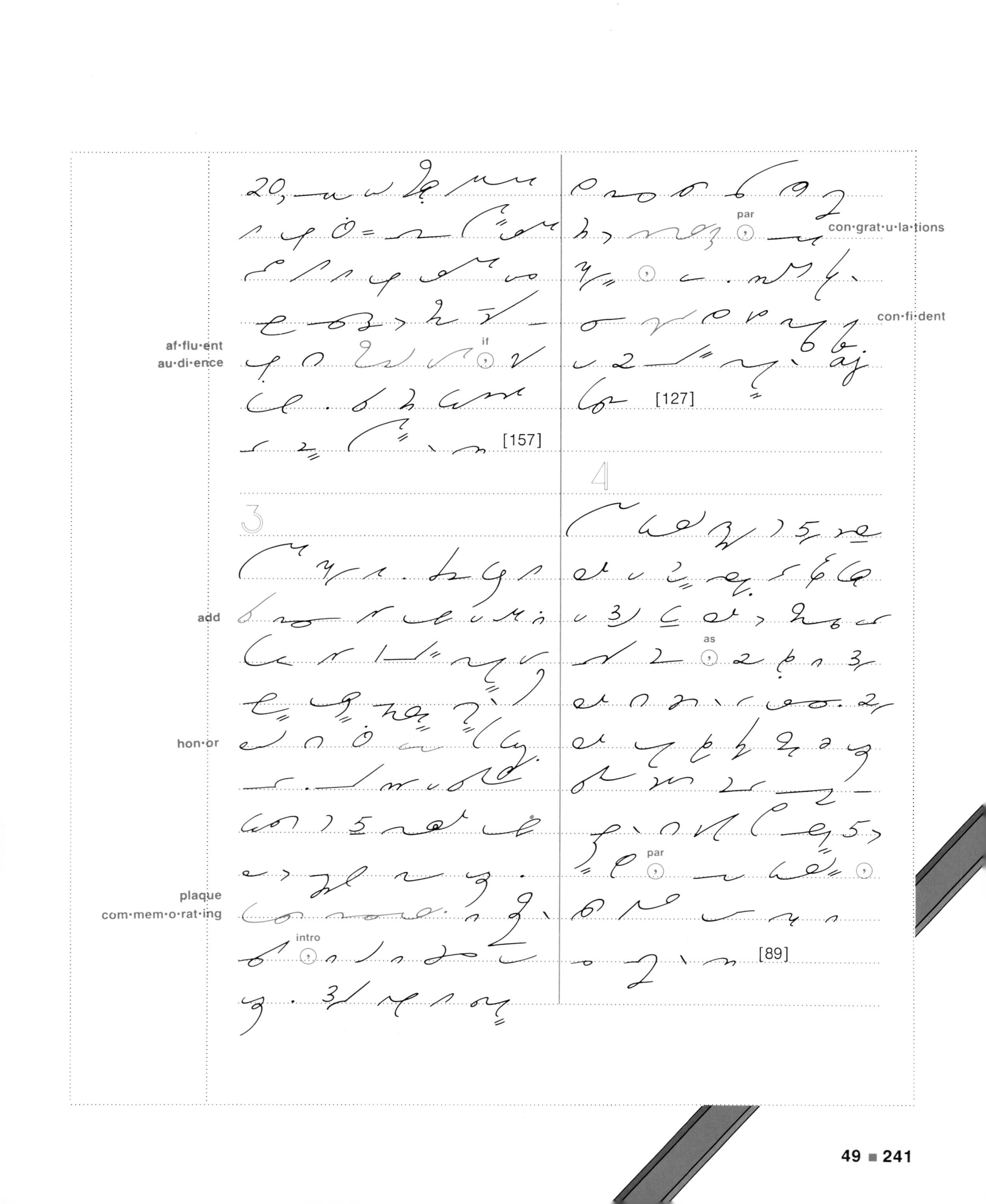

af·flu·ent
au·di·ence

if

[157]

par

con·grat·u·la·tions

con·fi·dent

[127]

3

add

hon·or

plaque
com·mem·o·rat·ing

intro

4

as

par

[89]

5

[97]

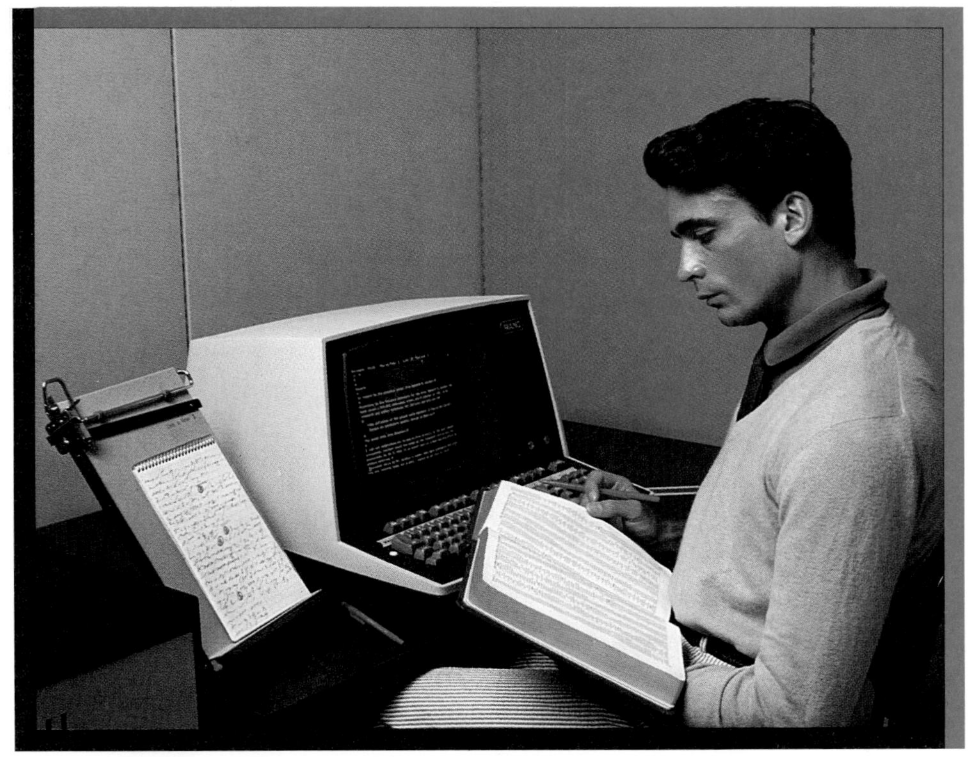

A legal secretary often has to confirm citations referred to in a court document.

Reading and Writing Practice

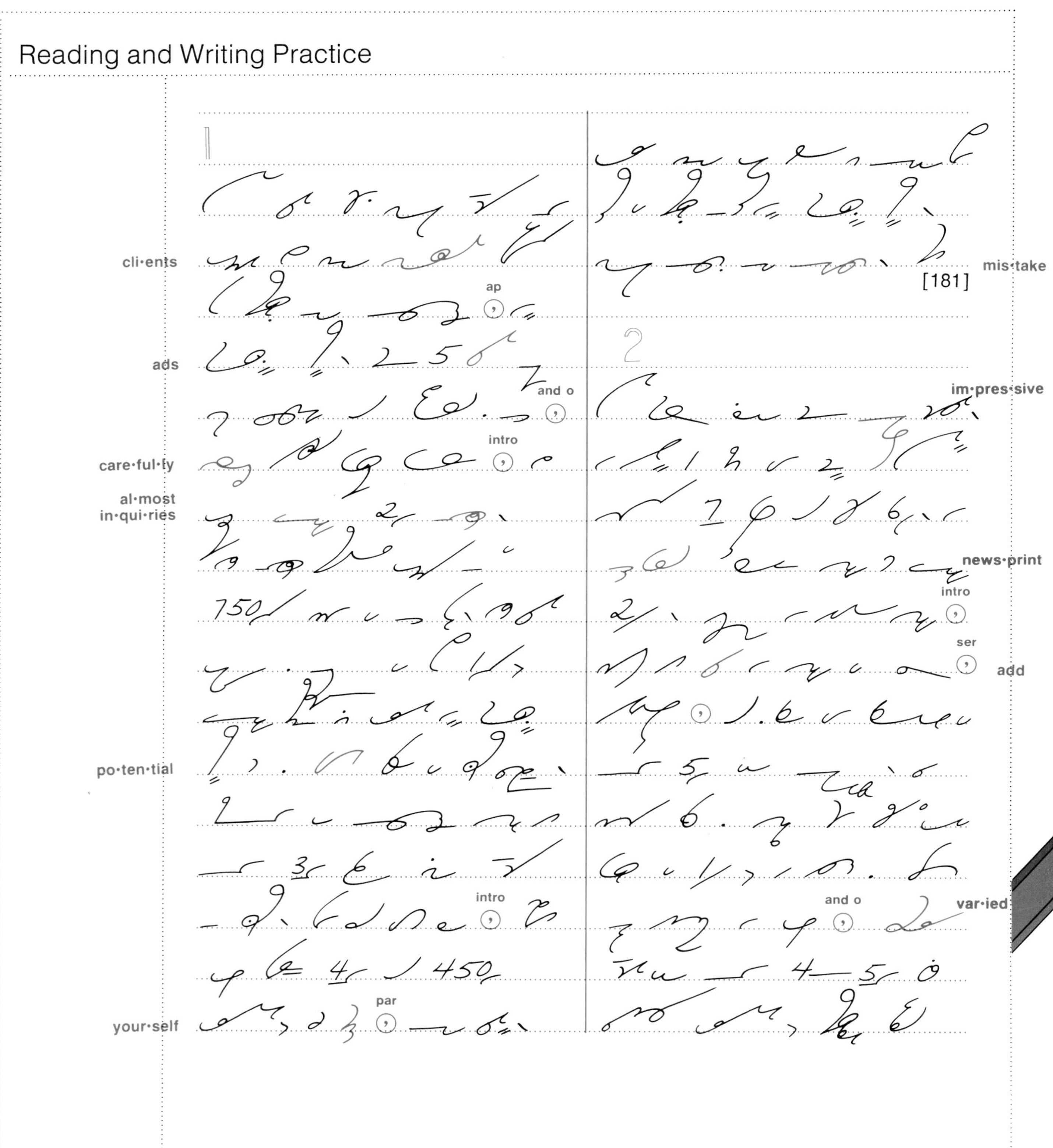

Principles

Brief Forms

When you have learned the following eight brief forms, you will have learned more than half the brief forms of Gregg Shorthand.

gentlemen	company	short
morning	manufacture	important, importance
where	next	

Word Beginnings Per-, Pur-

The word beginnings *per-, pur-* are represented by *p-r.*

Spell: pur-s-n, person; pur-chay-a-s, purchase

Per-

person	perfect	persist
personal	permanent	perhaps
permit	personnel	persuade

Pur-

purchase	purple	purpose

When you take dictation on a job, you will have to write many numbers. Because of the extreme importance of accuracy in transcribing numbers, you should take special care in writing numbers in your shorthand notes. The letters in the Reading and Writing Practice of this lesson will help you to review the devices of Gregg Shorthand used for expressing numbers and quantities.

Building Transcription Skills

Similar-Words Drill ■ ad, add

ad Short for *advertisement.*

Did you see the *ad* in the newspaper?

add To make an addition; to include.

Please *add* my name to your list of subscribers.

Business Vocabulary Builder

newsprint A relatively inexpensive paper made from wood pulp and used mostly for newspapers.

opulent Wealthy; rich.

plaque (pronounced plak) An inscribed tablet presented and displayed to note a special event.

Word Beginnings De-, Di-

The word beginnings *de-, di-* are represented by *d*.

Spell: de-l-a, delay; de-r-e-k-t, direct

De-

delay ...... deposit ...... decide ......
deserve ...... deliver ...... decision ......
desirable ...... depended ...... design ......

Di-

direct ...... direction ...... directly ......

Building Transcription Skills

Similar-Words Drill

The English language contains many groups of words that sound alike, but each member of the group is spelled differently and has its own meaning.

Example: sent (dispatched); scent (a smell); cent (a coin).

In addition, there are many groups of words that sound almost alike.

Example: defer (to put off); differ (to disagree).

The secretary who is not alert may, while transcribing, select the wrong member of the group, with the result that the transcript makes no sense.

In this lesson and in a number of other lessons that follow, you will find a Similar-Words Drill that will call to your attention similar words which may cause the unwary transcriber to stumble.

Study these words carefully.

Similar-Words Drill ■ personal, personnel

personal Individual; private; pertaining to the person or body.

He is traveling on *personal* business.
You should watch your *personal* appearance with care.

at·ten·dant

[149]

Transcription Quiz

For you to supply: 5 commas—2 commas apposition, 1 comma *as* clause, 1 comma introductory, 1 comma parenthetical.

Transcription Checklist

To get the full benefit from the spelling and punctuation helps in the Reading and Writing Practice, be sure to:

1 Circle the punctuation marks in your notes as you copy each Reading and Writing Practice.

2 Note the reason for the use of each punctuation mark to be sure that you understand why it was used.

3 Spell aloud at least once the spelling words given in the margin of the shorthand.

personnel The people who work for a firm; the staff.

Yesterday I read your *personnel* policies booklet.
You can rely on our *personnel* to give you good service.

Business Vocabulary Builder

wildcat strike A work stoppage that does not have the approval of the union.

imaginative Having creative ability.

deadline A time or date before which something must be done.

Reading and Writing Practice

Brief-Form Letter

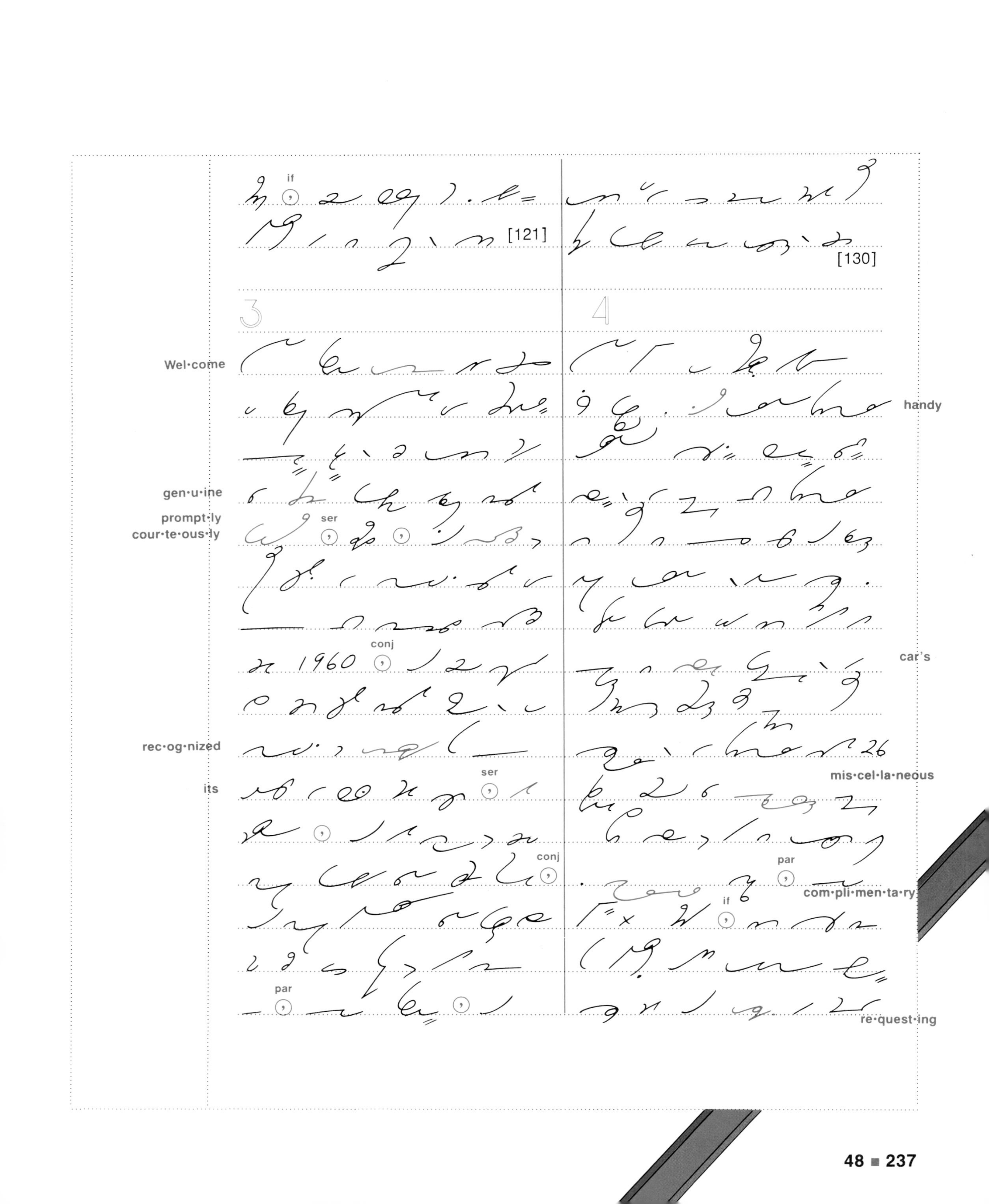

if

[121]

[130]

3

Wel·come

gen·u·ine

prompt·ly

cour·te·ous·ly

ser

1960 conj

rec·og·nized

its

ser

conj

par

4

handy

car's

26

mis·cel·la·ne·ous

par

com·pli·men·ta·ry

if

re·quest·ing

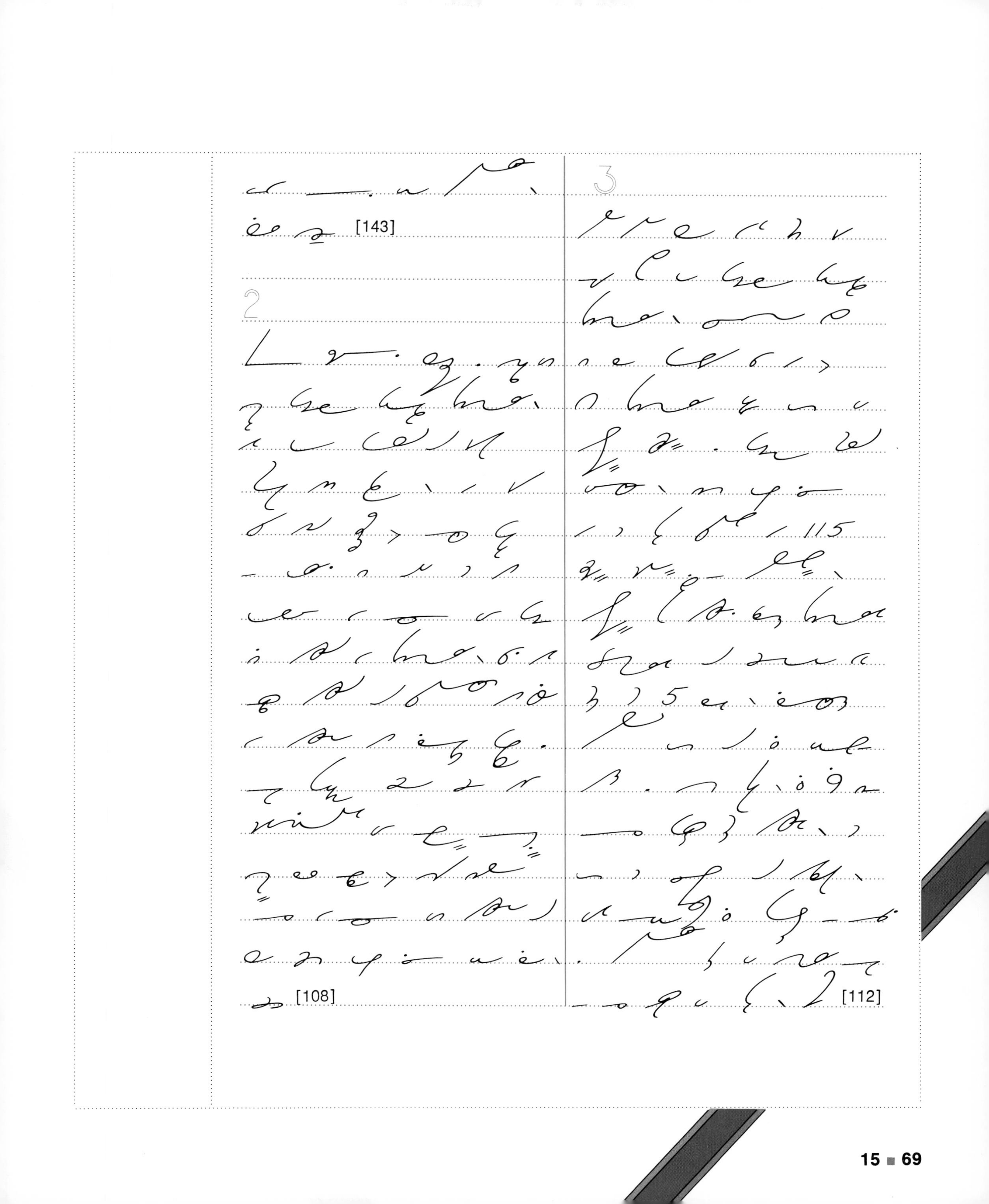

[143]

2

[108]

3

[112]

Reading and Writing Practice

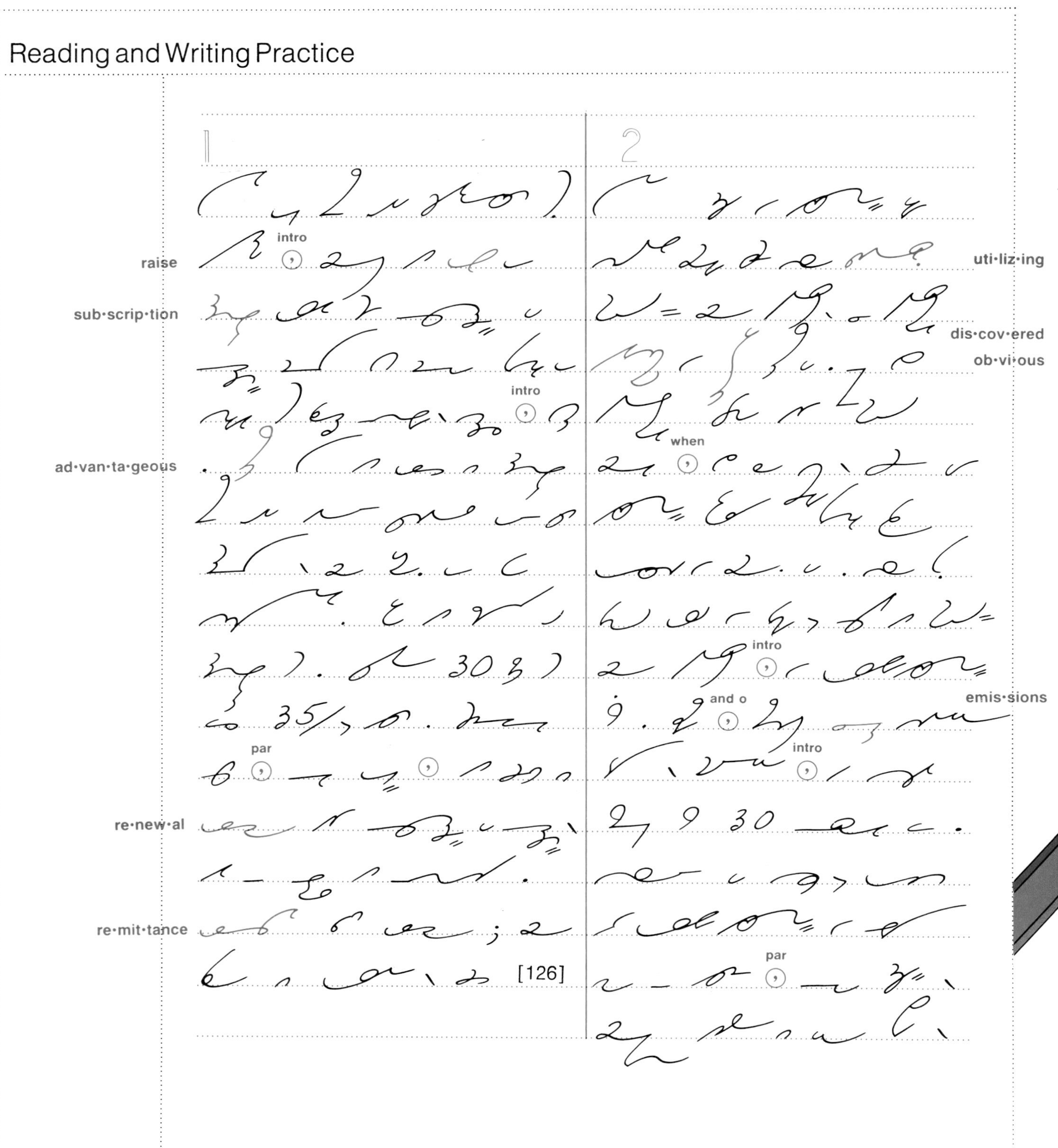

4

[79]

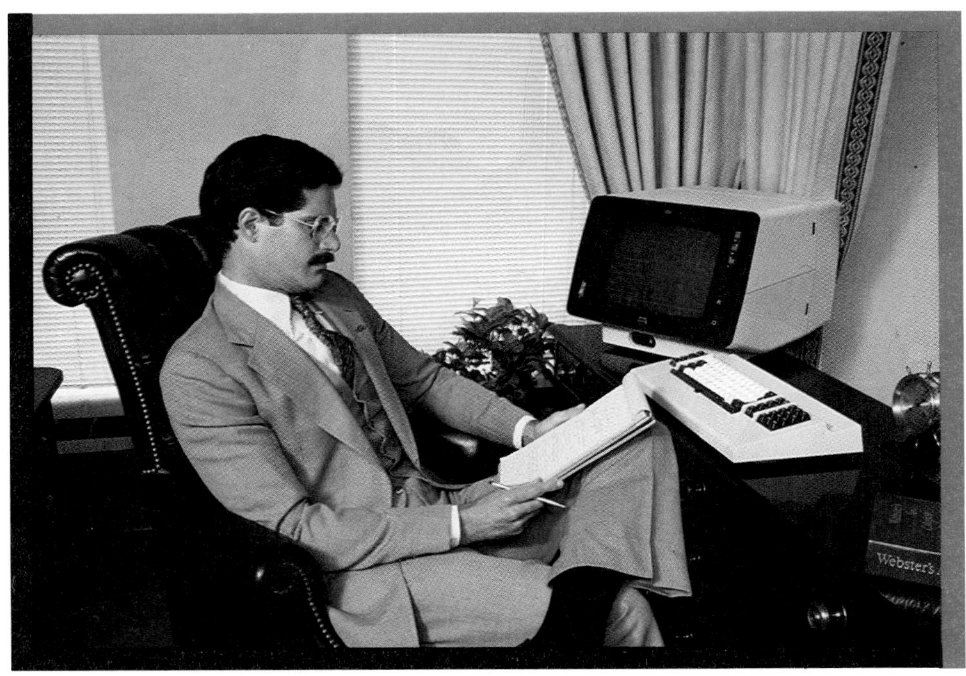

Executives who know how to write shorthand find it a useful skill when outlining responses to communications received via electronic mail.

As you learned during the early stages of your study of Gregg Shorthand, unnecessary vowels are omitted in some words to help you gain fluency in writing without sacrificing legibility. In the Reading and Writing Practice of this lesson, there are many illustrations of words from which unnecessary vowels are omitted.

Building Transcription Skills

Spelling Families ■ -ious, -eous

Words Ending in -ious

con-scious	gra-cious	pre-vi-ous
de-li-cious	in-ge-nious	se-ri-ous
de-vi-ous	ju-di-cious	te-dious
en-vi-ous	ob-vi-ous	var-i-ous

Words Ending in -eous

ad-van-ta-geous	er-ro-ne-ous	si-mul-ta-neous
cour-te-ous	mis-cel-la-neous	spon-ta-ne-ous

Business Vocabulary Builder

emissions Substances discharged into the air, such as smoke and gasoline fumes.

continuously Without interruption.

miscellaneous Consisting of many different things or members.

Principles

Brief Forms

Here is another group of brief forms—only six this time.

part ... Ms. ... opportunity ...
present ... advertise ... immediate ...

U

The sound of *u*, as in *use*, is represented by .

Spell: u-s, use

use ... review ... unite ...
few ... unit ... pure ...
view ... unique ... acute ...

Word Ending -ment

The word ending *-ment* is represented by *m*.

Spell: p-a-ment, payment

payment ... department ... settlement ...
management ... equipment ... treatment ...

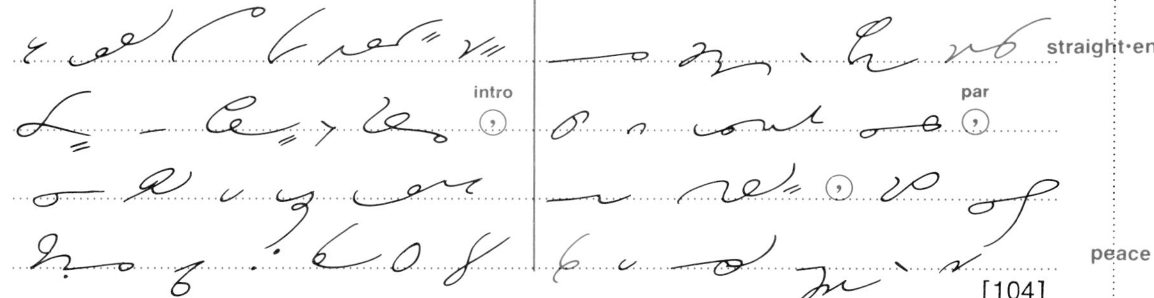

Transcription Quiz

The following letter requires 6 commas in order to be punctuated correctly—1 comma *as* clause, 1 comma apposition, 2 commas series, 1 comma introductory, 1 comma *if* clause.

Remember to indicate each comma in your shorthand notes and to give the reason for its use.

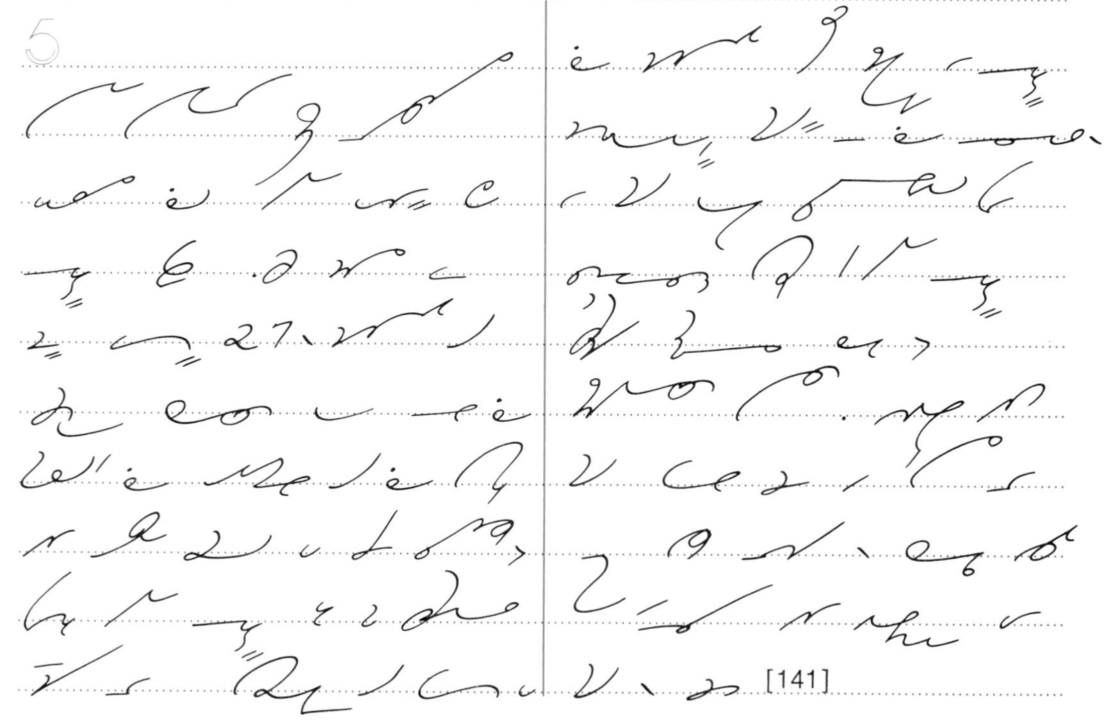

shipment	movement	element
advertisement	replacement	assignment

■ Observe that in *assignment,* the *m* is joined to the *n* with a jog.

Word Ending -tial

The word ending *-tial* (also spelled *-cial*) is represented by *ish.*

Spell: s-p-e-shul, special

special	financial	initial
especial	social	initially
partial	official	initialed

Building Transcription Skills

Spelling

When you look at the letter on page 73, you get a very favorable first impression. The letter is tastefully positioned; the right-hand margin is even; the date, inside address, and closing are all in their proper places. When you scan the letter casually, you find that it makes good sense and apparently represents what the dictator said.

But that favorable first impression will vanish when you read the letter carefully. In fact, you will quickly realize that it will never be signed and that the dictator will have some harsh words for the person who transcribed the letter. Why? It contains several misspelled words. No business executive will knowingly sign a letter that contains a misspelled word!

If you are to succeed as a secretary, your letters must not only be accurate transcripts of what your employer dictated, but they must also be free of spelling errors. A secretary who regularly submits letters for the employer's signature that contain spelling errors will not be a secretary long!

To make sure that you will be able to spell correctly when you have completed your shorthand course, you will from this point on give special attention to spelling in each Reading and Writing Practice.

As you read the Reading and Writing Practice, you will occasionally find shorthand outlines printed in color. These outlines represent words that stenographers and secretaries often misspell. When you encounter one of these outlines, finish reading the sentence in which it occurs; then glance at the margin, where you will find the word in type, properly spelled and syllabicated.

Spell the word aloud if possible, pausing slightly after each word division. (The word divisions indicated are those given in *Webster's New Collegiate Dictionary.)*

ab·sorb

par

sense

[161]

3

de·ter·mined

if

mod·est

ap·pro·pri·ate

sult·ed

if

al·ways

la·bels

par

in·gre·di·ents

[147]

4

dun·ning

Feb·ru·ary

re·ceived

when

prompt·ly

can·celed

1520 Arapahoe Street , Denver, Colorado 80202

November 18, 19XX

Mrs. Jane Carson
Western Systems Corporation
483 Market Street
San Francisco, California 94137

Dear Mrs. Carson:

We are sorry to tell you that the materiels you are produceing for our airplane seats do not exactly match the color specifications we agreed on. I know that you used the method we observed in your factory, but the blue thred does not dye quite as bright as expected. Even though we indicated that the fabric should match the color of the air craft carpeting, we feel that this discrepancy might not make too much differrence.

Please send us additionall samples of the dyed material for our inspection. We will compare them with the carpeting we have ordered and will let you know if it is satisfactory. If not, perhaps you will have to use another dye that would intensify the shade, or we may need to chose a new color.

Yours truely,

Gerald A. Bell

Gerald A. Bell
General Manager

Can you find all the errors in this letter?

Reading and Writing Practice

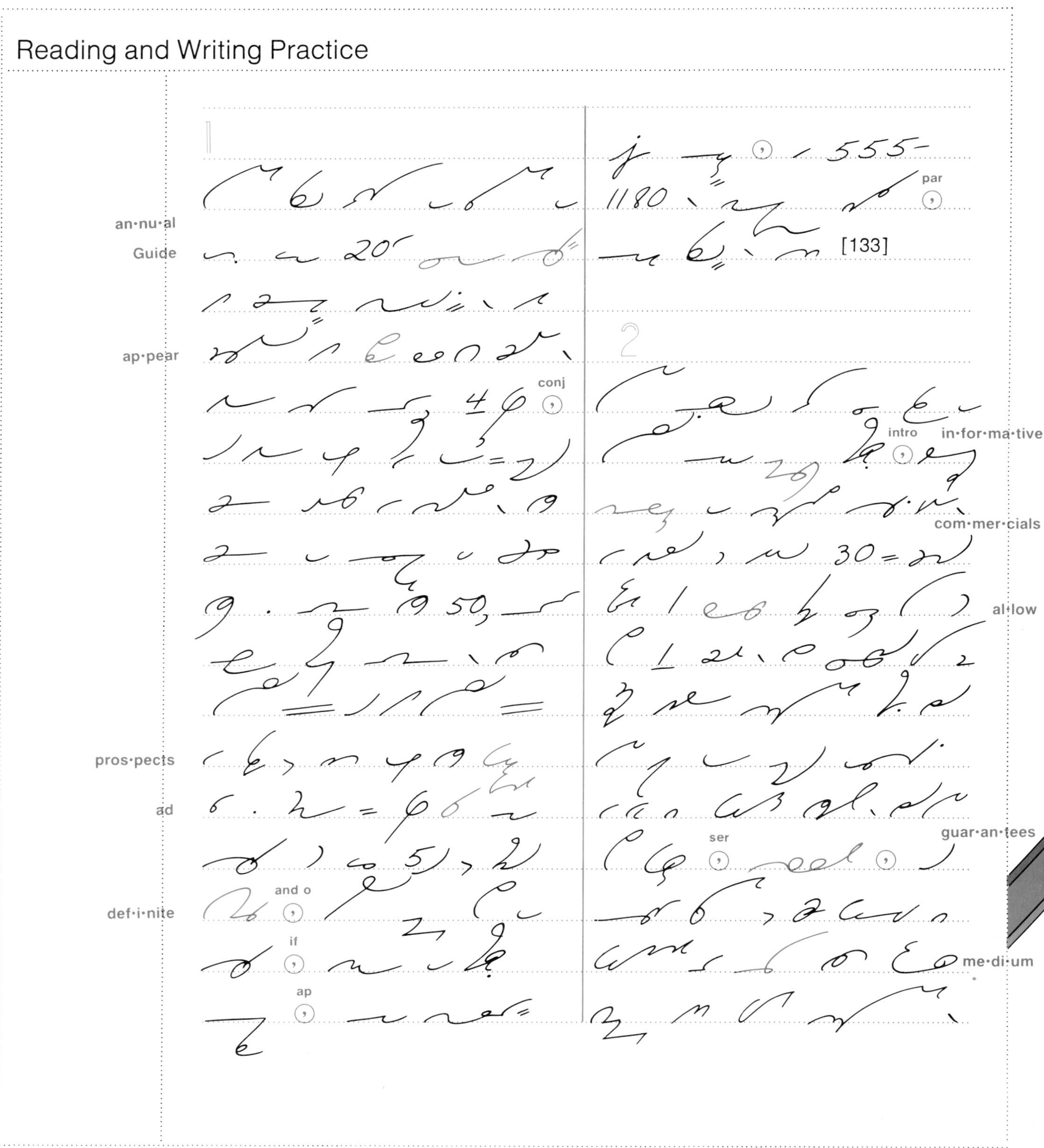

Business Vocabulary Builder

unique The only one of its kind.

car accessories Items such as radios, heaters, tire chains, and so on.

installment One part of a repayment plan.

Reading and Writing Practice

Brief-Form Letter

spe·cial

pur·chased

ac·ces·so·ries

[190]

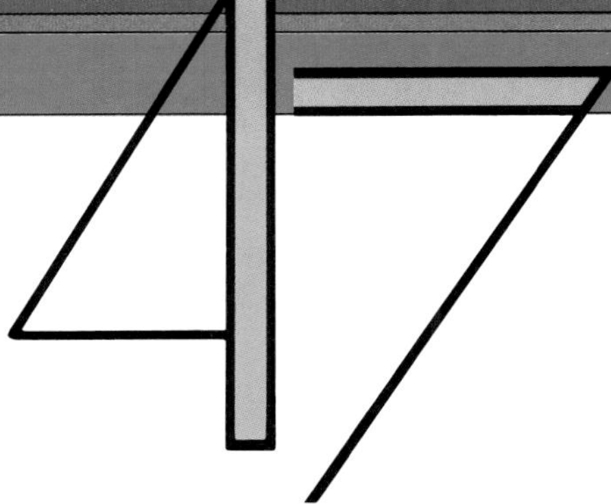

One of the major reasons why Gregg Shorthand can be written so rapidly and fluently is its blends—single strokes that represent two or more sounds. In the Reading and Writing Practice of this lesson, you will find many words and phrases that employ these blends.

Building Transcription Skills

Common Prefixes ■ pro-

pro- In many words in the English language, *pro-* means *before*, *ahead*, or *forward.*

progress A moving ahead; a going forward.
produce To bring forward; to make.
proceed To go ahead.
program A plan for the future.
promote To move ahead.

Business Vocabulary Builder

appropriate (adjective) Especially suitable or fitting.

ingredients Things that are parts of compounds or mixtures.

dunning Making persistent demands upon.

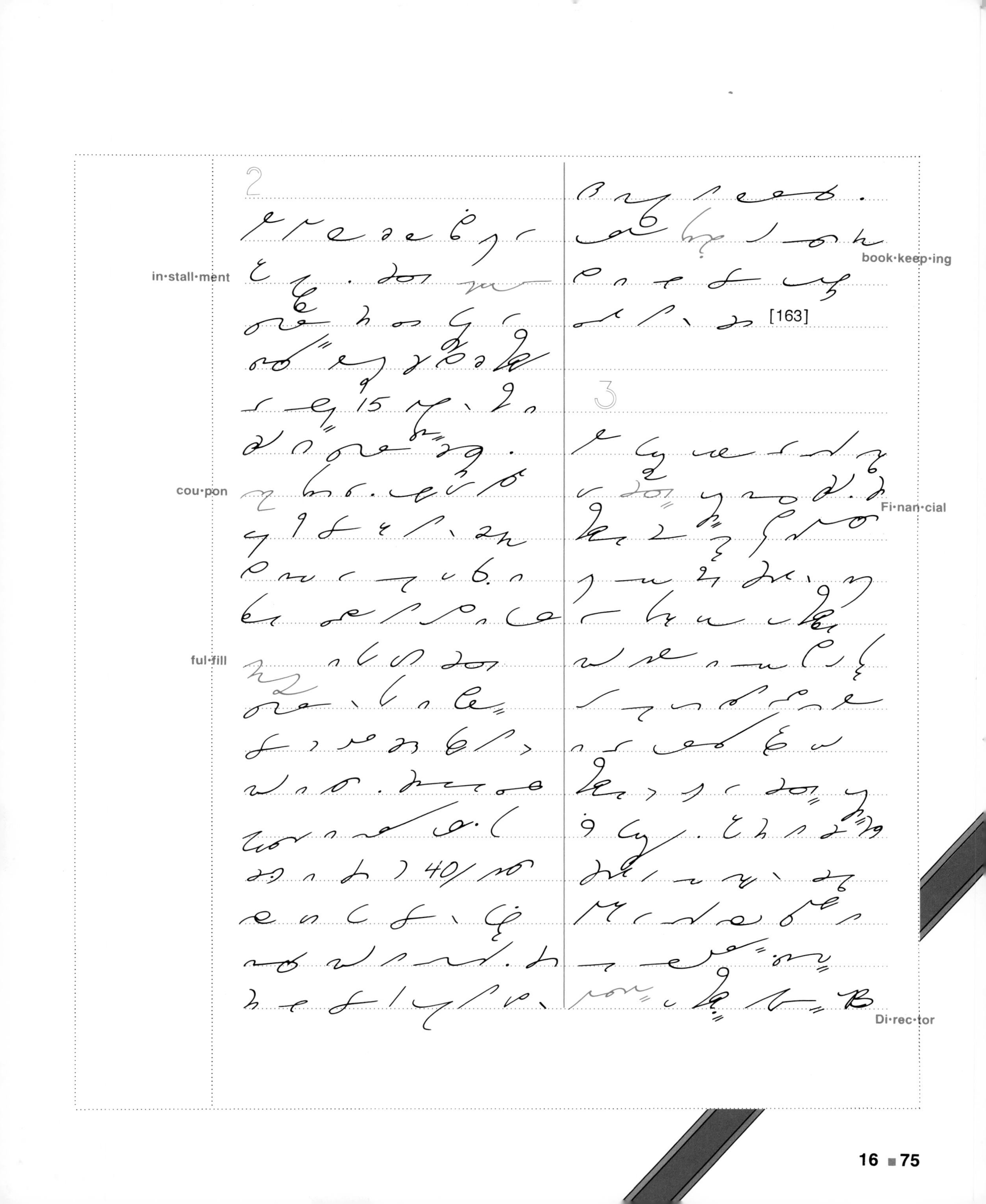

2

in·stall·ment

cou·pon

ful·fill

book·keep·ing

[163]

3

Fi·nan·cial

Di·rec·tor

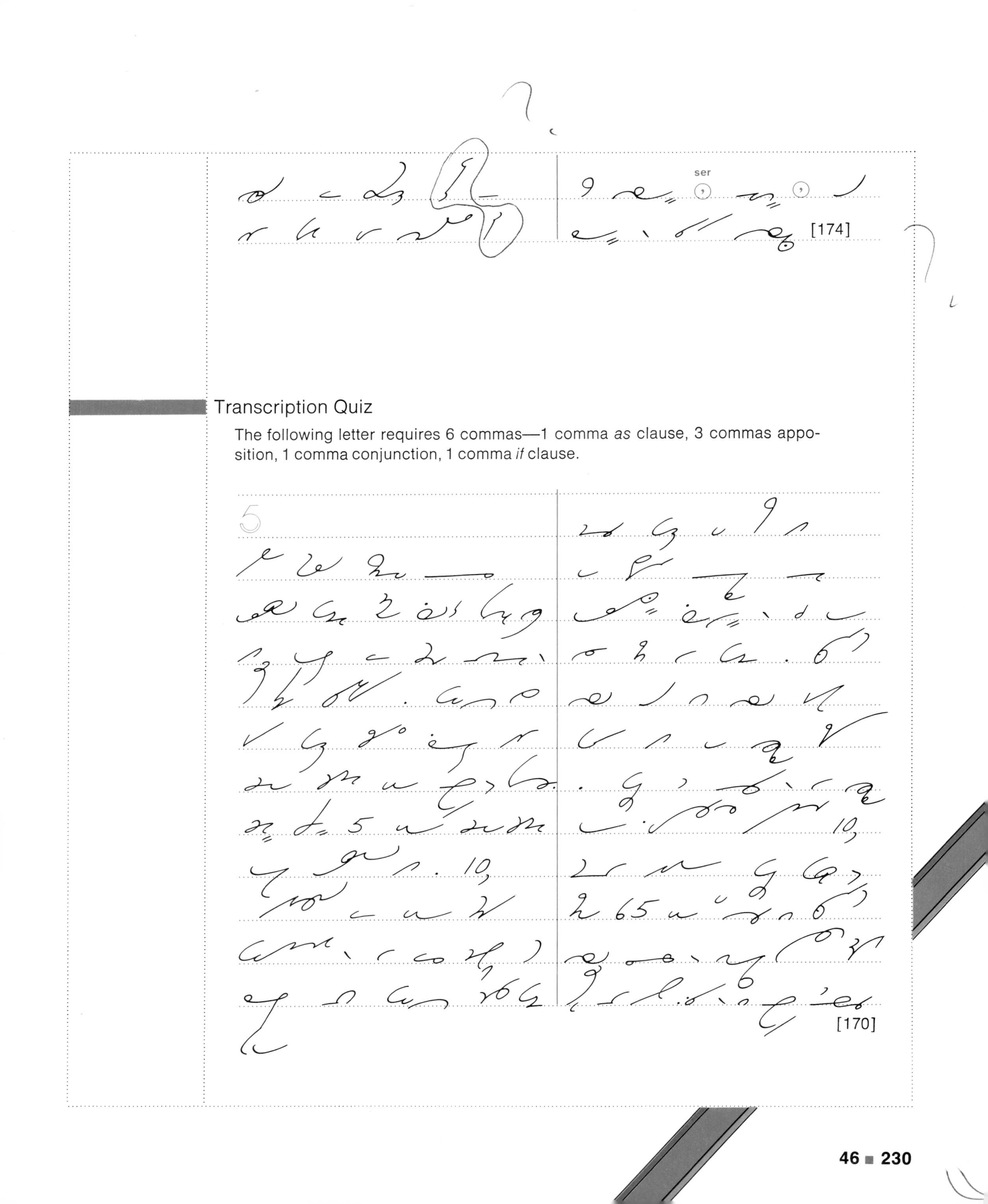

ser

[174]

Transcription Quiz

The following letter requires 6 commas—1 comma *as* clause, 3 commas apposition, 1 comma conjunction, 1 comma *if* clause.

5

[170]

ef·fi·cient

[146]

4

ad·ver·tis·ing

[61]

5

lug·gage

per·son·al

[94]

6

[124]

3

intro

intro

com·ply

and o

self-ad·dressed

par

[133]

4

ap

23

spon·sor

its

as

de·signed

4=

col·leges

mod·el

shop·ping

[104]

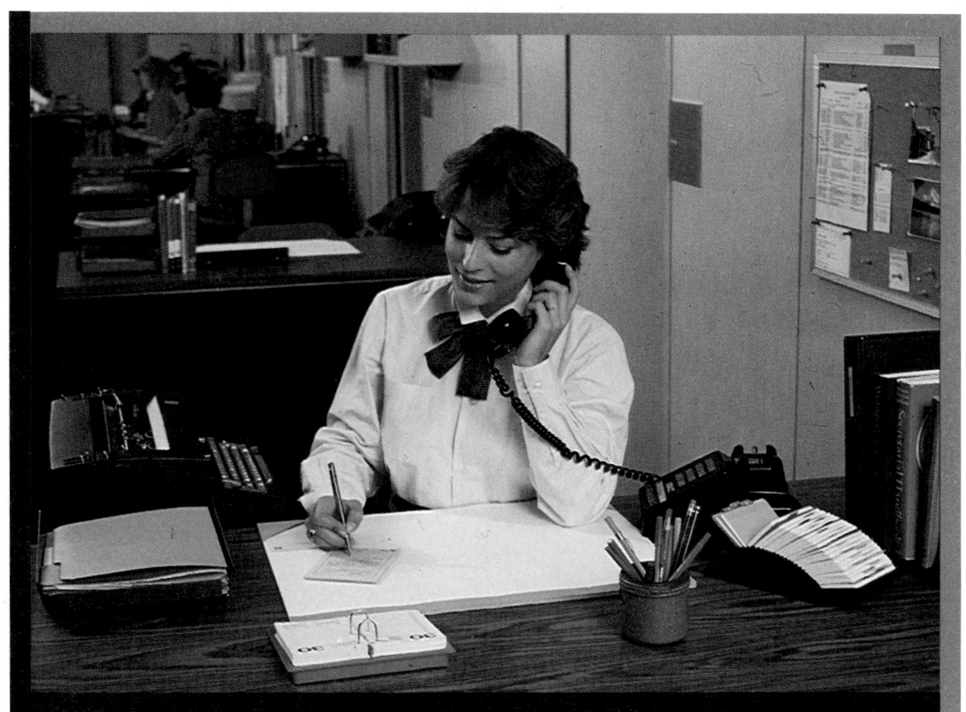

A secretary can use shorthand for more than just taking dictation—shorthand can be used to record telephone messages.

Reading and Writing Practice

[136]

2

ve·hi·cle

neigh·bor·hood

prac·ti·cal

amaz·ing·ly

qual·i·fi·ca·tions

sa·lient

wel·come

in·tro·duc·to·ry

re·ceive

vol·umes

ex·ceed·ing·ly

stim·u·lat·ing

intro

intro

intro

and o

as

if

when

par

17

Principles

Ow

The sound of *ow,* as in *now,* is written .

Spell: n-ow, now

now	south	how
down	loud	house
sound	account	ounce
found	round	crowd

Word Ending -ther

The word ending *-ther,* as in *other,* is represented by *ith.*

Spell: oo-ther, other

other	mother	either
another	gather	bother
whether (weather)	brother	bothered

Word Beginning Con-

The word beginning *con-,* as in *confer,* is represented by *k.*

Spell: con-f-e-r, confer

confer	considerable	concrete

In this lesson you will brush up on the disjoined word endings of Gregg Shorthand. The disjoined word endings are used a number of times in the Reading and Writing Practice.

Building Transcription Skills

Similar-Words Drill ■ county, country

county A political subdivision of a state.

Miami is in Dade *County.*

country A nation.

Our *country* produces a great deal of aluminum.

Business Vocabulary Builder

salient Standing out prominently.

seminar An advanced or graduate course featuring informality and discussion.

eligibility Qualification to be chosen.

concert ...... control ...... contract ......

convey ...... convince ...... contest ......

Word Beginning Com-

The word beginning *com-*, as in *complete*, is also represented by *k*.

Spell: com-p-l-e-t, complete

complete ...... compliment ...... combine ......

computer ...... compare ...... accomplish ......

Con-, Com- Followed by a Vowel

When *con-*, *com-* are followed by a vowel, these word beginnings are represented by *kn* or *km*.

connect ...... commit ...... commercial ......

connection ...... commerce ...... accommodate ......

Building Transcription Skills

Business Vocabulary Builder

complimentary Flattering; free.

convey Give or deliver to another.

conserve Avoid wasteful use of; save.

Reading and Writing Practice

Brief-Form Review Letter

ac·cept

Transcription Quiz

To punctuate the following letter correctly, you must supply 7 commas—2 commas series, 2 commas *when* clause, 2 commas parenthetical, 1 comma introductory.

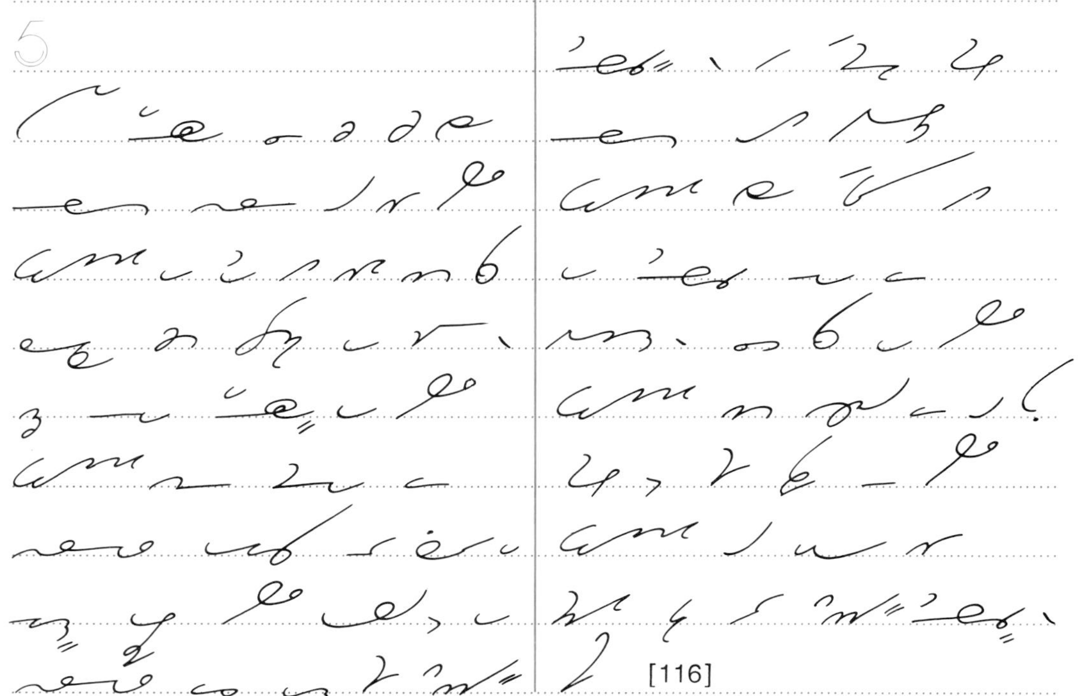

Brief-Form Checklist

Are you making good use of the brief-form chart that appears near the back of your textbook? Remember, the brief forms represent many of the most frequently used words in the language. The better you know them, the more rapid progress you will make in developing your shorthand speed.

Be sure to:

1 Spend a few minutes reading from the chart each day.

2 Time yourself and try to cut a few seconds off your reading time with each reading.

3 Read the brief forms in a different order each time—from left to right, from right to left, from top to bottom, from bottom to top.

re·ceived

com·plaints

[133]

2

con·ven·tion

an·nounce·ment

pro·fi·cien·cy

ac·com·plish·ments

[118]

3

unique

in·tro·duc·to·ry

par

mis·take

[174]

3

ap

is·sue

intro

ser

in·for·ma·tive

de·vel·op·ments

and o

con·ve·nience

[103]

4

su·pe·ri·or

re·solve

[116]

com·plete

con·crete

ma·jor

[143]

[119]

4

5

cri·sis

Reading and Writing Practice

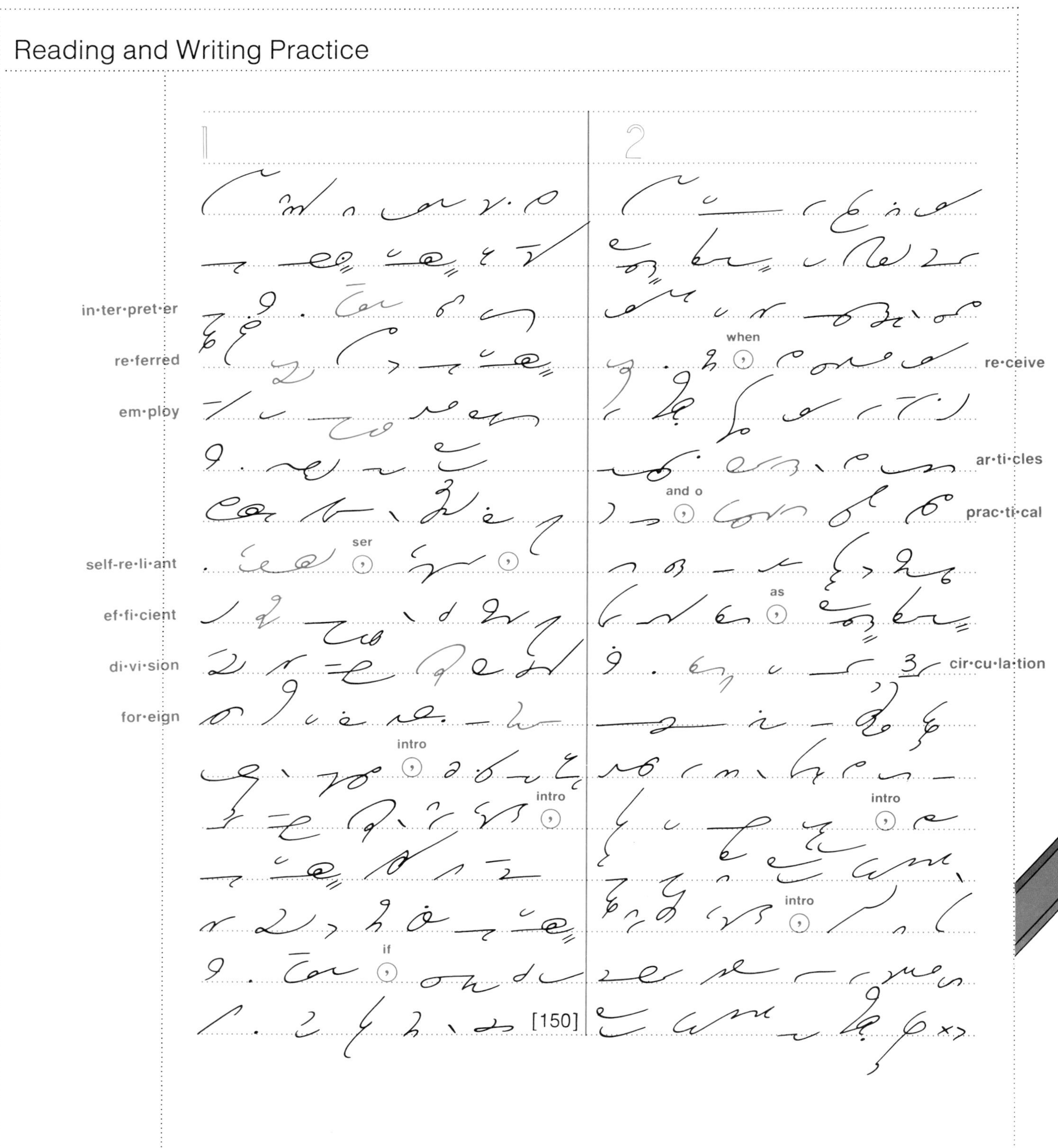

amounts 150 90

slipped

[93]

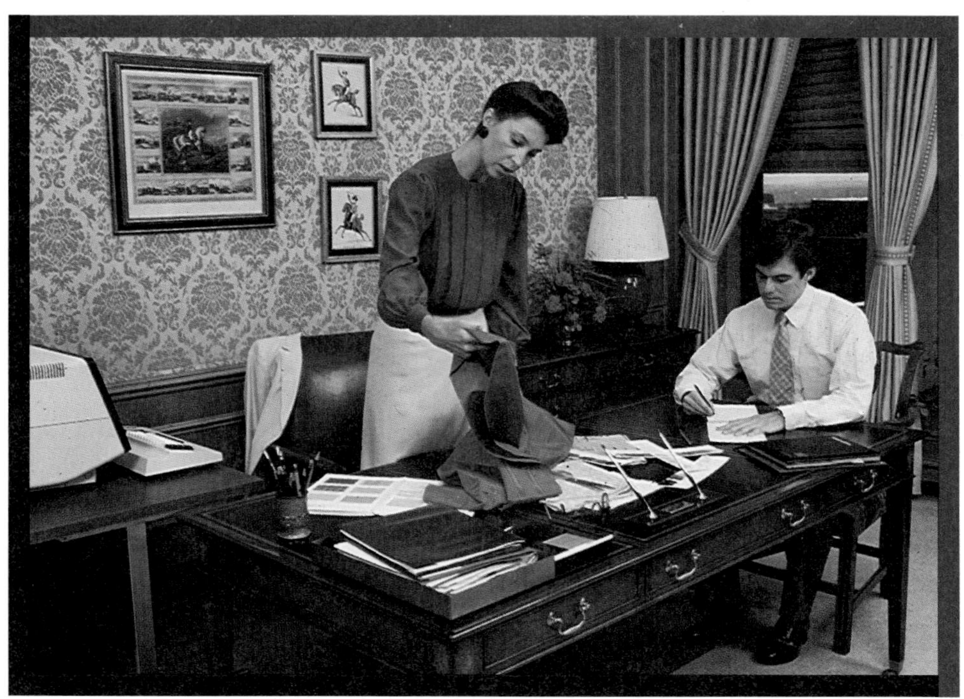

All industries—including the world of fashion design—have a need for shorthand-writing secretaries.

Disjoined word beginnings are given intensive treatment in Lesson 45. The letters in the Reading and Writing Practice contain many illustrations of the disjoined word beginnings of Gregg Shorthand.

Building Transcription Skills

Grammar Checkup ■ comparisons

The comparative degree of an adjective or adverb is used when reference is made to two objects; the superlative degree is used when reference is made to more than two objects.

comparative

Of the two students, Lee is the taller.
Which clerk is more efficient, Jane or Bill?
Mildred is the better qualified of the two pupils.

superlative

Of the three students, Lee is the tallest.
Which clerk is most efficient, Jane, Bill, or Kay?
Mildred is the best qualified of the three pupils.

Business Vocabulary Builder

interpreter A person who translates for people speaking different languages.

creamery A place where butter and cheese are made or where milk and cream are prepared or sold.

transforms Changes in character or condition.

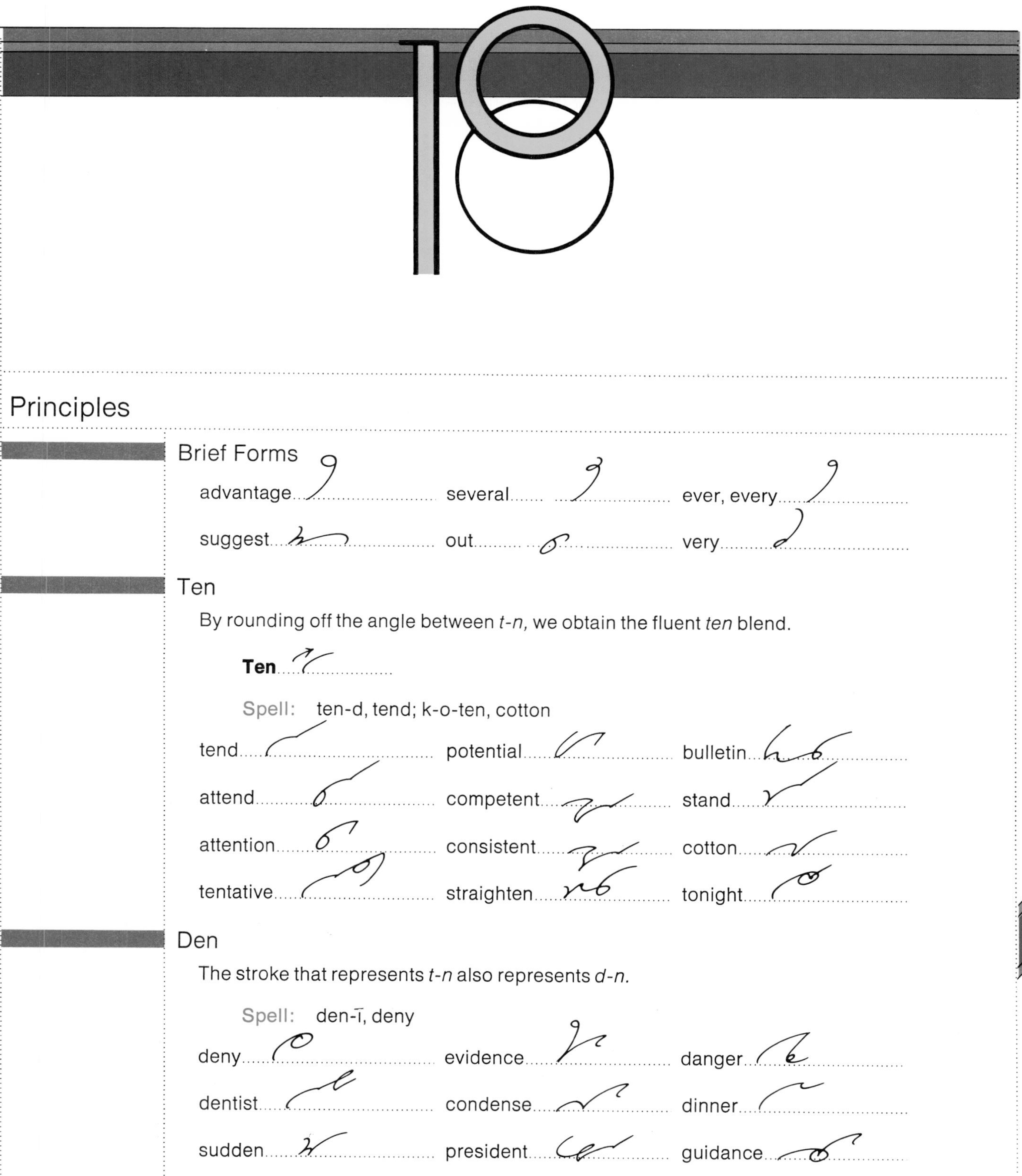

18

Principles

Brief Forms

advantage, several, ever, every, suggest, out, very

Ten

By rounding off the angle between *t-n,* we obtain the fluent *ten* blend.

Ten

Spell: ten-d, tend; k-o-ten, cotton

tend, potential, bulletin, attend, competent, stand, attention, consistent, cotton, tentative, straighten, tonight

Den

The stroke that represents *t-n* also represents *d-n.*

Spell: den-ī, deny

deny, evidence, danger, dentist, condense, dinner, sudden, president, guidance comma *if* clause.

As you copy the Transcription Quiz in your notebook, be sure to insert the necessary commas at the proper points and to indicate the reason for the punctuation.

Tain

The stroke that represents *t-n, d-n* also represents *-tain.*

Spell: o-b-tain, obtain

obtain .... attain .... pertain ....

contain .... retain .... certainly ....

maintain .... detain .... obtainable ....

Building Transcription Skills

Business Vocabulary Builder

residential Pertaining to the home or residence.

materialize Come into existence; appear.

anticipate Foresee and deal with in advance.

Reading and Writing Practice

Brief-Form Letter

in·stall·ing

over·due

grate·ful

here·af·ter

[89]

4

cur·tailed

pe·ti·tioned

re·lief

im·ple·ment

Be·gin·ning

dis·counts

amaze

[147]

Transcription Quiz

The correct punctuation of the following letter calls for 7 commas—1 comma introductory, 2 commas series, 2 commas apposition, 1 comma *and* omitted, 1

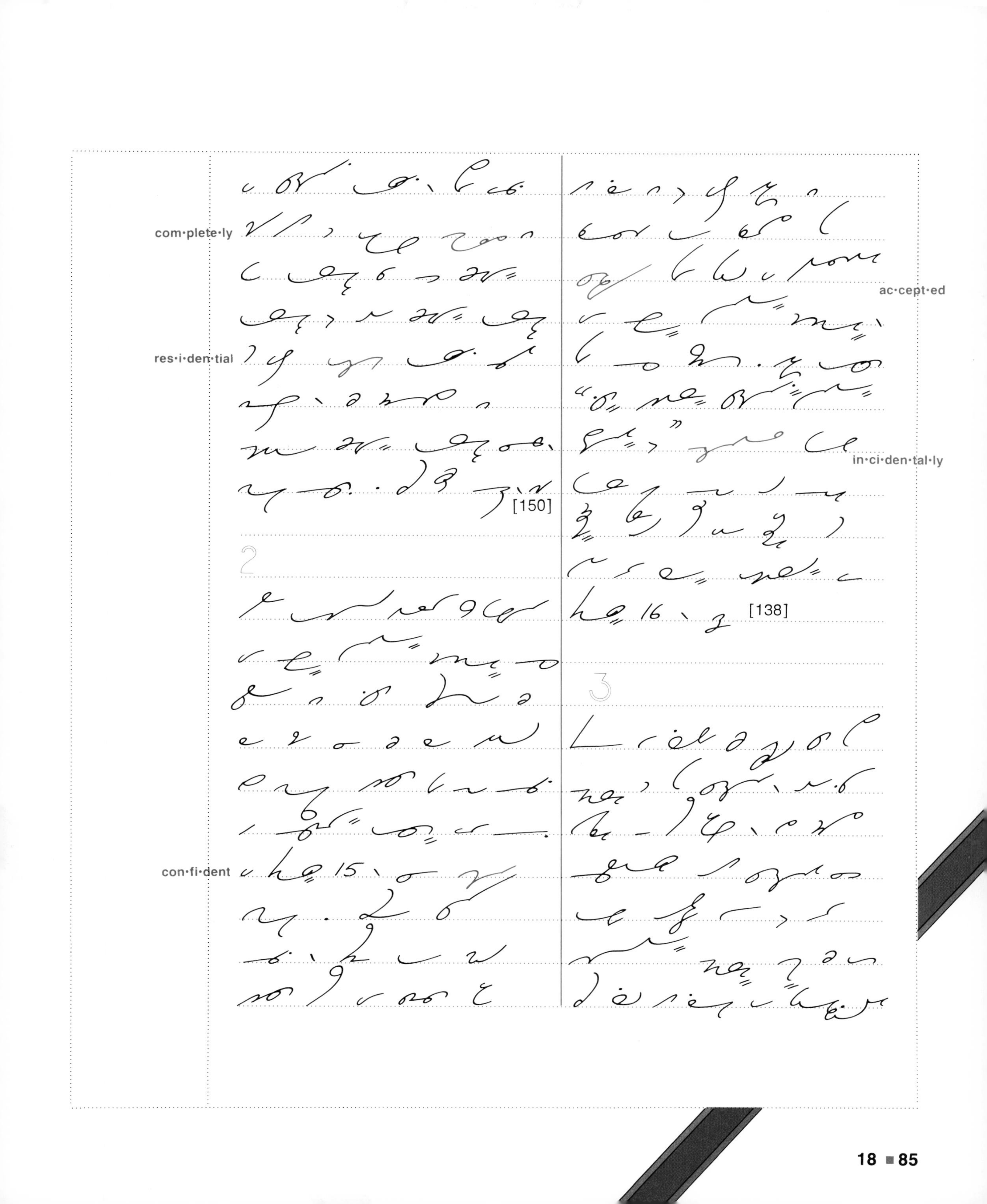

com·plete·ly

res·i·den·tial

[150]

2

con·fi·dent

ac·cept·ed

in·ci·den·tal·ly

[138]

3

re·ferred

and o

world's

clear

bot·tom

intro

pre·cau·tion

sew·age

conj

pol·lu·tion

pre·ven·tion

nom·i·nal

if

ac·cept·able

when

[165]

[133]

2

3

per·son

ev·ery·one

ef·fi·cient

ad·van·tages

coun·sel·or

555-9271 [164]

[141]

else·where

4

5

ship·ping

15

1930

Lesson 44 gives special attention to the joined word endings of Gregg Shorthand. The letters in the Reading and Writing Practice contain many illustrations of the joined word endings.

Building Transcription Skills

Common Prefixes ■ pre-

pre- before; beforehand; in advance

preliminary Before the main business or action.
predict To tell beforehand; forecast.
precaution Care taken in advance.
preventive Acting ahead of; to ward off.
preview An advance showing or viewing.

Business Vocabulary Builder

nominal Small; in name only.

curtail To cut off; shorten.

implement (verb) To carry out.

Reading and Writing Practice

1

ap

per·mis·sion

man·u·al

cir·cu·lars

at·tend·ing

[62]

At one time most secretaries were male. Gradually more and more women became secretaries until they dominated the field. Today, the electronic office is enticing men to return to secretarial careers.

[176]

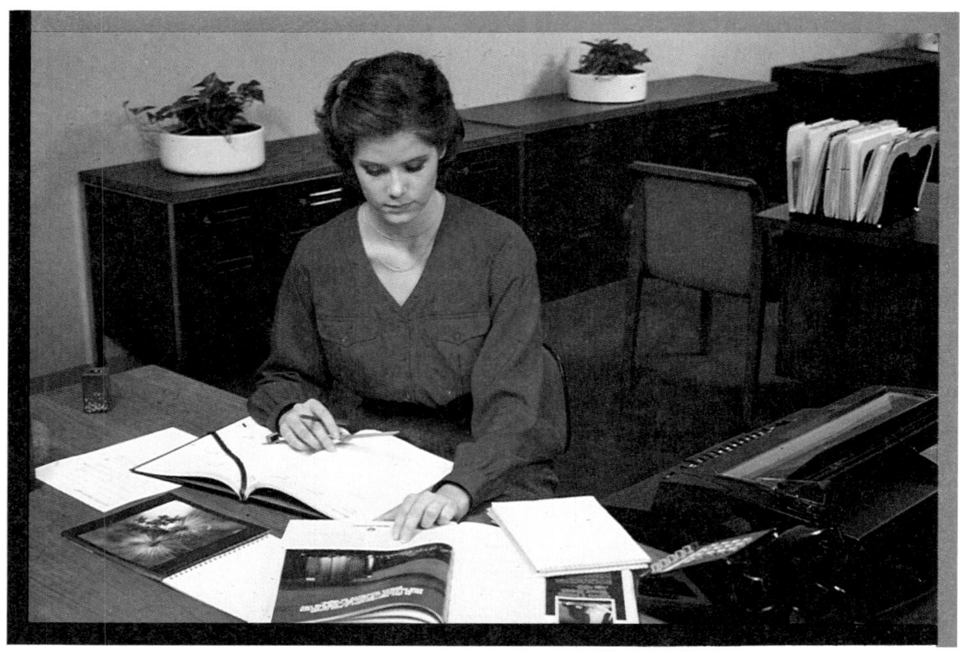

Following previously dictated instructions regarding travel plans, the secretary blocks out the appropriate time on the manager's calendar, makes transportation arrangements, and confirms hotel reservations.

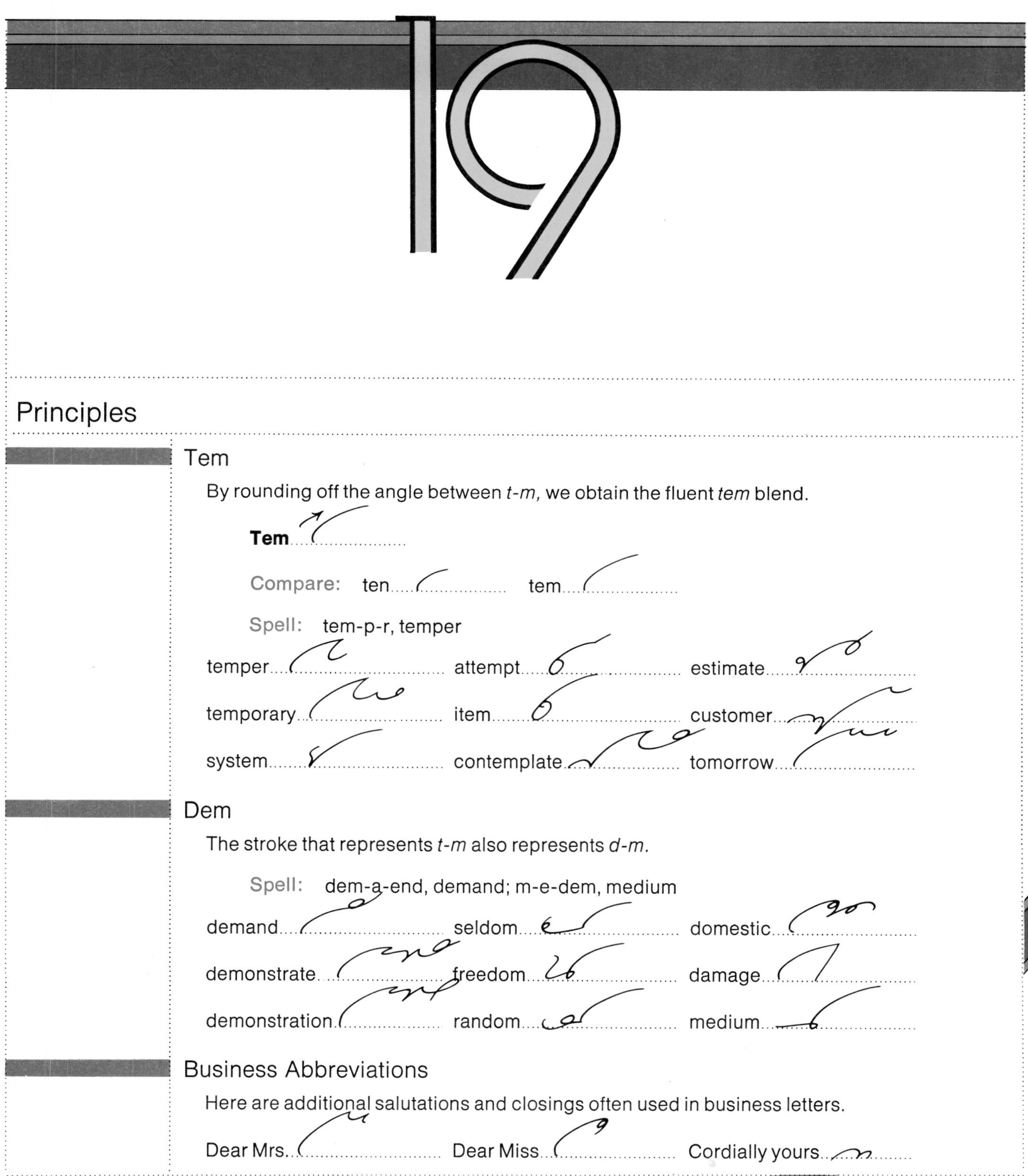

19

Principles

Tem

By rounding off the angle between *t-m,* we obtain the fluent *tem* blend.

Tem

Compare: ten tem

Spell: tem-p-r, temper

temper attempt estimate

temporary item customer

system contemplate tomorrow

Dem

The stroke that represents *t-m* also represents *d-m.*

Spell: dem-a-end, demand; m-e-dem, medium

demand seldom domestic

demonstrate freedom damage

demonstration random medium

Business Abbreviations

Here are additional salutations and closings often used in business letters.

Dear Mrs. Dear Miss Cordially yours

4

re·li·able

en·roll·ment

intro

and o

intro

Feb·ru·ary

intro

when

par

[158]

Transcription Quiz

The correct punctuation of the following letter calls for 6 commas—1 comma *as* clause, 2 commas series, 1 comma *and* omitted, 1 comma parenthetical, 1 comma *if* clause.

5

Dear Mr. .... Dear Ms. .... Yours sincerely ....

Useful Phrases

With the *ten* and *tem* blends, we can form three very useful phrases.

to know .... to me .... to make ....

Days of the Week

Sunday .... Wednesday .... Friday ....

Monday .... Thursday .... Saturday ....

Tuesday ....

Months of the Year

You are already familiar with the shorthand forms for several of the months as they are written in full. Here are all 12 months.

January .... May .... September ....

February .... June .... October ....

March .... July .... November ....

April .... August .... December ....

Building Transcription Skills

Business Vocabulary Builder

contemplate Consider; think of doing.

surpass Go beyond.

contagious Catching.

irreparably Permanently damaged; not able to be repaired.

ef·fi·cient

when

rep·re·sen·ta·tive

me·di·an

browse

if

dis·ap·pears

re·ap·pears

de·cid·ed

rea·son·able

if

intro

and o

en·joy·able

[154]

3

par

de·sign·er

[164]

Reading and Writing Practice

Brief-Form Review Letter

1

do·mes·tic

tem·po·rary

ten·ants

[187]

2

80 wpm

Reading and Writing Practice

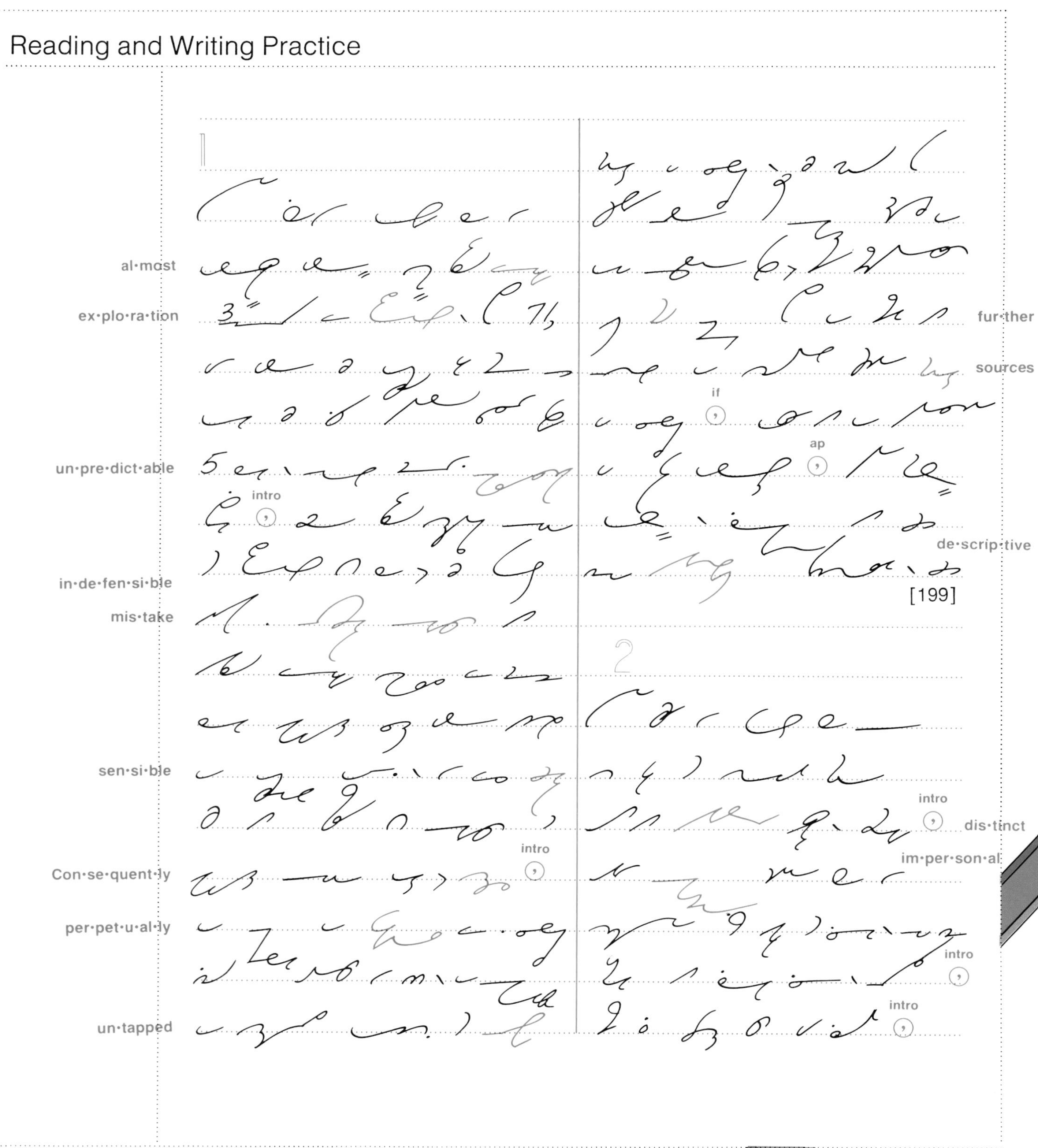

al·most

ex·plo·ra·tion

un·pre·dict·able

in·de·fen·si·ble

mis·take

sen·si·ble

Con·se·quent·ly

per·pet·u·al·ly

un·tapped

fur·ther

sources

de·scrip·tive

[199]

dis·tinct

im·per·son·al

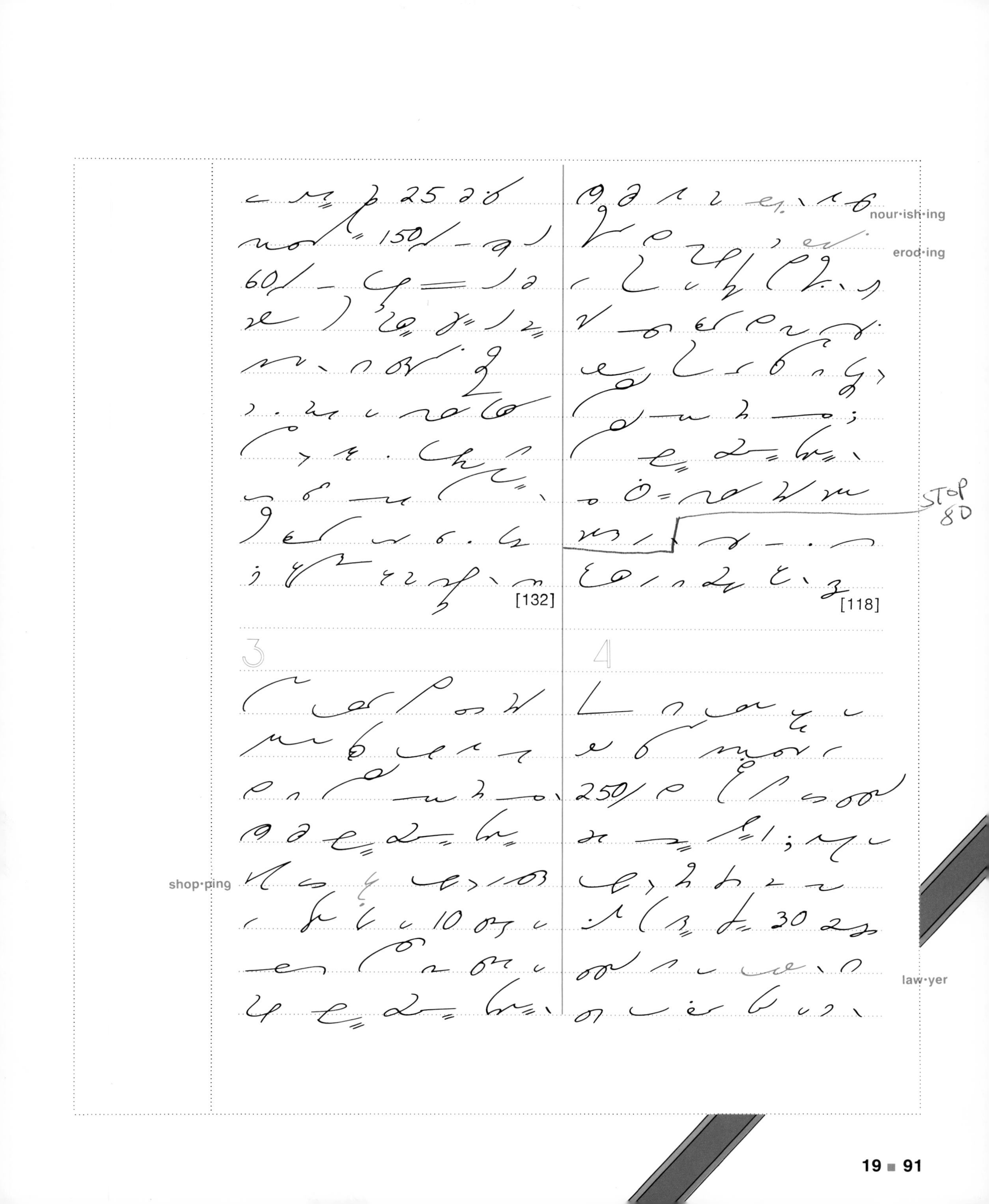

nour·ish·ing

erod·ing

STOP 80

[132]

[118]

3

4

shop·ping

law·yer

The letters in Lesson 43 give you an opportunity to review the joined word beginnings of Gregg Shorthand.

Building Transcription Skills

Spelling Families ■ -able, -ible

Words Ending in -able

avail-able	con-sid-er-able	un-for-get-ta-ble
ca-pa-ble	re-li-able	un-pre-dict-able
com-fort-able	suit-able	un-rea-son-able

Words Ending in -ible

ad-mis-si-ble	im-pos-si-ble	leg-i-ble
de-duct-ible	in-cred-i-ble	re-spon-si-ble
flex-i-ble	in-de-fen-si-ble	sen-si-ble

Business Vocabulary Builder

unpredictable Not capable of being foretold.

perpetually Continuing forever; everlasting.

interior designer One who plans and supervises the design or construction of rooms and their furnishings.

median (adjective) Being in the middle.

ir·rep·a·ra·bly

[105]

5

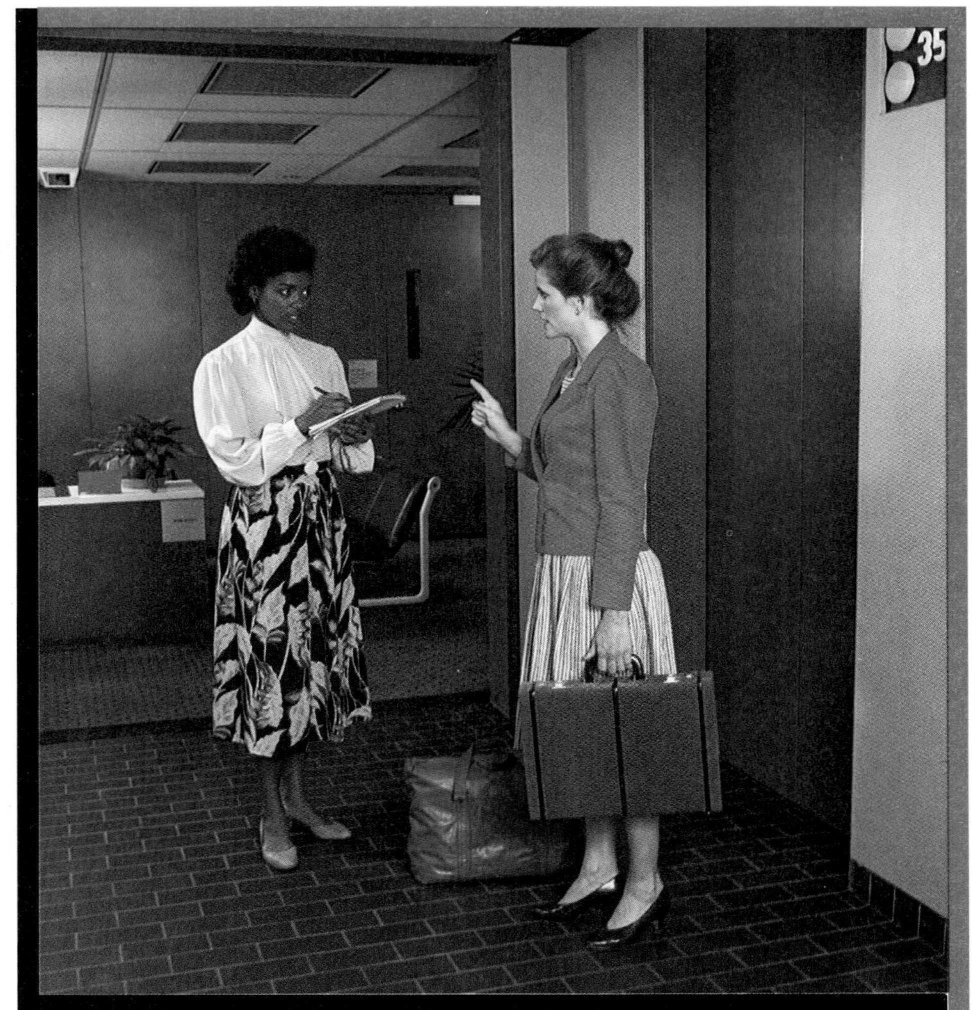

Shorthand is a portable skill and busy executives often dictate on the run.

[107]

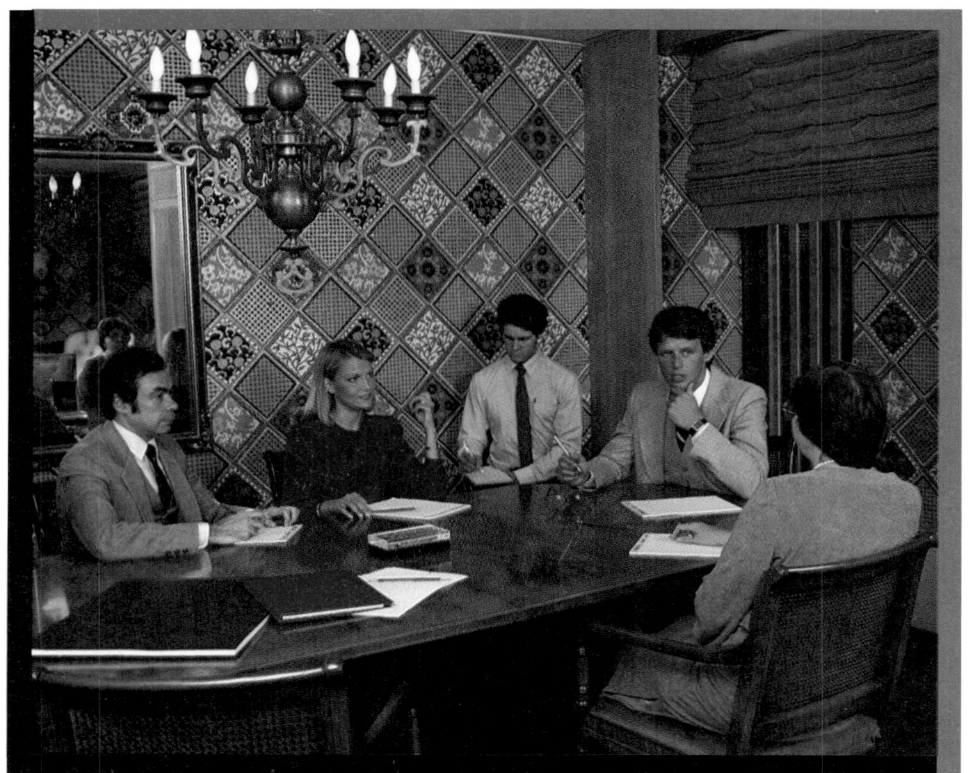

Secretaries are often required to attend important meetings in order to record the minutes.

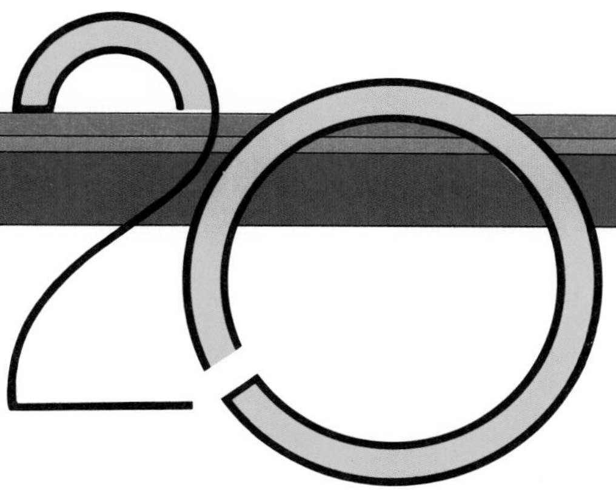

Principles

Brief Forms

After this group, you have only four more groups to learn.

acknowledge .... time .... organize ....

general .... question .... over* ....

*The outline for *over* is written above the following shorthand stroke. It is also used as a prefix form, as in:

oversight .... overdo .... overcame ....

Def, Dif

By rounding off the angle between *d-f,* we obtain the fluent *def, dif* blend.

Def, Dif ....

Spell: def-ī, defy; def-r, differ

defy .... define .... differ ....

defied .... definite .... different ....

defeat .... defect .... difference ....

Div, Dev

The stroke that represents *def, dif* also represents *div* and *dev.*

Spell: div-ī-d, divide; dev-o-t, devote

divide .... dividend .... division ....

re·ceive

intro

ser

if

when

if

when

[146]

4

ser

ex·pe·di·tious·ly

[90]

Transcription Quiz

To punctuate the following letter correctly, you must supply 6 commas—1 comma as clause, 1 comma apposition, 1 comma introductory, 1 comma conjunction, 2 commas parenthetical.

5

devote .... develop .... devotion ....

Ea, Ia

The sounds of *ea,* as in *create,* and *ia,* as in *piano,* are represented by a large circle with a dot placed within it.

Spell: k-r-eah-t, create

create .... appropriate .... piano ....

area .... appreciate .... brilliant ....

recreation .... aviation .... initiate ....

Building Transcription Skills

Similar-Words Drill ■ to, too, two

to (preposition) In the direction of. (*To* is also the sign of the infinitive.)

I gave the book *to* Kay.
I will go back *to* work on May 15.

too Also; more than enough.

I, *too,* have a college degree.
You make *too* many telephone calls.

two One plus one.

I will need *two* days to finish the job.

if

and o

[149]

intro

coupon

gallon

par

[127]

2

lemon

neighborhood

flavors

favorite

intro

appreciation

thoughtfulness

3

intro

accomplish

and o

competent

ser

friendliest

par

Business Vocabulary Builder

creative Having the ability to produce through imagination.

recreational Relating to the refreshment of strength or spirit after work.

appropriation An amount of money set aside for a specific purpose.

Reading and Writing Practice

Brief-Form Letter

1

OVERMAN

may·or

cam·paign·ing

cit·i·zens

[141]

2

1950

its

com·plete·ly

It is especially important to keep parallel all ideas in a tabulation.

no

The main duties were:

1. Typing letters
2. Answering the telephone
3. To take dictation

yes

The main duties were:

1. Typing letters
2. Answering the telephone
3. Taking dictation

Business Vocabulary Builder

rotate To alternate in a series.

dedicated (adjective) Committed to a cause, ideal, or purpose.

expeditiously Promptly and efficiently.

Reading and Writing Practice

as

and o

ap

conj

ex·cel·lent

re·pairs

par

urge

mis·take

par

ex·pen·sive

copy·ing

[170]

3

owned

As·so·ciates

urge

[164]

4

Lesson 42 provides you with an opportunity to increase your skill in writing the frequently used phrases of Gregg Shorthand. The following letters are packed with phrases. Several illustrations of the phrasing principles of Gregg Shorthand appear in the letters.

Building Transcription Skills

Grammar Checkup ■ sentence structure

Parallel ideas should be expressed in parallel form.

no
The class was interesting, informative, and of value to all of us.

yes
The class was interesting, informative, and valuable to all of us.

no
As soon as we verify your credit, your account will be opened and we will send your order.

yes
As soon as we verify your credit, your account will be opened and your order will be sent.

de·vel·op·ing

too

[101]

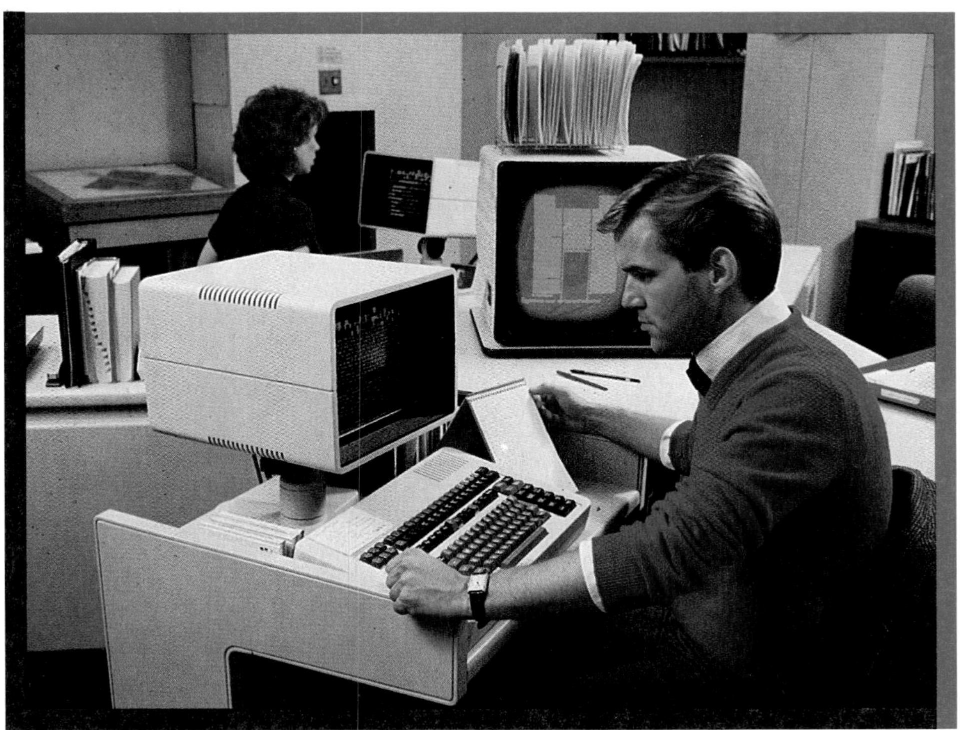

After a newspaper or magazine journalist keyboards a story into a terminal, the copy is checked against the shorthand notes that were written on location.

Transcription Quiz

In Lessons 26 through 37 you have been learning to apply nine rules for the correct use of the comma. In Lessons 41 through 60 you will have an opportunity to test your mastery of these rules through a Transcription Quiz—a letter in which no commas are indicated in the shorthand. It will be your job, as you copy the letter in shorthand in your notebook, to insert the commas in the proper places and to give the reasons why the commas are used. The shorthand in your notebook should resemble the following example:

At the head of each Transcription Quiz you will find the number and types of commas you should supply.

The correct punctuation of the following letter calls for 4 commas—1 comma *and* omitted, 2 commas series, 1 comma parenthetical.

6

[94]

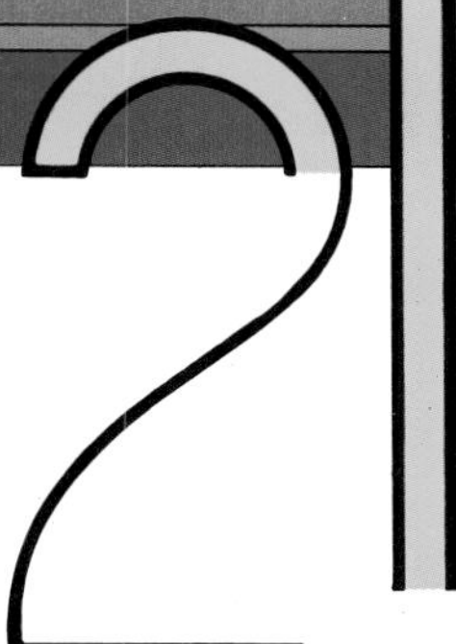

Principles

Brief Forms

envelope	state	success
difficult	satisfy, satisfactory	wish
progress	request	under*

*The outline for *under* is written above the following shorthand stroke. It is also used as a prefix form, as in:

underneath	undertake	undermine

Cities and States

In your work as a secretary, you will frequently have occasion to write geographical expressions. Here are a few important cities and states.

Cities

New York	Boston	Los Angeles
Chicago	Philadelphia	St. Louis

States

Michigan	Massachusetts	Missouri
Illinois	Pennsylvania	California

[214]

4

cor·re·spon·dence

ap

as

bi·month·ly

self-ad·dressed

and o

7:30

9:30

[113] de·ci·sion

5

intro

intro

roll·ing

Useful Business Phrases

The following phrases are used in business so frequently that special forms have been provided for them.

as soon as ... to do ... let us ...

as soon as possible ... of course ... I hope ...

Building Transcription Skills

Business Vocabulary Builder

influential Having the power to sway or convince.

tentative Not final; uncertain.

tailored Made to fit a special need or purpose.

Reading and Writing Practice

Brief-Form Letter

el·i·gi·ble

achieve

ul·ti·mate

def·i·nite

par

di·vi·sion

[184]

3

re·ceived

ap

per·son·nel

suc·cess·ful

cor·re·spon·dent

as

and o

or·ga·ni·za·tion

char·ac·ter·is·tic

when

ac·knowl·edge

oc·ca·sion

ocean

intro

voy·age

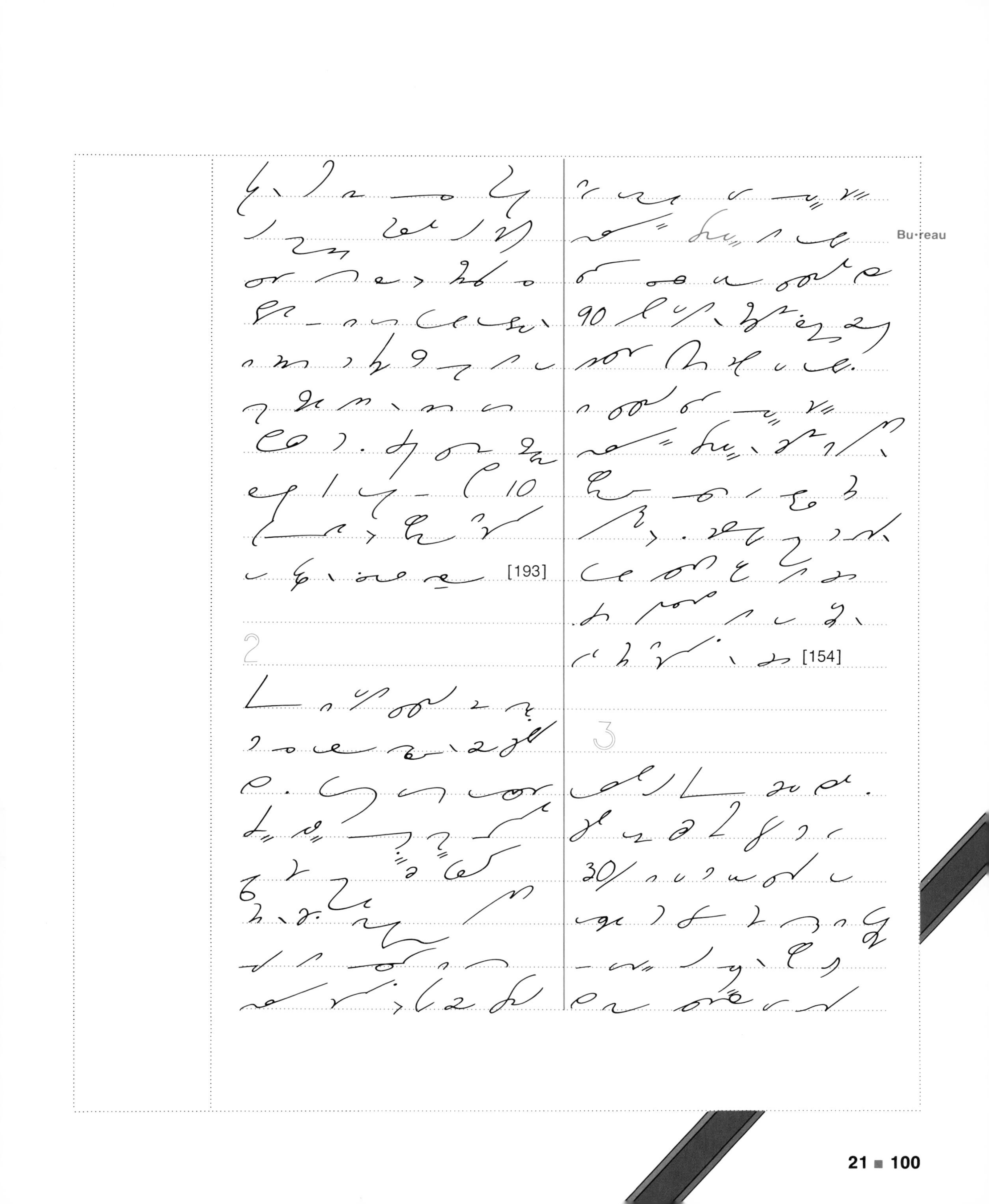

[193]

2

[154]

3

Bu·reau

Reading and Writing Practice

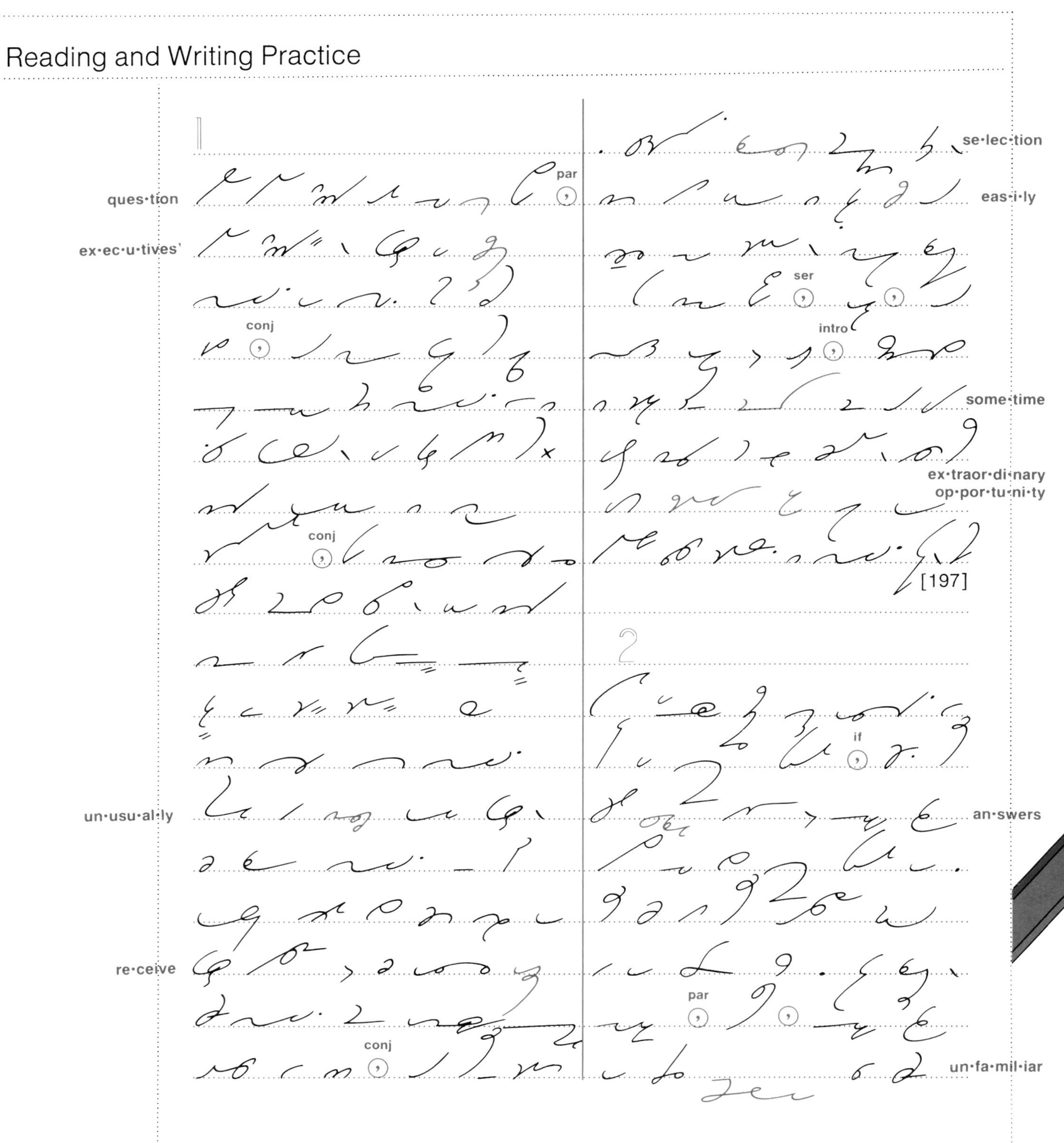

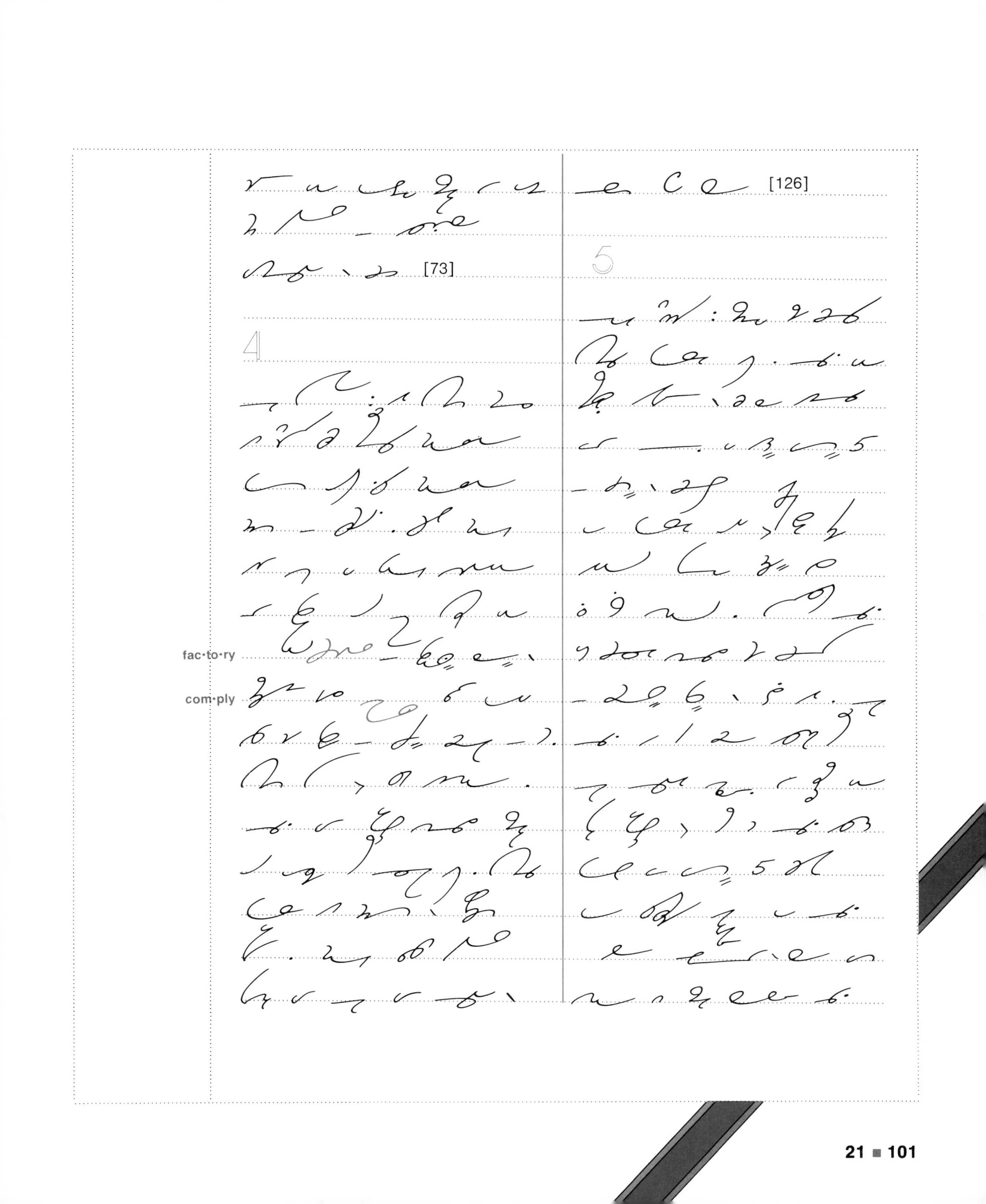

[73]

4

fac·to·ry

com·ply

[126]

5

The letters in Lesson 41 contain many of the brief forms and brief-form derivatives of Gregg Shorthand. Because you have seen and written the brief forms of Gregg Shorthand many, many times, you should be able to read the letters in this lesson in record time!

Building Transcription Skills

Spelling Families ■ -tion, -sion

Words Ending in -tion

ap-pli-ca-tion
cir-cu-la-tion
con-tri-bu-tion
in-for-ma-tion
or-ga-ni-za-tion
pro-tec-tion
ques-tion
sat-is-fac-tion
se-lec-tion

Words Ending in -sion

con-clu-sion
de-ci-sion
oc-ca-sion
per-mis-sion
pro-fes-sion
ses-sion

Business Vocabulary Builder

mature (verb) Become due or payable.

vandals Those who willfully destroy or damage property.

trespassers Those who enter another's property unlawfully.

[131]

6

kitch·en

[105]

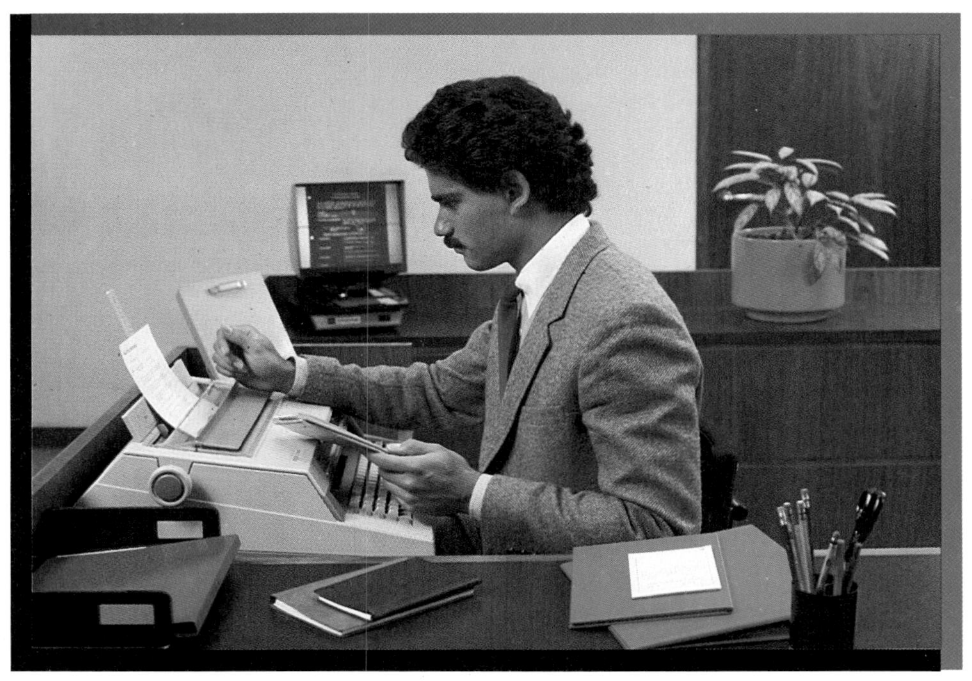

Today secretaries are using a wide variety of equipment in the performance of their jobs.

SECTION 2

Principles

Long I and a Following Vowel

Any vowel following long i is represented by a small circle within a large circle.

Compare: signs .... science ....

Spell: t-r-īah-l, trial

trial .... drier .... compliance ....

dial .... client .... reliance ....

prior .... quiet .... appliances ....

Word Beginnings En-, Un-

The word beginnings *en-, un-* are represented by *n.*

En-

Spell: en-j-oi, enjoy

enjoy .... engagement .... endanger ....

engrave .... engine .... encourage ....

endeavor .... enlarge .... encouragement ....

Un-

Spell: un-t-e-l, until

until .... unfair .... unfilled ....

for·ward

par

ser

when

ap

au·tho·riz·ing

conj

[136]

intro

it's

plau·si·ble

intro

intro

sin·cer·i·ty

conj

intro

intro

par

ap

[137]

unless ... unpaid ... unreasonable ...

undue ... uncertain ... undoubtedly ...

In-, En-, Un- Followed by a Vowel

When *in-, en-, un-* are followed by a vowel, they are written in full.

innovation ... enact ... unable ...

Useful Business Phrases

Here are six more frequently used business phrases.

more than ... to us ... your order ...

we hope ... let me ... you ordered ...

Building Transcription Skills

Business Vocabulary Builder

enlarged Made bigger.

fragile Easily broken or destroyed.

enlightening Furnishing knowledge or information.

Reading and Writing Practice

Brief-Form Review Letter

un·doubt·ed·ly

oc·ca·sion

③ par ④ if and o par [170]

5

as over·whelm·ing·ly par intro Con·se·quent·ly re·plen·ish and o conj par col·umns [125]

6

if

en·joy·able

chef

cal·en·dar

[176]

2

bag·gage

un·ques·tioned

guar·an·tee

if

max·i·mum

ef·fi·cien·cy

ser

and o

if

when

if

[207]

3

as

intro

great

in·sig·nif·i·cant

par

par

par

con·sult

ap

neigh·bor·hood

[144]

4

intro

intro

frayed

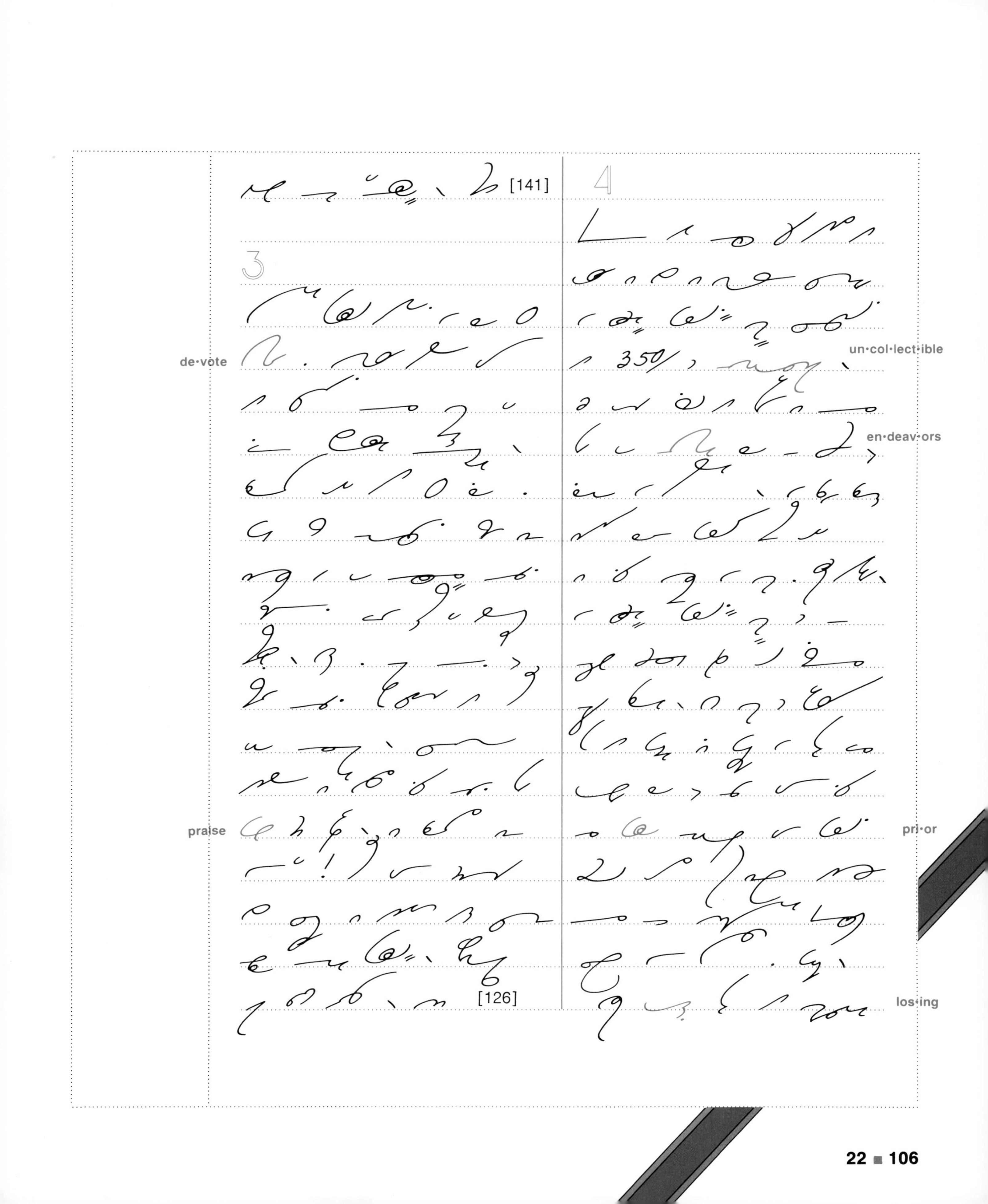

[141]

3

de·vote

praise

[126]

4

350

un·col·lect·ible

en·deav·ors

pri·or

los·ing

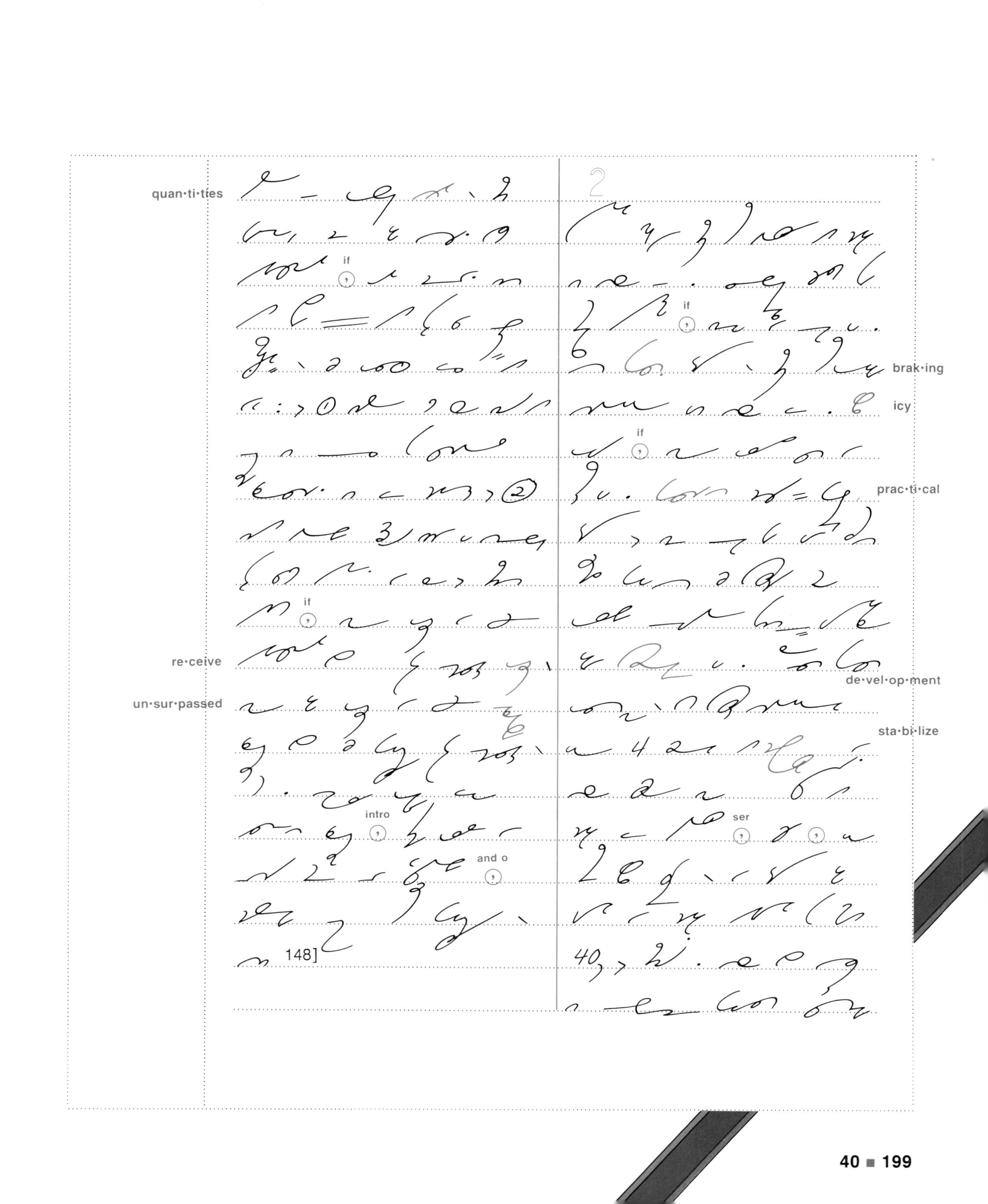

quan·ti·ties

if

if

re·ceive

un·sur·passed

intro

and o

148]

2

if

brak·ing

icy

if

prac·ti·cal

de·vel·op·ment

sta·bi·lize

ser

de·mise
in·ev·i·ta·ble

[193]

5

[48]

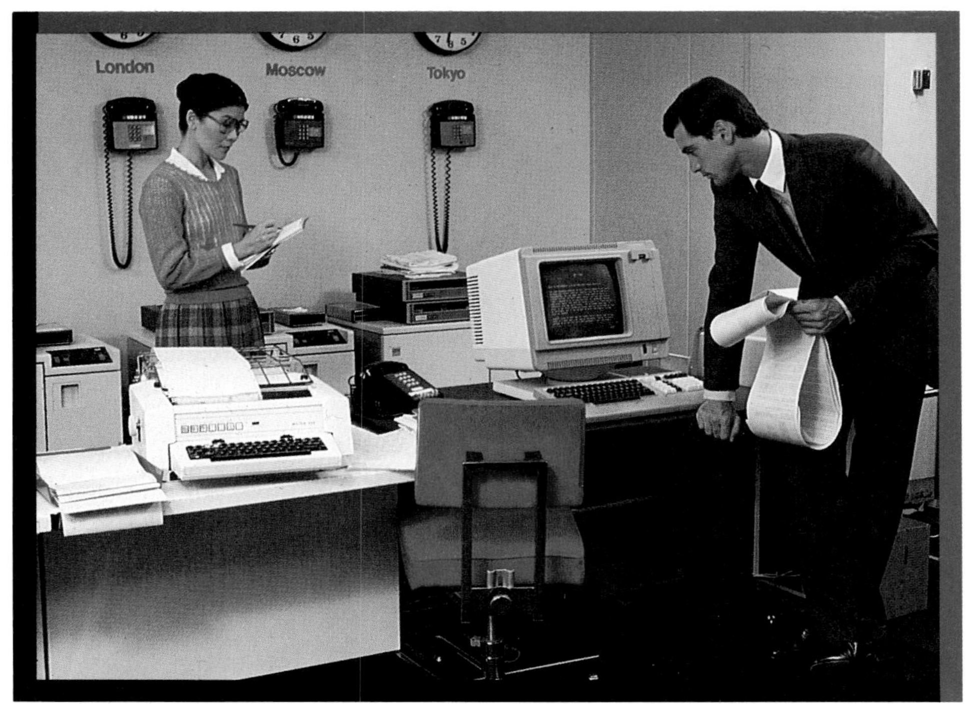

Stockbrokers obtain up-to-the-minute financial data from all over the world via Telex and other telecommunications devices.

Building Transcription Skills

Grammar Checkup

Most business executives have a good command of the English language; some rarely make an error in grammar. There are times, though, when even the best dictators will inadvertently use a plural verb with a singular noun or use the objective case when they should use the nominative. They usually know better, but in concentrating intently on expressing a thought or idea, they occasionally suffer a grammatical lapse.

It will be your job as secretary to catch these occasional errors in grammar and to correct them when you transcribe.

From time to time in the lessons ahead, you will be given an opportunity to brush up on some of the rules of grammar that are frequently violated.

Grammar Checkup ■ subject and verb

A verb must agree with its subject in number.

Our president is on vacation.
The receipts are being processed now.

The inclusion of a phrase such as *in addition to, as well as,* or *along with* after the subject does not affect the number of the verb. If the subject is singular, use a singular verb; if the subject is plural, use a plural verb.

Our president, as well as the treasurer, is on vacation.
The receipts, along with the invoice, are being processed now.

Business Vocabulary Builder

unsurpassed Cannot be exceeded or outdone.

stabilize To hold steady.

overwhelmingly Overcome by force of numbers; crushingly.

Reading and Writing Practice

Brief-Form Review Letter

when

com•mer•cial

Principles

Brief Forms

After you have learned the following brief forms, you will have only two more groups to go!

particular	speak	newspaper
probable	subject	opinion
regular	regard	idea

Ng

The sound of *ng,* as in *sing,* is written

Compare: seen sing

Spell: s-e-ing, sing

sing	bring	length
sang	rang	strength
song	wrong	single

Ngk

The sound of *ngk,* as in *sink*, is written

Compare: seem sink

Spell: r-a-ink, rank

rank	drink	uncle

Principles

Geographical Expressions and Names

In geographical expressions and proper names, the ending *-burg* is represented by *b*; the ending *-ville,* by *v*; the ending *-ington,* by a disjoined *ten* blend; the ending *-ingham*, by a disjoined *m.*

-burg

Spell: h-a-r-e-s-burg, Harrisburg

Harrisburg .... Pittsburgh .... Hamburg ....

-ville

Spell: n-a-ish-ville, Nashville

Nashville .... Jacksonville .... Evansville ....

-ington

Spell: oo-o-ish-ington, Washington

Washington .... Wilmington .... Harrington ....

-ingham

Spell: f-r-a-m-ingham, Framingham

Framingham .... Buckingham .... Cunningham ....

frank shrink banquet

bank ink anxious

Omission of Vowel Preceding -tion

When *t, d, n,* or *m* is followed by *-ition* or *-ation,* the circle is omitted.

addition quotation permission

edition combination commission

notation reputation estimation

Building Transcription Skills

Business Vocabulary Builder

greenhouses Glassed buildings used for cultivating and protecting plants.

automation A technique often using electronic devices that take the place of human effort.

heirs Those who are entitled to inherit.

Reading and Writing Practice

Brief-Form Letter

yes·ter·day's

be·gin·ning

[179]

4

via

ap

mis·spelled

par

[102]

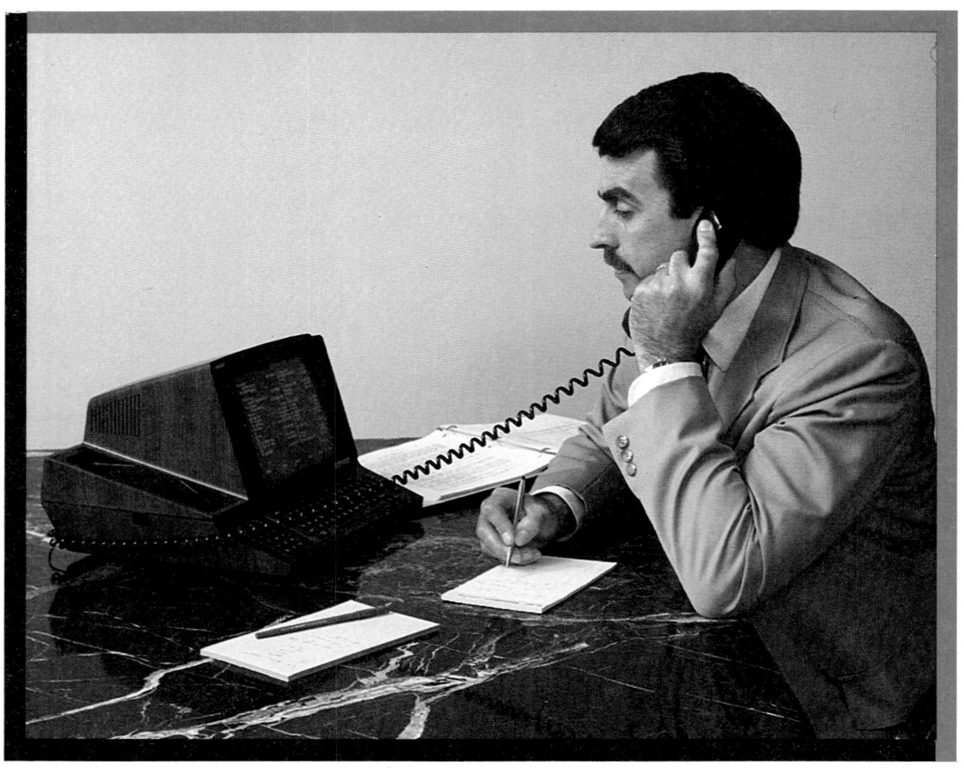

During a telephone conversation in which important information is being discussed, an executive who uses shorthand is able to record all facts without holding up the conversation.

green·houses

[177]

2

heirs

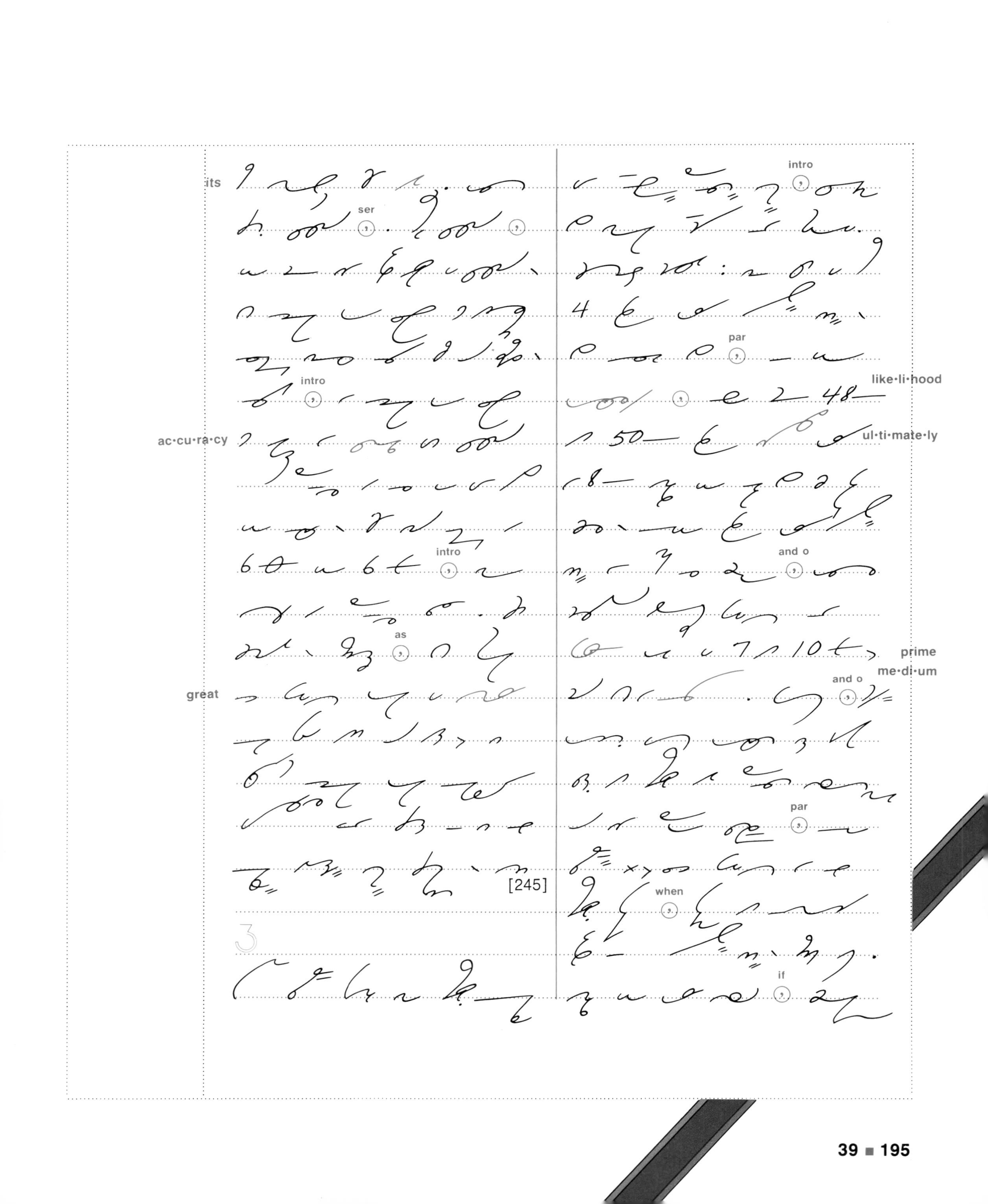

its

ser

intro

ac·cu·ra·cy

intro

as

great

[245]

3

intro

par

like·li·hood

ul·ti·mate·ly

and o

prime

me·di·um

and o

par

when

if

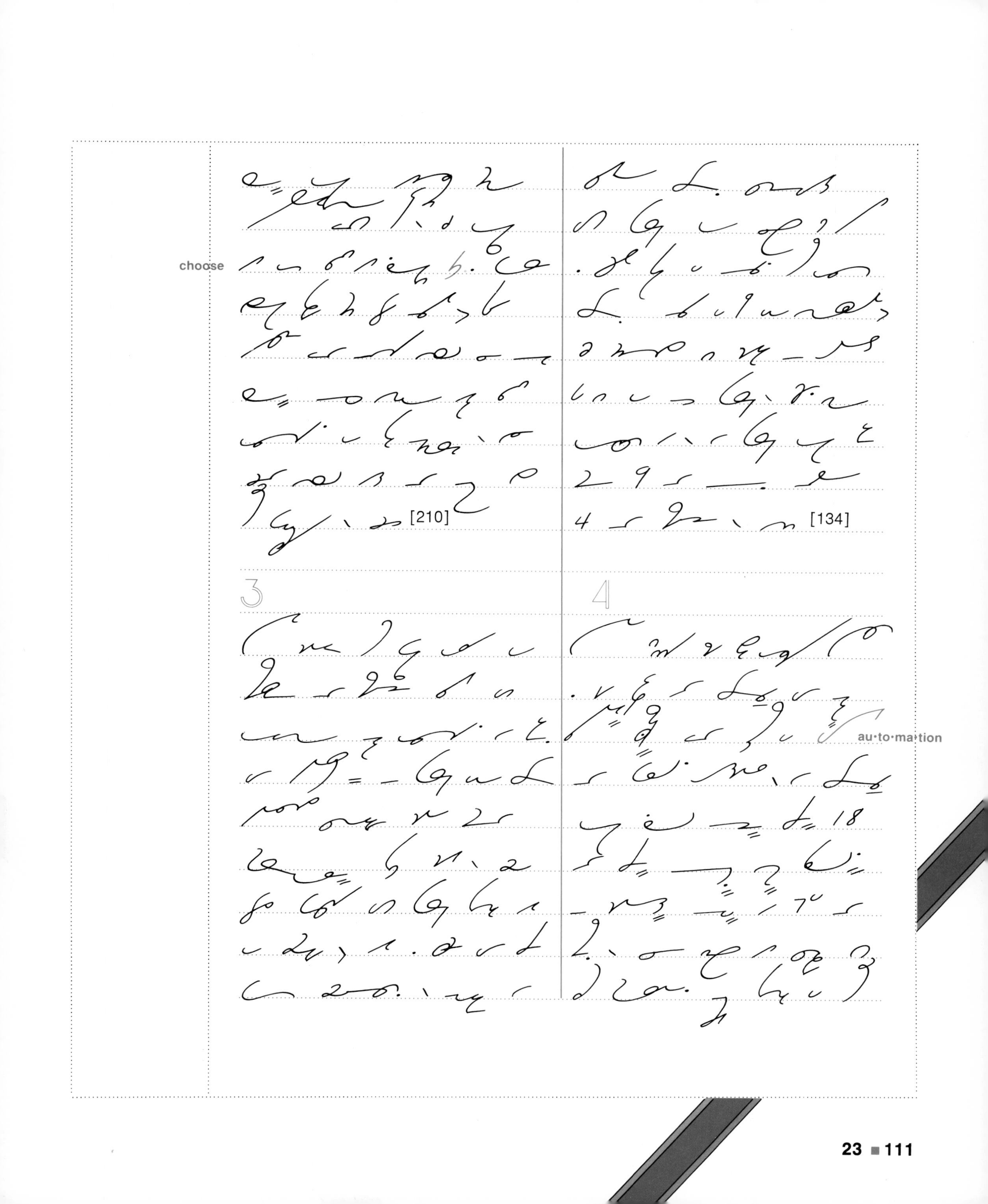

choose

[210]

[134]

3

4

au·to·ma·tion

Reading and Writing Practice

Brief-Form Review Letter

1

[158]

2

conj

grapevine

intro

our·selves

in·stall·ing

and o

ef·fi·cient

its

sub·sid·iar·ies

intro

intro

ad·van·tage

help·ful

char·ac·ter·is·tic

when

intro

as·signed

[179]

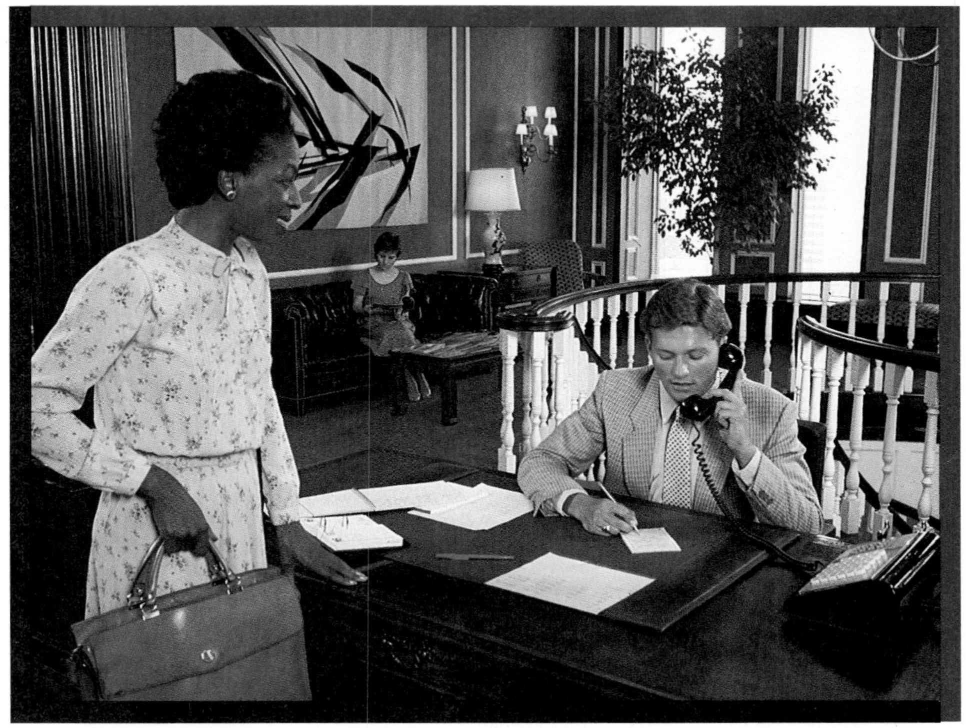

In order to properly announce a visitor, the receptionist should write down necessary information; if written in shorthand, it can be done more quickly and more efficiently.

OR if A businessman – ASK for A business card

anywhere ... worthwhile ... withstand ...

thereupon ... however* ... notwithstanding ...

*The dot may be omitted in *however.*

Intersection

Intersection, or writing of one shorthand character through another, is sometimes useful for special phrases. This principle may be used when constant repetition of certain combinations of words in your dictation makes it clearly worthwhile to form special outlines for them.

a.m. ... vice versa ...

p.m. ... Chamber of Commerce ...

Building Transcription Skills

Similar-Words Drill ■ it's, its

it's Contraction for *it is.*

It's not necessary to bring all your books to class.

its Possessive form of *it.*

You will be pleased with *its* efficiency.

Business Vocabulary Builder

grapevine An informal person-to-person means of passing information.

via By means of; by way of.

subsidiaries Companies wholly controlled by other companies.

Principles

Ah, Aw

A dot is used for *a* in words that begin *ah* and *aw.*

Spell: a-h-e-d, ahead; a-oo-a, away

ahead	awaken	awoke
away	awakened	award

X

The letter *x* is represented by an *s* written with a slight backward slant.

Compare: miss mix

fees fix

Spell: t-a-ex, tax; t-a-exes, taxes

tax	relax	indexes
taxes	relaxes	approximate
box	relaxation	complex

Omission of Short U

In the body of a word, the sound of short *u,* as in *fun,* is omitted before *n, m,* or a straight downstroke.

Principles

Word Ending -gram

The word ending *-gram* is represented by a disjoined *gay*.

Spell: t-e-l-gram, telegram

telegram .... monogram .... programs ....

diagram .... monogrammed .... programmer ....

Word Beginning Electric

The word beginning *electric-* (and the word *electric*) is represented by a disjoined *el.*

Spell: electric-l, electrical

electric .... electrically .... electric wire ....

electrical .... electric typewriter .... electric motor ....

Word Beginning Electr-

The word beginning *electr-* is also represented by a disjoined *el.*

Spell: electro-n-e-k, electronic

electronic .... electrician .... electricity ....

Compounds

Most compound words are formed simply by joining the outlines for the words that make up the compound. In some words, however, it is desirable to modify the outline for one of the words in order to obtain an easier joining.

anyhow .... someone .... within ....

Before N

fun .... done .... lunch ....
begun .... son (sun) .... front ....

Before M

sum (some) .... come .... income ....
summer .... become .... column ....

Before a Straight Downstroke

rush .... touch .... judged ....
brushed .... much .... budget ....

Building Transcription Skills

Business Vocabulary Builder

perplexing Baffling; difficult to solve.

conscientious Governed by the desire to do the right and proper thing.

Reading and Writing Practice

Brief-Form Review Letter

aware

ex·ceed

10

[180]

6

18

ap

18

re·gard·ing

li·brary

3104 18

as

mi·nor

550

intro

item·ized

and o

[161]

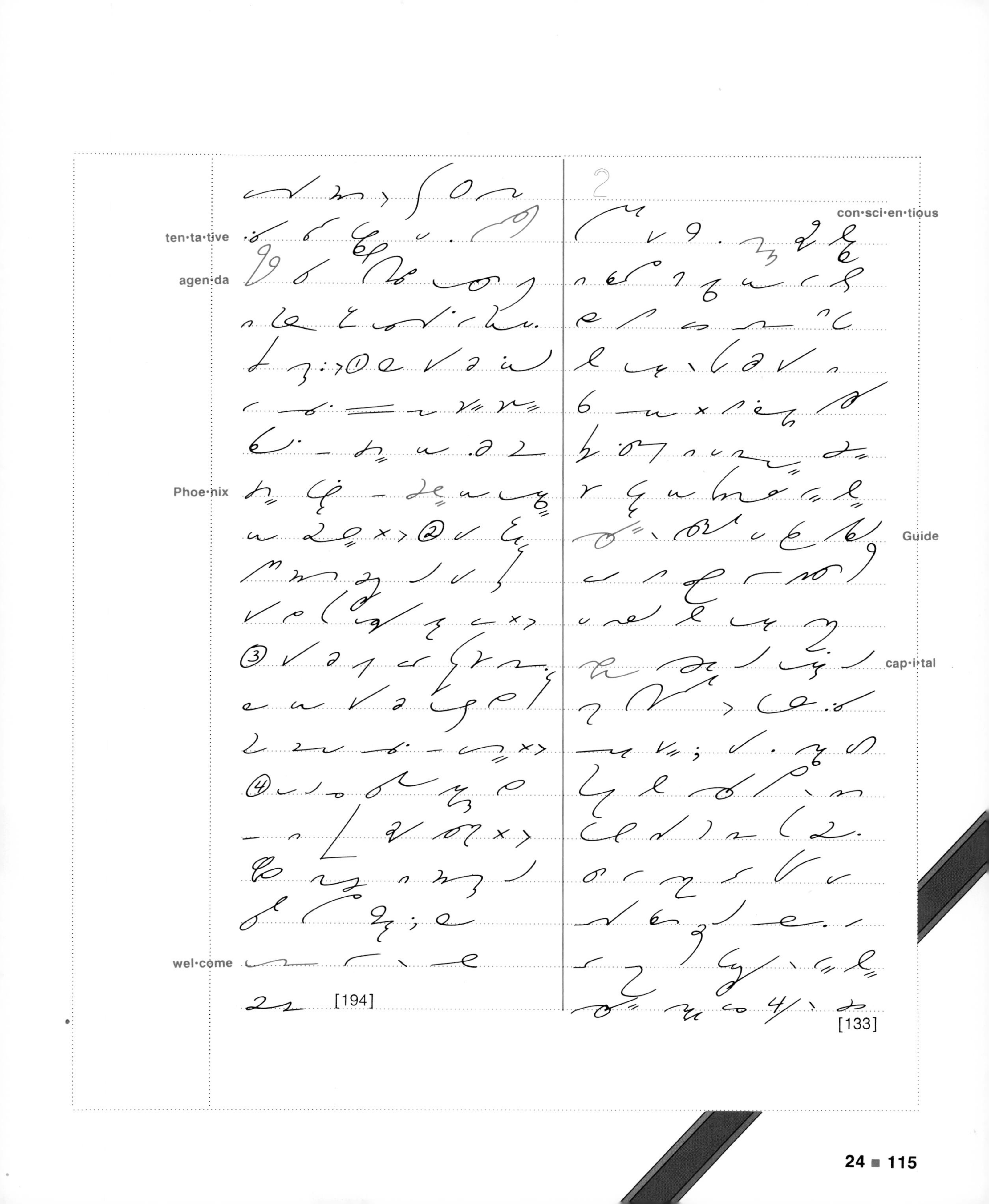

ten·ta·tive

agen·da

Phoe·nix

wel·come

[194]

2

con·sci·en·tious

Guide

cap·i·tal

[133]

in·di·cated

par

ex·traor·di·nary

when

ul·ti·mate·ly

par

[183]

5

as

ap

intro

pe·ri·od

if

intro

guar·an·tee

3

be·lieve

ris·ing

max·i·mum

sim·ply

[153]

4

spa

de·vot·ed
com·plete·ly

deemed

conj

mak·ing

ecol·o·gy

[202]

3

par

intro

ap

ser

as

prob·a·bly

and o

rec·og·nized

mul·ti·tude

intro

serv·ing

par

if

con·ve·nient

[177]

4

gov·ern·ment

ser

neigh·bor·hoods

[156]

5

as·sis·tant

[78]

Double-checking content when proofreading is easily done when shorthand is the input medium—the notes are right at hand.

Reading and Writing Practice

Brief-Form Review Letter

1

ap

su·per·vis·ing

de·vel·op·ment

An·thol·o·gy

as

mem·o·ran·dum

ac·qui·si·tion

and o

[97]

2

rough·ly

intro

al·le·vi·ate

par

mi·nor

par

su·per·fi·cial

ser

Principles

Brief Forms

responsible	publish, publication	usual
worth	ordinary	world
public	experience	recognize

Word Beginning Ex-

The word beginning *ex-* is represented by *e-s.*

Spell: ex-t-r-a, extra

extra	expenses	excuse
examine	expert	extensive
extremely	excellent	exception

Word Ending -ful

The word ending *-ful* is represented by *f.*

Spell: k-a-r-ful, careful

careful	useful	helpful
doubtful	thoughtful	helpfully
grateful	beautiful	helpfulness

Quantities and Amounts

Here are a few more helpful abbreviations for quantities and amounts.

600	$5,000,000,000	several hundred
$600	a dollar	5 pounds
$8,000,000	a million	8 feet

■ Observe that the *n* for *hundred* is written under the figure as a positive distinction from *million,* in which the *m* is written beside the figure.

Building Transcription Skills

Spelling Families ■ silent e dropped before -ing

An effective device to improve your ability to spell is to study words in related groups, or spelling families, in which all the words contain a common spelling problem.

To get the most benefit from these spelling families, practice them in this way:

1. Spell each word aloud, pausing slightly after each syllable.
2. Write the word once in longhand, spelling it aloud as you write it.

Words in Which Silent E Is Dropped Before -ing

chal-leng-ing	mak-ing	sav-ing
hav-ing	man-u-fac-tur-ing	stim-u-lat-ing
hous-ing	pre-par-ing	su-per-vis-ing
in-creas-ing	re-ceiv-ing	typ-ing

You will find a number of the words in this spelling family used in the Reading and Writing Practice of this lesson.

Business Vocabulary Builder

anthology A collection of literary pieces or passages.

alleviate Ease.

superficial Shallow; concerned only with the obvious.

Word Endings -cal, -cle

The word endings *-cal, -cle* are represented by a disjoined *k.*

Spell: k-e-m-ical, chemical

chemical .... logical .... technical ....

medical .... political .... physically ....

identical .... typical .... articles ....

Building Transcription Skills

Similar-Words Drill ■ write, right

write To put words on paper.

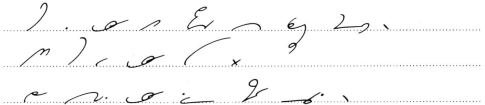

I will *write* you about my plans.

right (noun) Something to which one has a just claim; **(adjective)** correct; **(adverb)** directly.

You have a *right* to expect good service from us.
Do you have the *right* time?
They are going *right* home after the meeting.

Also Rite - Ritual

Business Vocabulary Builder

remote Far away; out of the way.

atlas A book of maps.

endorsement Approval.

Principles

Word Ending -hood

The word ending *-hood* is represented by a disjoined *d.*

Spell: n-a-b-r-hood, neighborhood

neighborhood .... boyhood .... likelihood ....

childhood .... girlhood .... parenthood ....

Word Ending -ward

The word ending *-ward* is also represented by a disjoined *d.*

Spell: o-n-ward, onward

onward .... outward .... rewarding ....

backward .... upward .... forward ....

afterward .... inward .... forwarded ....

Ul

Ul is represented by *oo* when it precedes a forward or upward stroke.

Spell: re-s-ul-t, result

result .... consultant .... cultured ....

consult .... ultimately .... culminate ....

insult .... multitude .... simultaneous ....

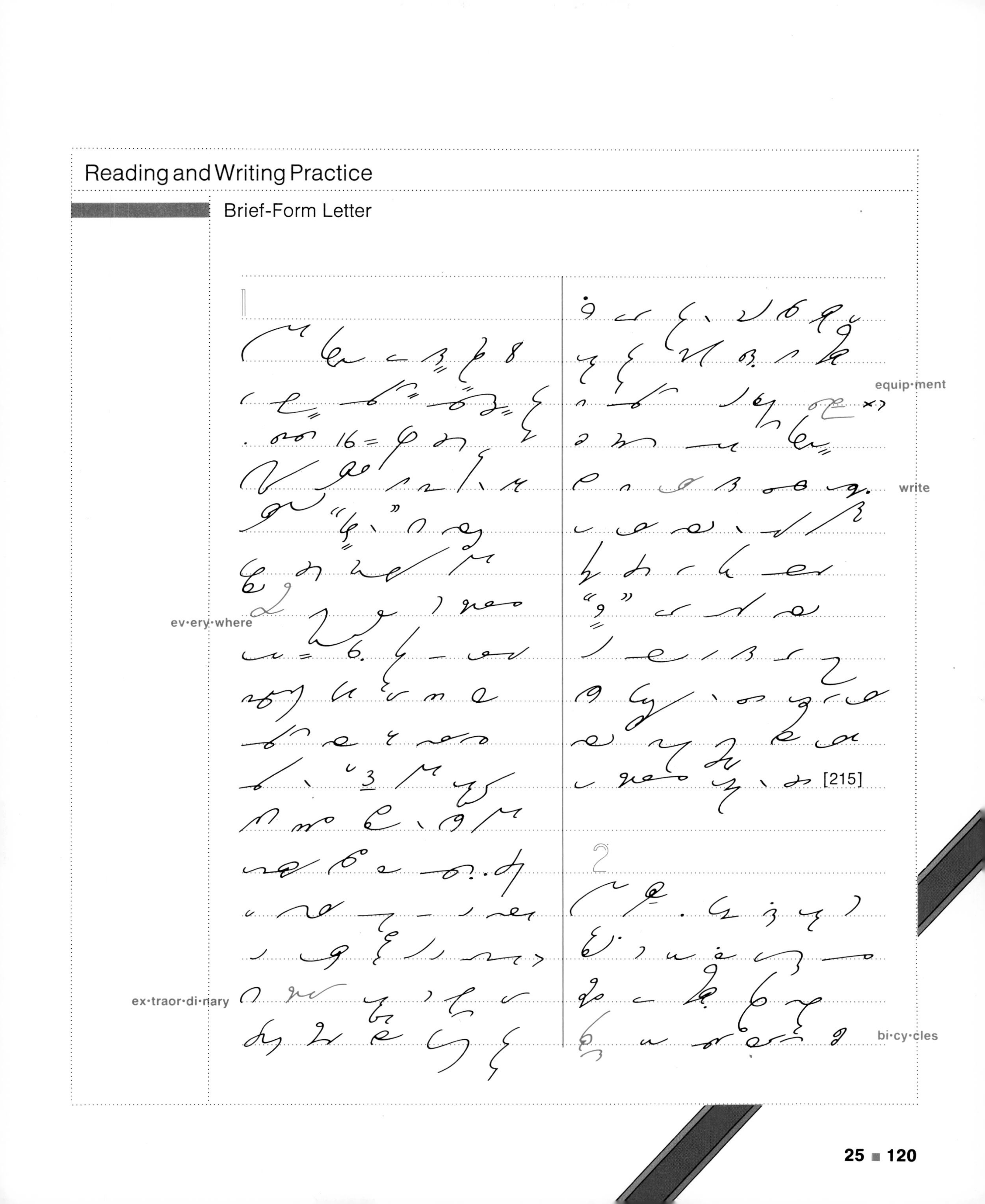

Reading and Writing Practice

Brief-Form Letter

1

equip·ment

write

ev·ery·where

[215]

2

ex·traor·di·nary

bi·cy·cles

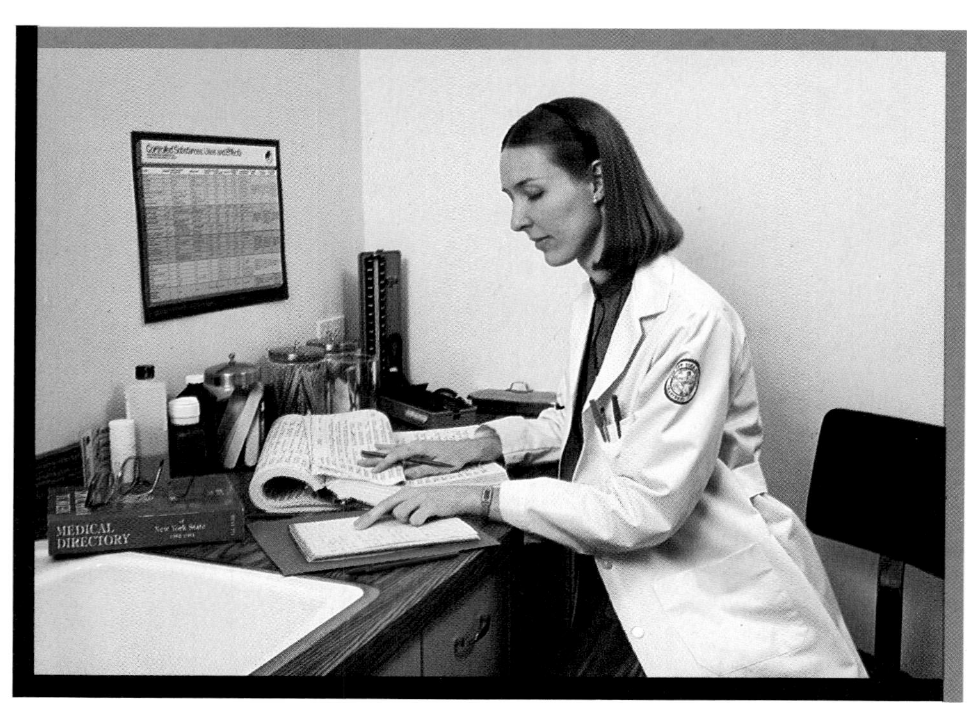

Regardless of their chosen careers, many people study shorthand because they recognize its usefulness in any job.

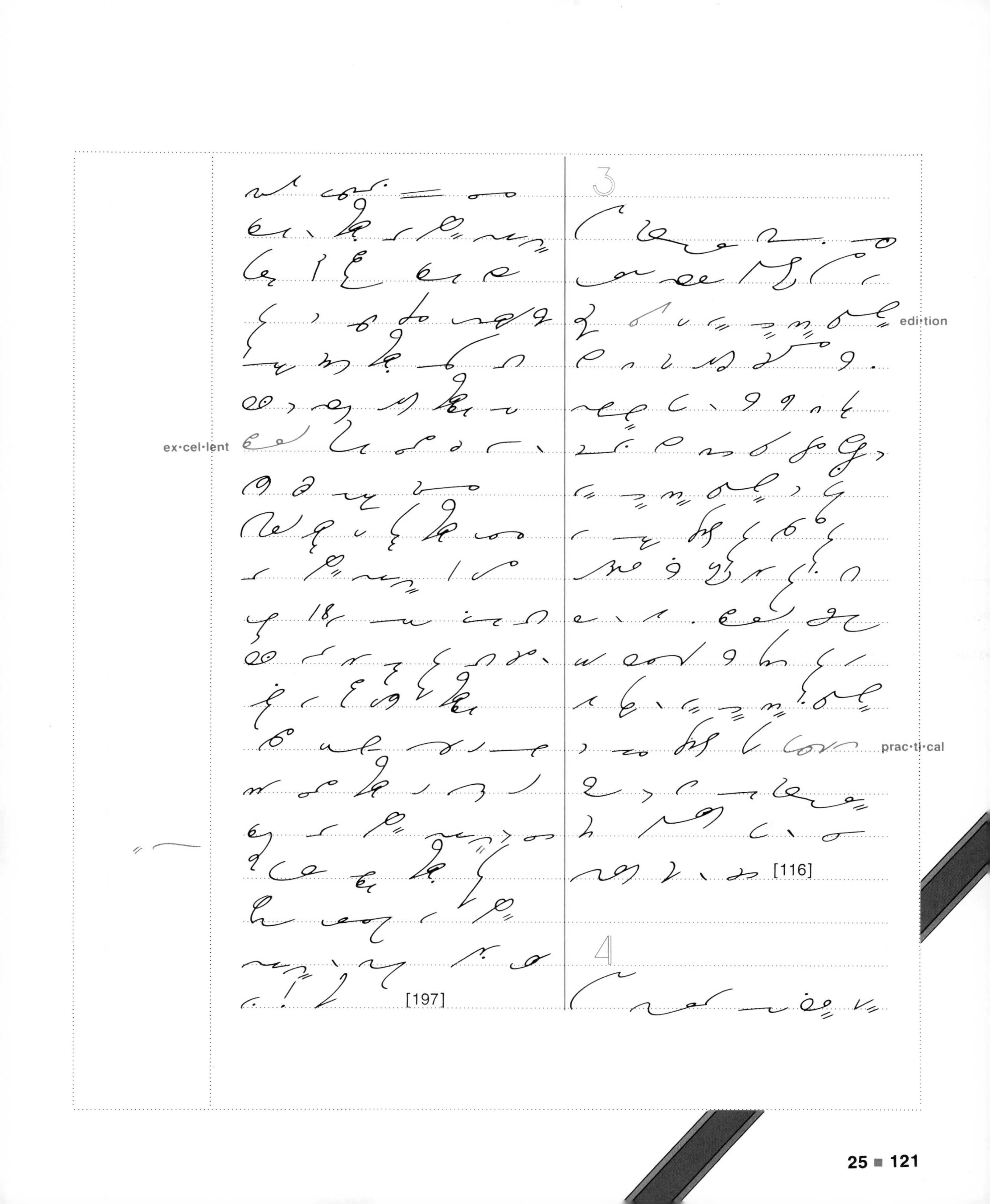

ex·cel·lent

[197]

3

edi·tion

prac·ti·cal

[116]

4

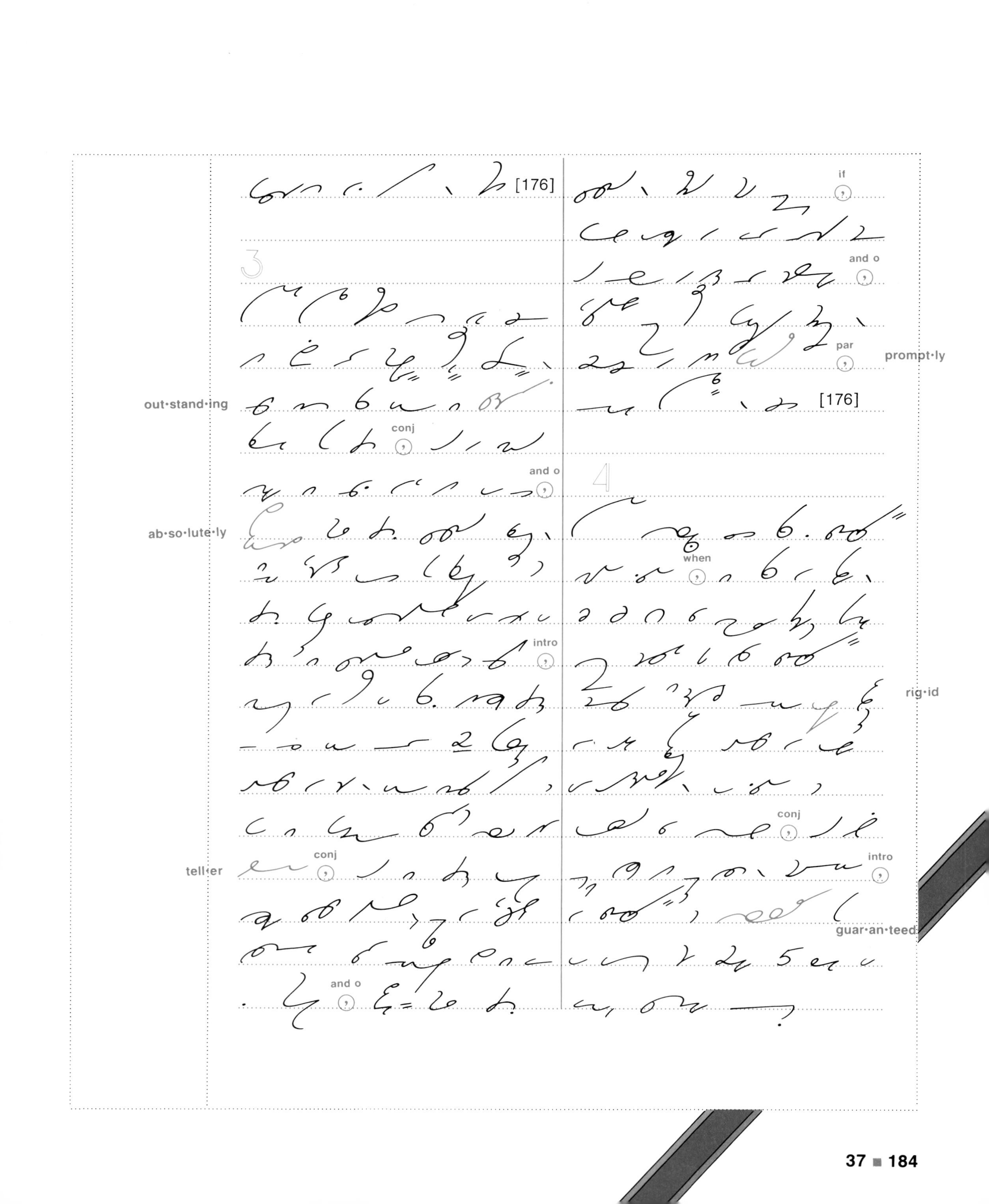

[176]

3

out·stand·ing

conj

and o

ab·so·lute·ly

intro

conj

tell·er

and o

if

and o

par

prompt·ly

[176]

4

when

rig·id

conj

intro

guar·an·teed

de·but

as·sur·ance

en·cour·age·ment

right

[167]

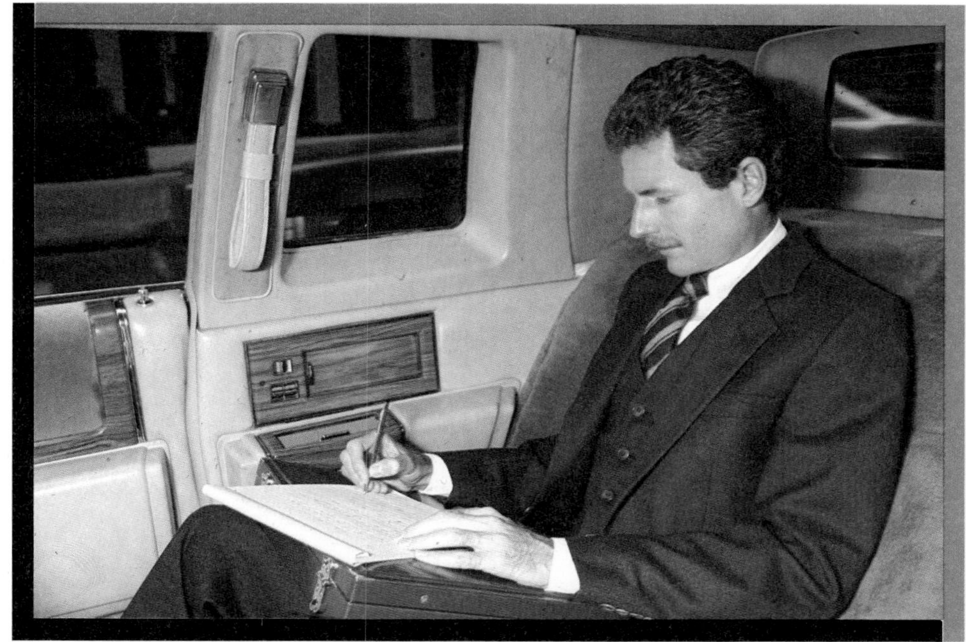

A busy executive saves time when outlining or drafting business communications in shorthand—whenever and wherever he can.

ser

self-suf·fi·cien·cy

an·noy·ing
em·bar·rass·ing
and o

dis·cov·er

un·de·vel·oped
and o

intro

cir·cum·stances
intro

[198]

2

Self-em·ploy·ment

intro

if

when

al·most

par

pen·al·ty
with·draw·al

par

and o
sen·si·ble

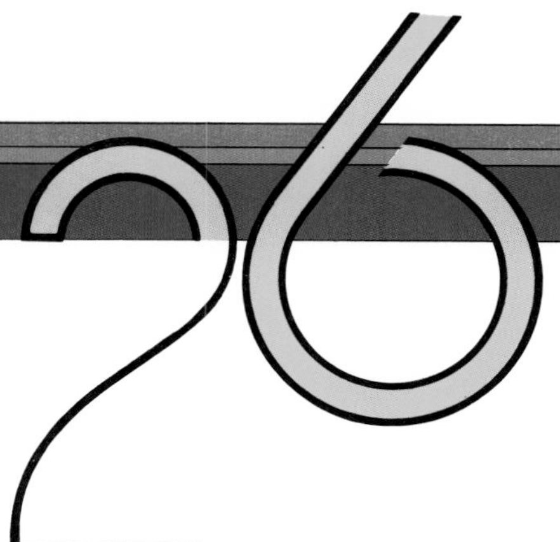

Principles

Brief Forms

This is the last group of brief forms you will learn!

never	throughout	govern
quantity	object	correspond, correspondence
executive	character	

Word Ending -ure

The word ending *-ure* is represented by *r*.

Spell: f-a-l-r, failure

failure	feature	nature
future	featured	natural

Word Ending -ual

The word ending *-ual* is represented by *l*.

Spell: a-k-t-l, actual

actual	schedule	equal
gradual	scheduled	equally

Building Transcription Skills

Punctuation Practice ■ , and omitted

When two or more consecutive adjectives modify the same noun, they are separated by commas.

Enclosed is a stamped, self-addressed envelope.

However, the comma is not used if the first adjective modifies the combined idea of the second adjective plus the noun.

The suit is made of beautiful blue material.

Note: You can quickly determine whether to insert a comma between two consecutive adjectives by mentally placing *and* between them. If the sentence makes good sense with *and* inserted between the adjectives, then the comma is used.

For example, the first sentence would make good sense if it read:

Enclosed is a stamped and self-addressed envelope.

Each time this use of the comma occurs in the Reading and Writing Practice, it will be indicated thus in the shorthand: and o

Business Vocabulary Builder

motivate Provide a need or desire for a person to act.

rigid Strictly observed; inflexible.

controller A financial officer of a company.

Reading and Writing Practice

Brief-Form Review Letter

tech·ni·cal

de·vel·op

en·roll·ing

Punctuation Practice

An efficient secretary must, as you have already learned, be able to take dictation at a reasonable speed and be able to spell. Another "must" for the efficient secretary is the ability to punctuate correctly. Most business executives rely on their secretaries to supply the proper punctuation when they transcribe. Because the inclusion or omission of a punctuation mark may completely alter the meaning of a sentence, it is important that you know when and where to use each punctuation mark.

To sharpen your punctuation skill, you will hereafter give special attention to punctuation in each Reading and Writing Practice.

In the lessons ahead you will review nine of the most common uses of the comma. Each time one of these uses of the comma occurs in the Reading and Writing Practice, it will be encircled in the shorthand, thus calling it forcefully to your attention.

Practice Suggestions If you follow these simple suggestions in your homework practice, your ability to punctuate should improve noticeably.

1 Read carefully the explanation of each comma usage (for example, the explanation of the parenthetical comma given below) to be sure that you understand it. You will encounter a number of illustrations of each comma usage in the Reading and Writing Practice exercises, so that eventually you will acquire the knack of applying each of them correctly.

2 Continue to read and copy each Reading and Writing Practice as you have done before. However, add these two important steps:

a Each time you see an encircled comma in the Reading and Writing Practice, note the reason for its use, which is indicated directly above the comma.

b As you copy the Reading and Writing Practice in your shorthand notebook, insert the commas in your shorthand notes, encircling them as was done in the textbook.

Punctuation Practice ■ parenthetical

A word or a phrase or a clause that is used parenthetically (that is, one not necessary to the grammatical completeness of the sentence) should be set off by commas.

If the parenthetical expression occurs at the end of the sentence, only one comma is necessary.

There is, *of course,* a small application fee.

Never hesitate to let us know, *Mr. Smith,* when our organization can help you.

We will be happy to serve you, *Mrs. Martinez.*

Each time a parenthetical expression occurs in the Reading and Writing Practice, it will be indicated thus in the shorthand: par (,)

Principles

Word Beginning Self-

The word beginning *self-* is represented by a disjoined left *s.*

Spell: self-m-a-d, self-made

self-made .... self-addressed .... selffish ....

self-control .... self-improvement .... selfishness ....

self-reliance .... self-explanatory .... unselfishly ....

Word Beginning Circum-

The word beginning *circum-* is also represented by a disjoined left *s.*

Spell: circum-s-ten-s, circumstance

circumstance .... circumstances .... circumstantial ....

Word Ending -ification

The word ending *-ification* is represented by a disjoined *f.*

Spell: r-a-t-ification, ratification

ratification .... notification .... modifications ....

classification .... gratification .... qualifications ....

justification .... identification .... specifications ....

Business Vocabulary Builder

deprived Taken from; denied something.

ravages Violent, destructive effects.

pursue Go after.

Reading and Writing Practice

Brief-Form Letter

Cor·re·spon·dence

suf·fi·cient

ex·haust

par

great

par

though

par

nat·u·ral·ly

par

sched·ule

[190]

4

if

[118]

ser

mis·ap·pre·hen·sions

en·thu·si·asm

When writing shorthand near the bottom of the page, slide the page up with the fingers of your nonwriting hand instead of moving your writing arm down.

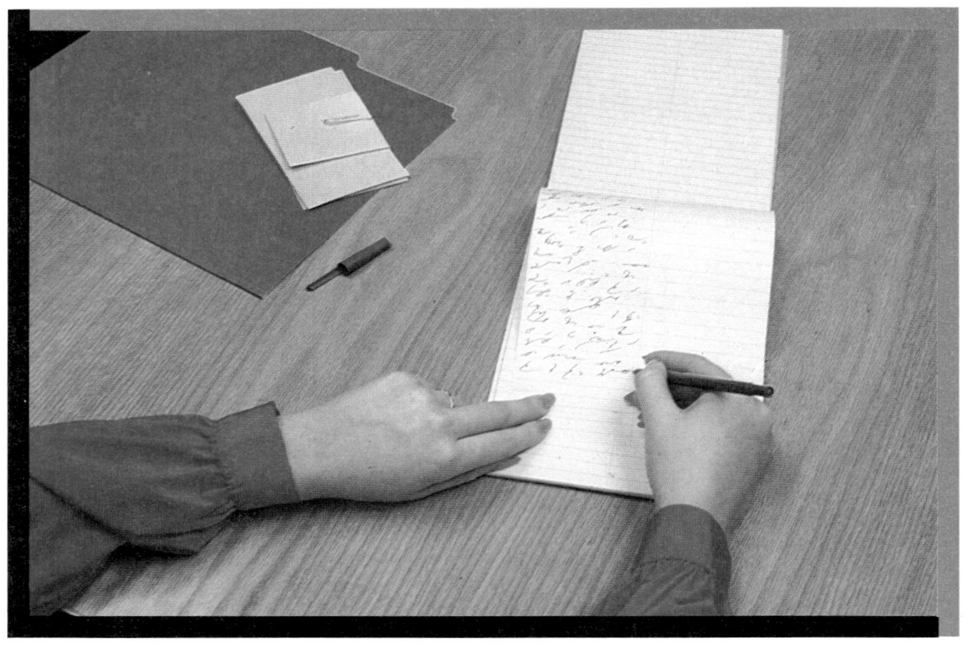

[218]

2

ex·cel·lent

prob·a·bly

pur·sue

[114]

3

sec·tion

par

par

par

ar·range

ap·point·ment

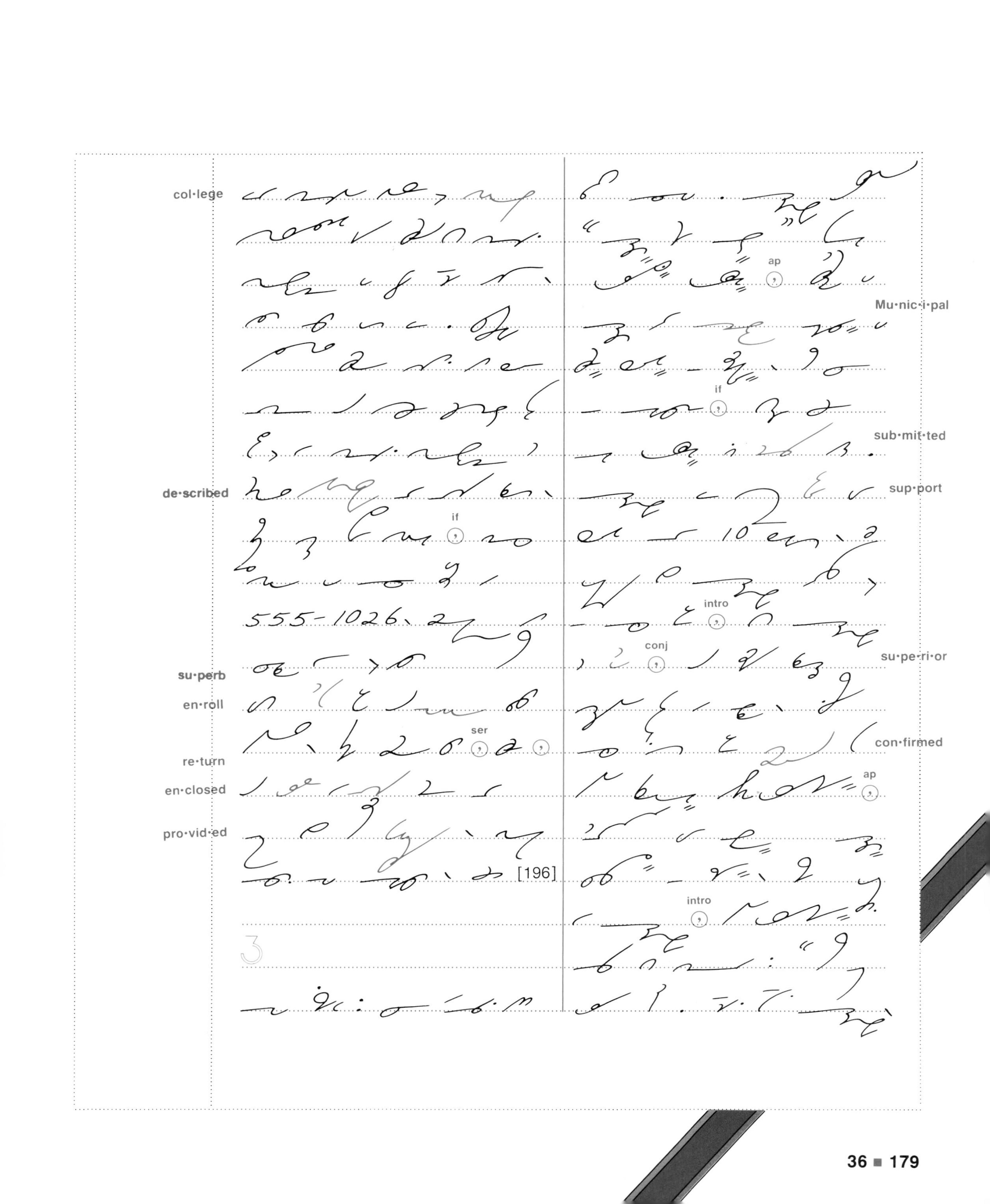

col·lege

de·scribed

555-1026

su·perb
en·roll
re·turn
en·closed
pro·vid·ed

[196]

3

Mu·nic·i·pal

sub·mit·ted
sup·port

su·pe·ri·or

con·firmed

ap
if
ser
intro
conj

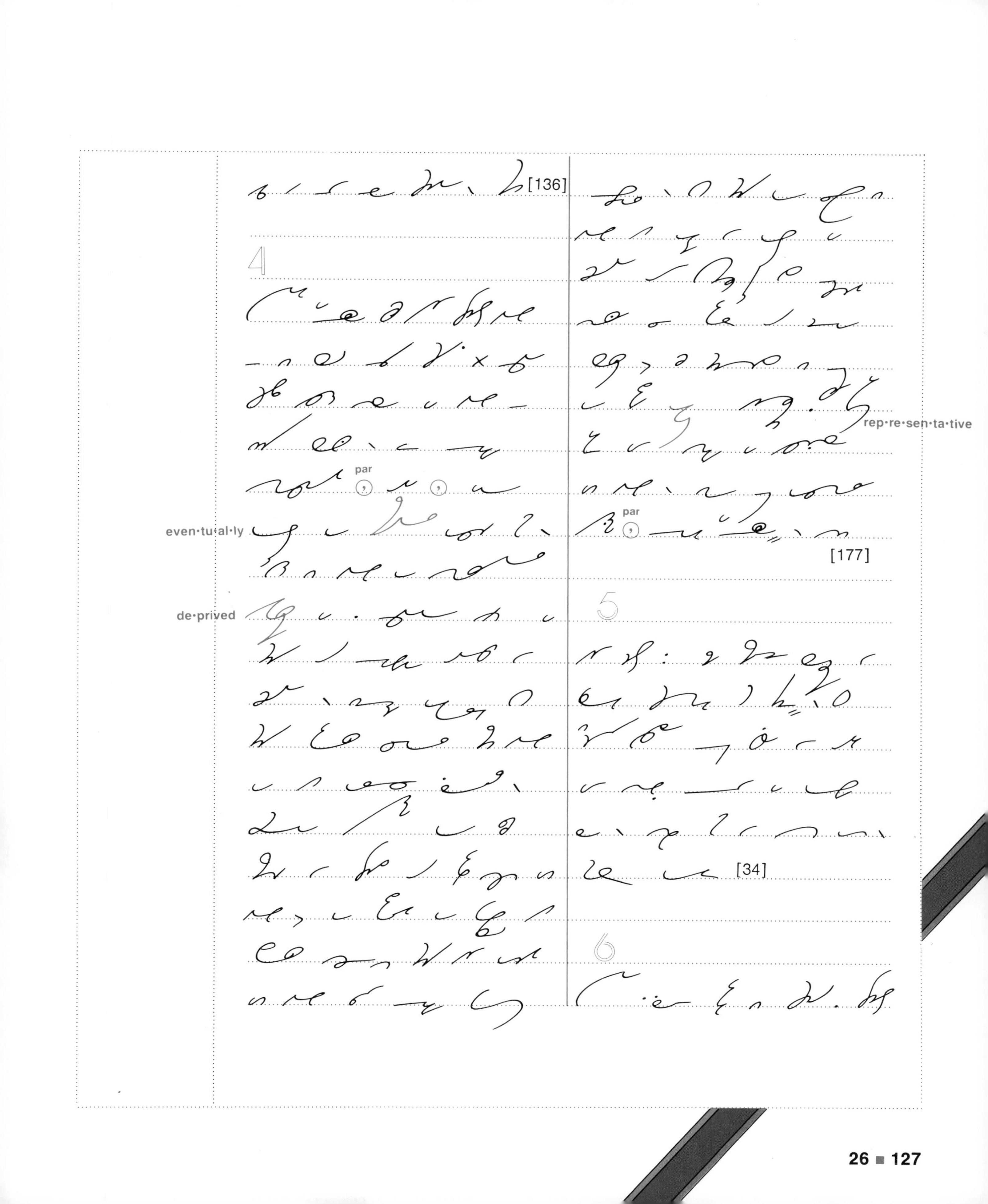

[136]

4

par

eventually

deprived

representative

par

[177]

5

[34]

6

Reading and Writing Practice

Brief-Form Review Letter

1

when

ap

ap

Mis·con·cep·tions

conj

ap

dis·cov·ered

mis·spelled

mis·take

oc·curred

conj

pho·to·graph·ic

intro

intro

[166]

2

ex·cel·lent

equiv·a·lent

conj

bud·get

loan

strain

[115]

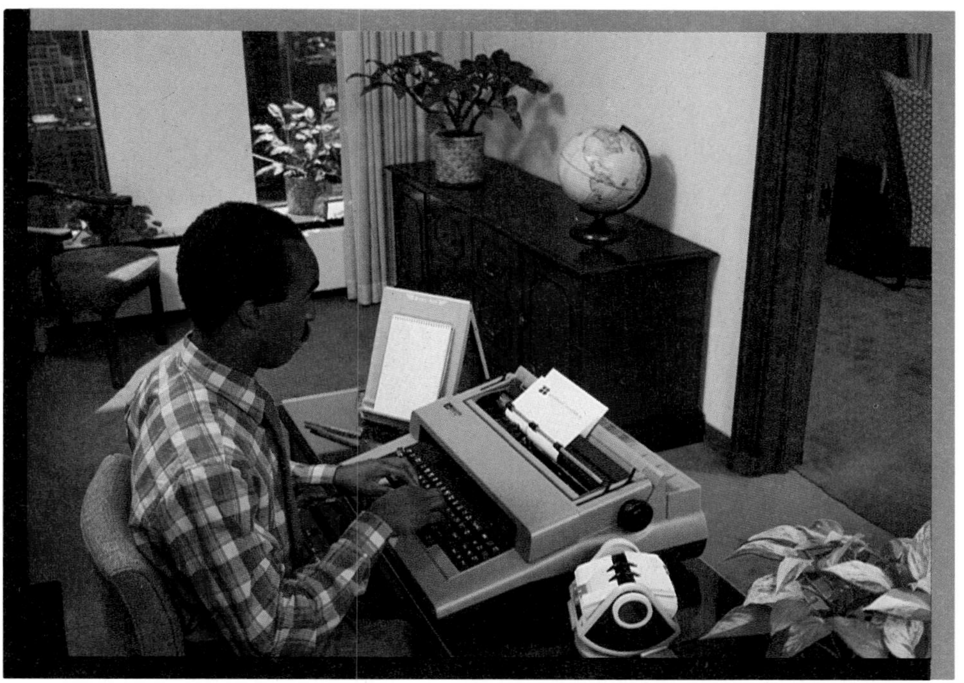

Many electronic typewriters have a linear display above the keyboard that enables a secretary to proofread and correct a document while it is being typed.

mutual communicate continue

manuscript monument discontinue

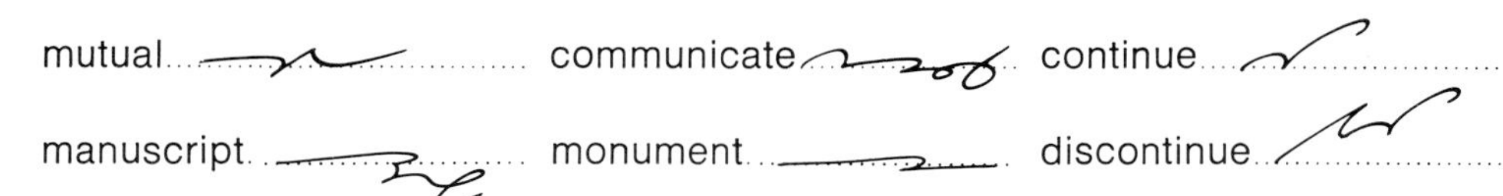

Building Transcription Skills

Punctuation Practice ■ , conjunction

A comma is used to separate two independent clauses that are joined by one of the following conjunctions: *and, but, or, for, nor.*

An independent clause (sometimes called a main or a principal clause) is one that has a subject and a predicate and that could stand alone as a complete sentence.

We have nine students in the organization, but only six of them can attend the meeting.

The first independent clause is:

We have nine students in the organization.

And the second independent clause is:

Only six of them can attend the meeting.

Both clauses could stand as separate sentences, with a period after each. Because the thoughts of the two clauses are closely related, however, the clauses were joined to form one sentence. Because the two independent clauses are connected by the conjunction *but,* a comma is used between them and is placed before the conjunction.

Each time this use of the comma occurs in the Reading and Writing Practice, it will be indicated thus in the shorthand: conj (,)

Business Vocabulary Builder

misconceptions Wrong impressions; misunderstandings.

commuter One who travels back and forth regularly, as between a suburb and a city.

rejected Refused to accept.

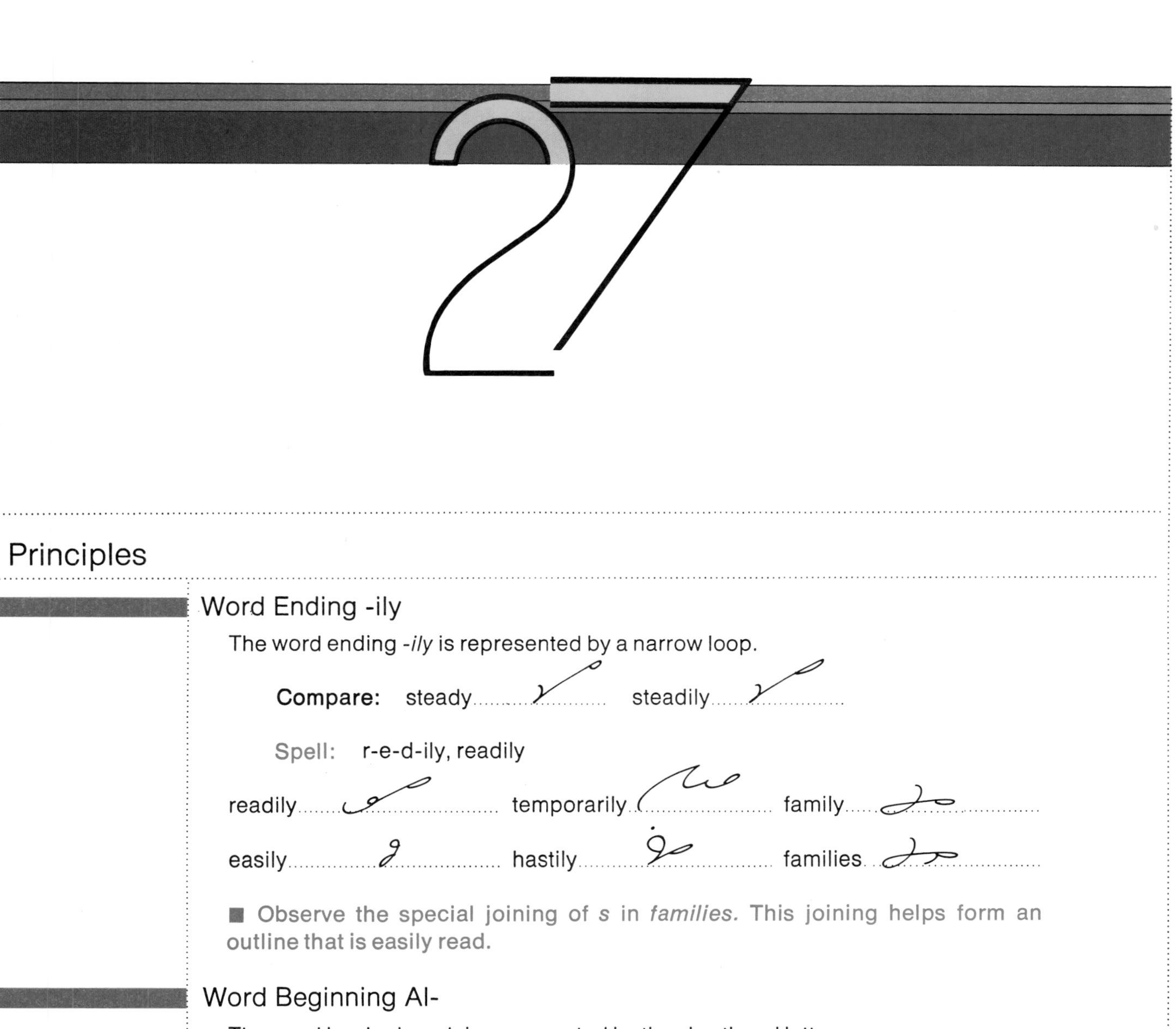

Principles

Word Ending -ily

The word ending *-ily* is represented by a narrow loop.

Compare: steady .... steadily ....

Spell: r-e-d-ily, readily

readily .... temporarily .... family ....

easily .... hastily .... families ....

■ Observe the special joining of *s* in *families.* This joining helps form an outline that is easily read.

Word Beginning Al-

The word beginning *al-* is represented by the shorthand letter *o.*

Spell: all-t-r, alter

alter .... altogether .... also ....

altered .... almost .... almanac ....

Word Beginnings Dis-, Des-

The word beginnings *dis-, des-* are represented by *d-s.*

Spell: dis-k-oo-s, discuss; dis-k-r-i-b, describe

Principles

Word Beginning Mis-

The word beginning *mis-* is represented by *m-s.*

Spell: mis-t-a-k, mistake

mistake	misplaced	misunderstand
misconception	mislaid	misunderstood
misprint	misapprehension	mystery

Word Beginning Super-

The word beginning *super-* is represented by a disjoined right *s.*

Spell: super-v-i-s, supervise

supervise	superintendent	superior
supervisor	superhuman	superb
supervision	superimpose	supersede

U Represented by OO

The *oo* hook may be used after *n* and *m* to represent the sound of *u,* as in *music.*

Spell: m-oo-s-e-k, music

music	musical	municipal

Dis-

discuss .... discourage .... distance ....
discover .... dismiss .... dispose ....

Des-

describe .... despite .... desperate ....
description .... destination .... destroy ....

Building Transcription Skills

Punctuation Practice ■ , apposition

An expression in apposition (that is, a word or a phrase or a clause that identifies or explains another word or term) should be set off by commas. When the expression in apposition occurs at the end of a sentence, only one comma is necessary.

My employer, *Ms. Mildred H. O'Brien,* is out of town.
The book, *Human Relations,* is now for sale.
The meeting is scheduled for Wednesday, *June 23.*

Each time an expression in apposition appears in the Reading and Writing Practice, it will be indicated thus in the shorthand: ap (,)

Business Vocabulary Builder

bench The office or dignity of a judge.

extensive Wide; considerable.

unbiased Not favoring one side or the other; fair.

temporarily For a short time; not permanently.

[187]

5

ap

ser

anal·y·sis

when

au·to·graph

[111]

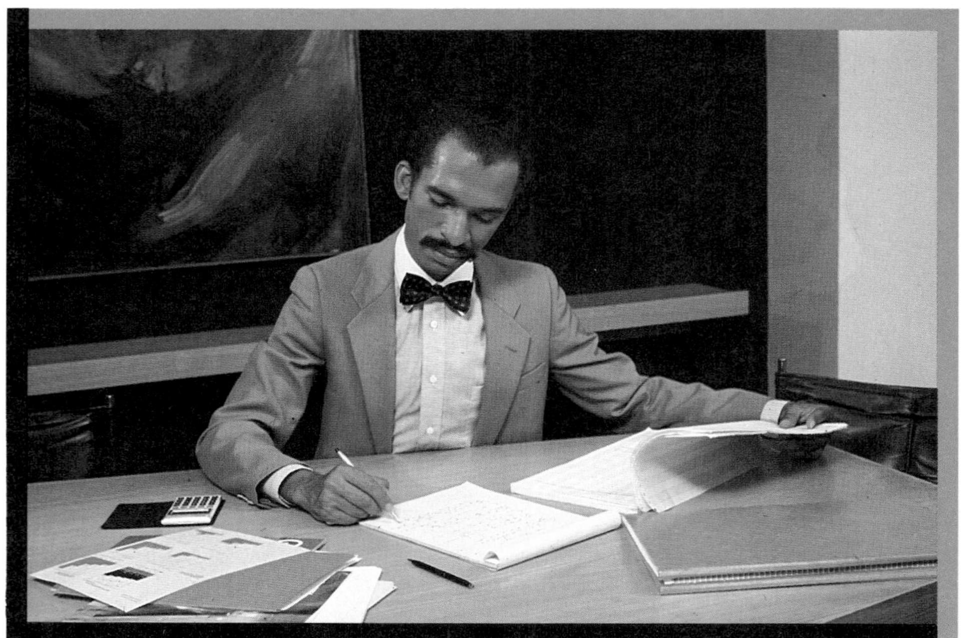

A business executive may draft a report in shorthand, gathering data from a variety of sources, including computer-generated documents.

Reading and Writing Practice

Brief-Form Review Letter

1

ap

gov·er·nor

opin·ion

ap

ex·ten·sive

dis·tinc·tion

cor·re·spond·ing

ap

[134]

2

al·most

ap

dis·cov·er·ing

pol·lu·tion

un·bi·ased

4

grat·i·tude

gen·u·ine

intro

par

when

if

[193]

tran·sis·tor

crit·i·cal

intro

ap

par

if

par

eas·i·ly

dis·pose

[167]

3

dis·turbed

ap

be·gin·ning

ap

def·i·nite

al·ready

re·plen·ished

31

par

[169]

4

ap

com·pre·hen·sive

sta·tis·tics

ap

18

fac·ul·ty

dis·cuss

con·ve·nient

[152]

2

intro 26

ser

en·light·en·ing

per·formed

if

treat

intro

per·ti·nent

ser

rec·og·nized

as

ben·e·fit

[158]

3

ap 18

sig·nif·i·cant

re·veals

de·scrib·ing

ef·fi·cien·cy

ap

[140]

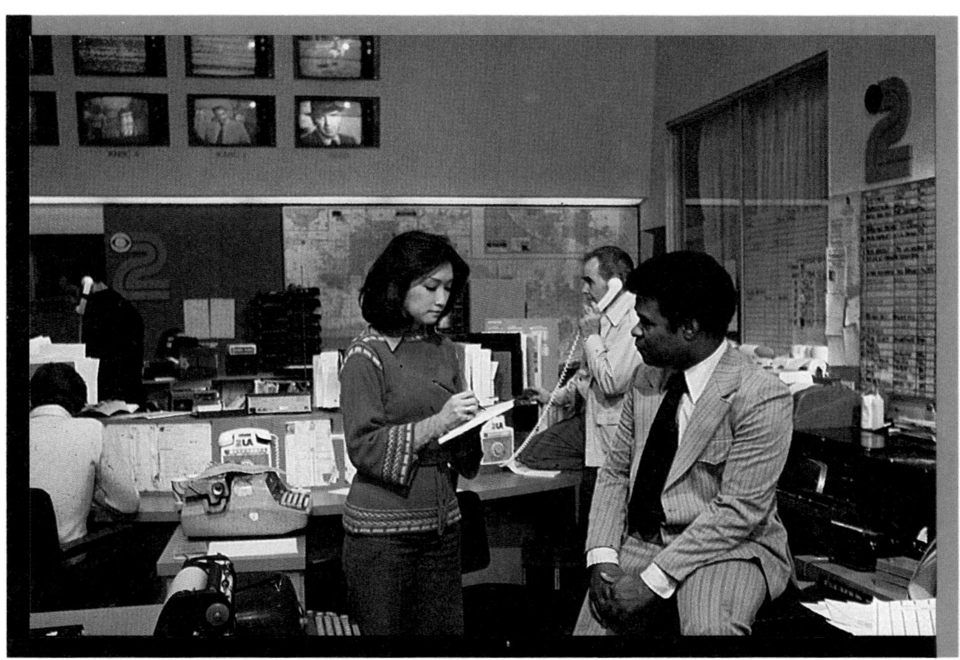

Things can get hectic in a television newsroom. If a reporter uses shorthand, instructions from the news director can be jotted down quickly.

transact .... transportation .... transit ....

transaction .... transfer .... transistor ....

Building Transcription Skills

Similar-Words Drill ■ accept, except

accept To Take.

Did you *accept* the offer?

except (preposition) Omitted; left out.

All the listed states, *except* one, border on the ocean.

Business Vocabulary Builder

alternative A choice.

pertinent Having direct bearing on the matter at hand; relevant.

autograph A person's handwritten signature.

Reading and Writing Practice

Brief-Form Review Letter

al·most

intro

con·sist·ing

Principles

Word Beginnings For-, Fore-

The word beginnings *for-, fore-* are represented by *f.*

Spell: for-gay-e-t, forget

forget	form	forerunner
forgive	inform	forlorn
effort	information	forever

■ Observe: 1 The *f* is joined with an angle to *r* or *l,* as in *forerunner* and *forlorn,* to indicate that it represents a word beginning.

2 The *f* is disjoined if the following character is a vowel, as in *forever.*

Word Beginning Fur-

The word beginning *fur-* is also represented by *f.*

Spell: fur-n-ish, furnish

furnish	furniture	further
furnished	furnace	furthermore

Ago in Phrases

In expressions of time, *ago* is represented by *gay.*

days ago	years ago	several days ago
weeks ago	months ago	few days ago

Principles

Abbreviated Words—in Families (Continued)

-graph

photograph	stenographer	paragraph
photographic	autographed	paragraphed
photographically	typographical	telegraphing

Abbreviated Words—Not in Families

The ending may be omitted from long words even though they do not fall into a family.

anniversary	significant, significance	reluctant, reluctance
memorandum	statistic	privilege
convenient, convenience	statistics	privileged
equivalent	statistical	privileges

Word Beginning Trans-

The word beginning *trans-* is represented by a disjoined *t*.

Spell: trans-m-e-t, transmit

transmit	transport	translation

Building Transcription Skills

Punctuation Practice ■ , series

When the last member of a series of three or more items is preceded by *and* or *or*, place a comma before the conjunction as well as between the other items.

I need *a desk, a chair, and a table.*
I saw Kay *on July 18, on July 19, and again on July 30.*
I need someone *to take dictation, to answer the telephone, and to greet callers.*

Note: Some authorities prefer to omit the comma before the conjunction. In your shorthand books, however, the comma will be inserted before the conjunction.

Each time a series occurs in the Reading and Writing Practice, it will be indicated thus in the shorthand: ser (,)

Business Vocabulary Builder

informally Casually; without ceremony.

gracious Having charm and good taste; pleasing.

forecasting Predicting.

Reading and Writing Practice

Brief-Form Review Letter

Cor·re·spon·dence

dis·ap·point·ing

ex·hausted

6

bud·get·ary

intro

ex·hausted

char·i·ties

intro

[139]

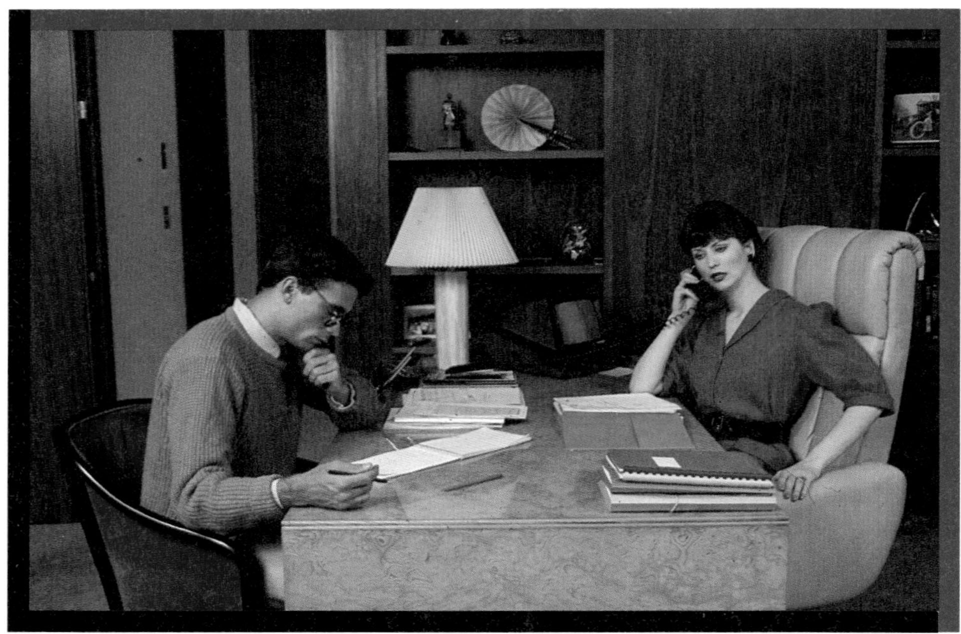

If the executive is interrupted during a dictation session, the secretary should use that time to review the shorthand notes and to insert punctuation.

ware·houses

ser

readi·ly

par

[198]

2

par

per·son·al

for·mer

ap

ac·cept·ed

re·spon·si·ble

gov·ern·ment

ser

par

some·time

[113]

3

ser

ex·traor·di·nary

per·suade

though

ac·knowl·edge

debt

opin·ions

[164]

5

Neu·ro·log·i·cal

cler·i·cal

pro·cess

cap·i·tal

con·se·quent·ly

[164]

gra·cious

ser

de·sign·er

par

[130]

4

fur·ther·more

else

de·scribe

[114]

5

an·nu·al

ap

ser

de·vel·oped

psy·cho·log·i·cal·ly

hours'

el·e·men·ta·ry

les·son

[137]

3

in·spi·ra·tion

world's

en·vi·able

fre·quent·ly

[132]

4

morn·ing's

con·sid·er·able

au·di·ence

[156]

en·gage·ment

6

ap

ap

ap

[44]

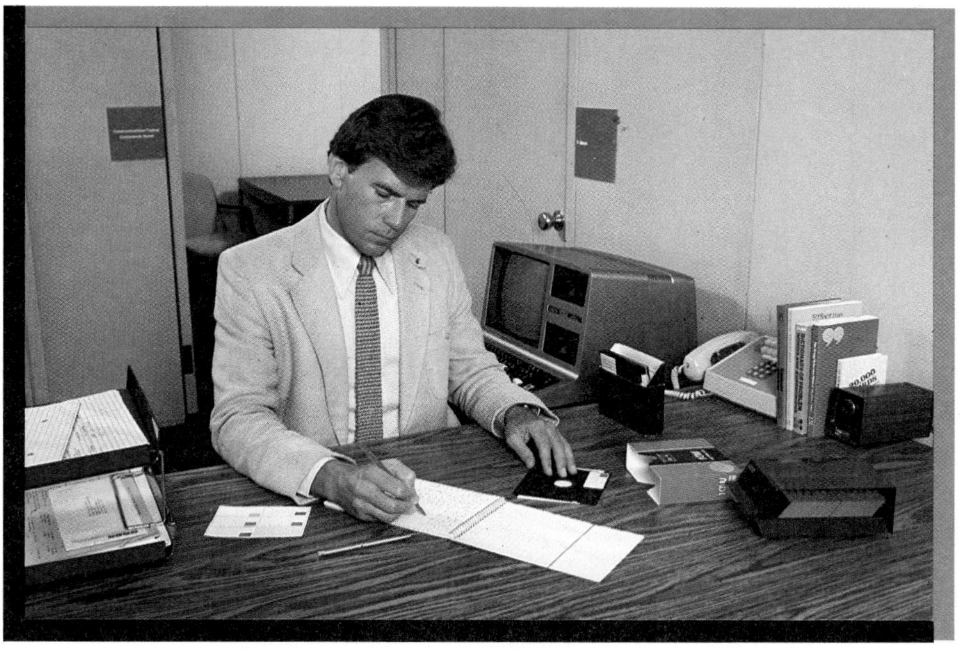

Documents stored on magnetic media, such as floppy disks, should be labeled—both on the disk and in the shorthand notes.

Business Vocabulary Builder

aptitude A natural ability; talent.

gratitude Appreciation of benefits received.

enviable Highly desirable.

formative Developing; taking shape.

Reading and Writing Practice

Brief-Form Review Letter

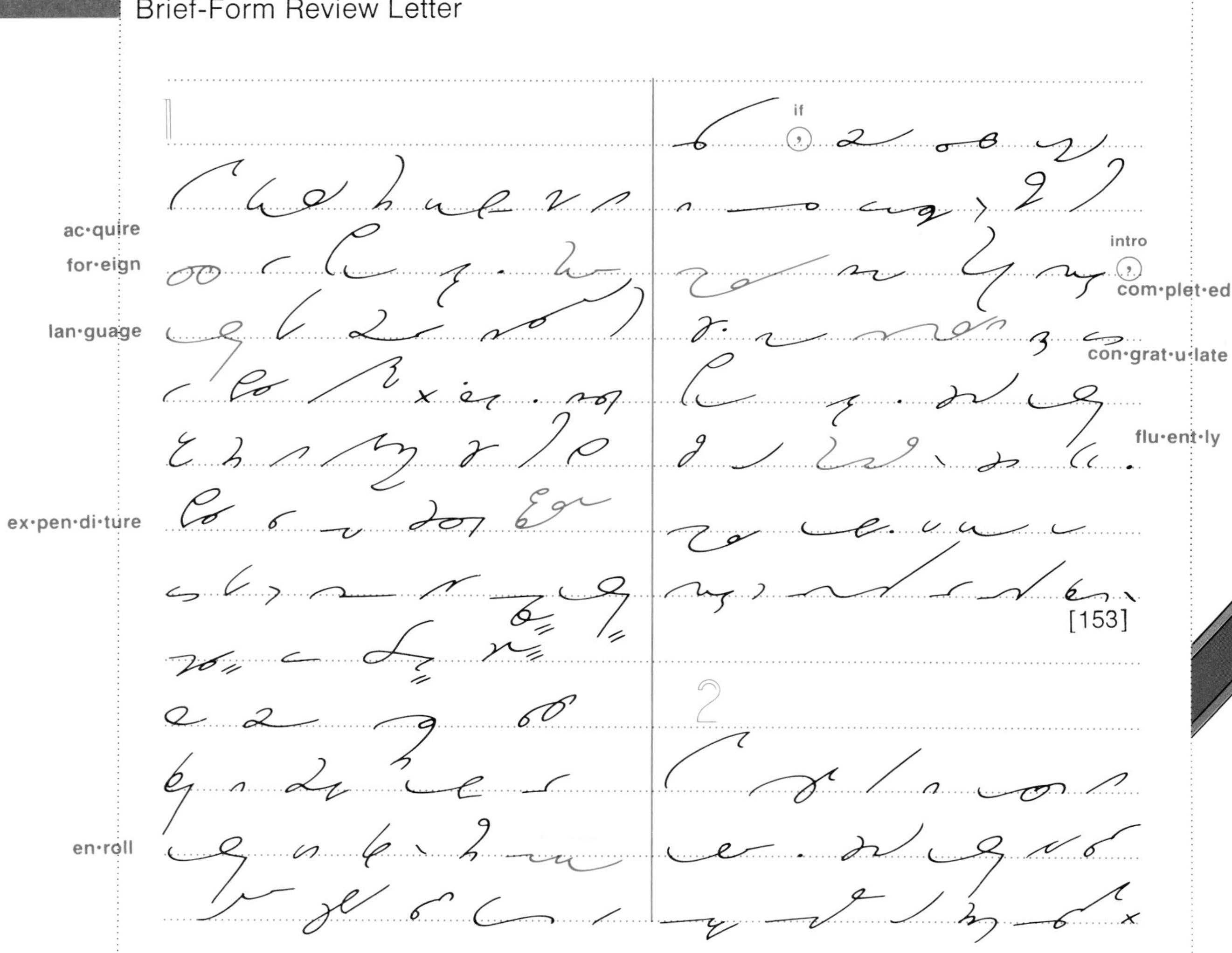

Principles

Want in Phrases

In phrases, *want* is represented by the *nt* blend.

I want .... I wanted .... if you want ....

you want .... he wants .... do you want ....

Ort

The *r* is omitted in the sound *ort.*

Spell: re-p-o-t, report

report .... quart .... sort ....

export .... quarterly .... portable ....

R Omitted in -ern, -erm

The *r* is omitted in the combinations *tern, term, thern, therm, dern.*

Spell: t-e-n, turn

turn .... term .... southern ....

return .... termed .... thermometer ....

western .... determined .... modern ....

-titute

substitute	institute	constitute
substitution	institution	constitution

-titude

aptitude	gratitude	latitude

-ology

psychology	sociology	apology
psychological	sociological	apologies

Building Transcription Skills

Punctuation Practice ■ , introductory

A comma is used to separate a subordinate introductory clause from a following main clause. You have already studied the application of this rule to subordinate clauses introduced by *if, as,* and *when.* Here are examples of subordinate clauses introduced by other subordinating conjunctions.

Although the price is high, I believe we should purchase the land.
Before you leave, please stop in to see me.
Unless we hear from you, we must cancel your subscription.
While I am eager to finish the work, I do not believe we should compromise its quality.

A comma is also used after introductory words or phrases such as *furthermore, on the contrary,* and *for instance.*

Furthermore, the letter contained a typographical error.
On the contrary, you are to be commended for your effort.
For instance, the company was late with its last payment.

Each time a subordinate introductory word, phrase, or clause other than one beginning with *if, as,* or *when* occurs in the Reading and Wrting Practice, it will be indicated thus in the shorthand: intro (,)

Note: If the subordinate clause or other introductory expression *follows* the main clause, the comma is usually not necessary.

I am enclosing an envelope for your convenience in sending me your answer.

Md

By rounding off the angle between *m-d,* we obtain the fluent *md* blend.

Md

Compare: blame ... blamed

Spell: b-l-a-emd, blamed

tamed ... named ... confirmed

claimed ... seemed ... framed

Mt

The stroke that represents *md* also represents *mt.*

Spell: p-r-o-emt, prompt

prompt ... promptly ... empty

Building Transcription Skills

Business Vocabulary Builder

quarterly Four times a year.

contention A point advanced in an argument or debate.

terminal A carrier station or depot or airport.

Reading and Writing Practice

Brief-Form Review Letter

ap

Principles

Abbreviated Words—in Families

Many long words may be abbreviated in shorthand by dropping the endings. This device is also used in longhand, as *Jan.* for *January.* The extent to which you use this device will depend on your familiarity with the words and with the subject matter of the dictation. When in doubt, write it out! The ending of a word is not dropped when a special shorthand word ending has been provided, such as *-lity,* in *ability.*

Notice how many of the words written with this abbreviating device fall naturally into families of similar endings.

-quent

consequent, consequence .... subsequent .... eloquent, eloquence ....
consequently .... subsequently .... frequent ....

-tribute

tribute .... contribute .... distribute ....
attribute .... contributed .... distributor ....
attributes .... contribution .... distribution ....

-quire

require .... inquire .... inquiries ....
requirement .... inquired .... acquire ....

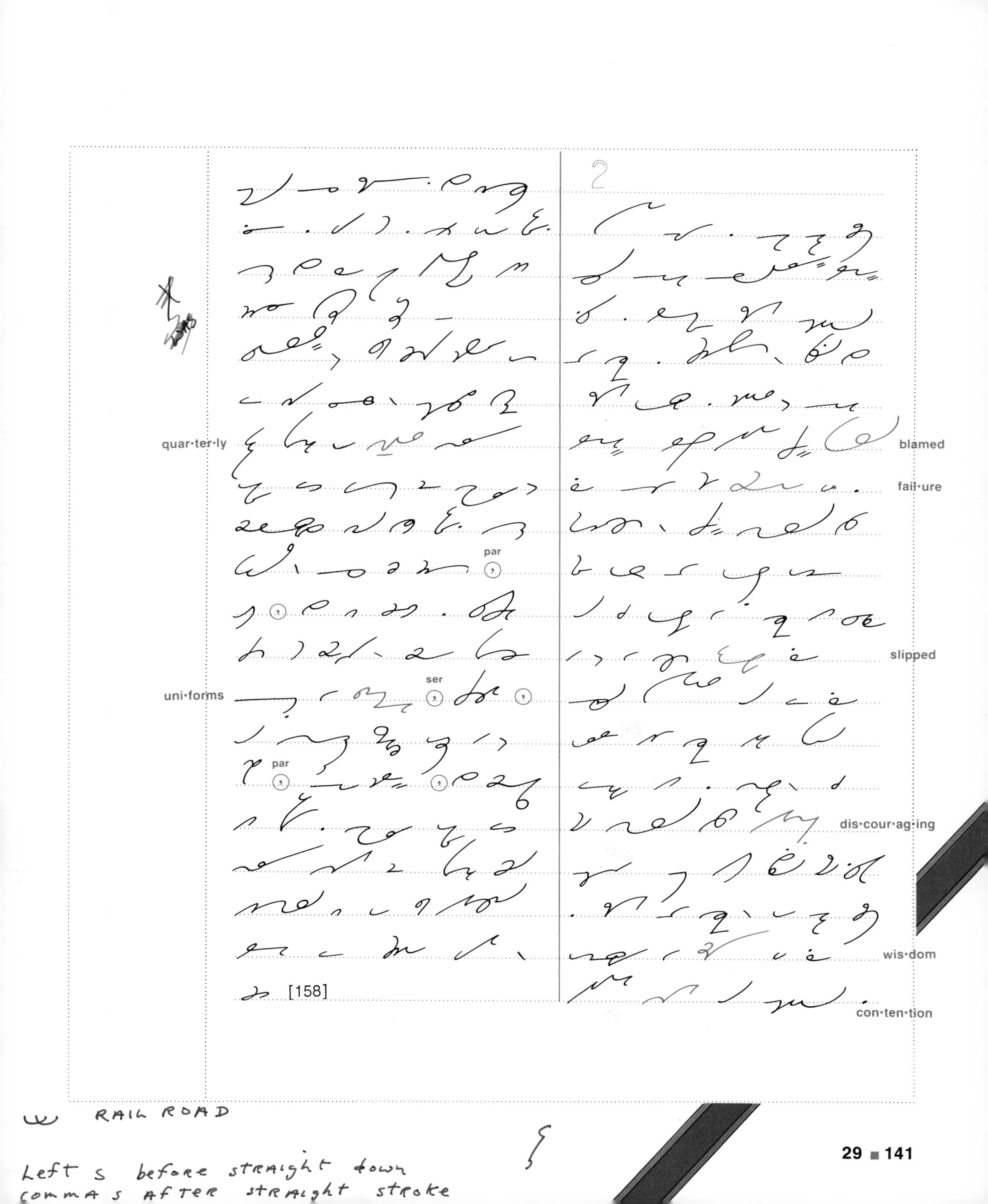

quar·ter·ly

par

uni·forms

ser

par

[158]

2

blamed

fail·ure

slipped

dis·cour·ag·ing

wis·dom

con·ten·tion

[134]

5

agree

as

ques·tion

[136]

when

ap

quan·ti·ties

if

par

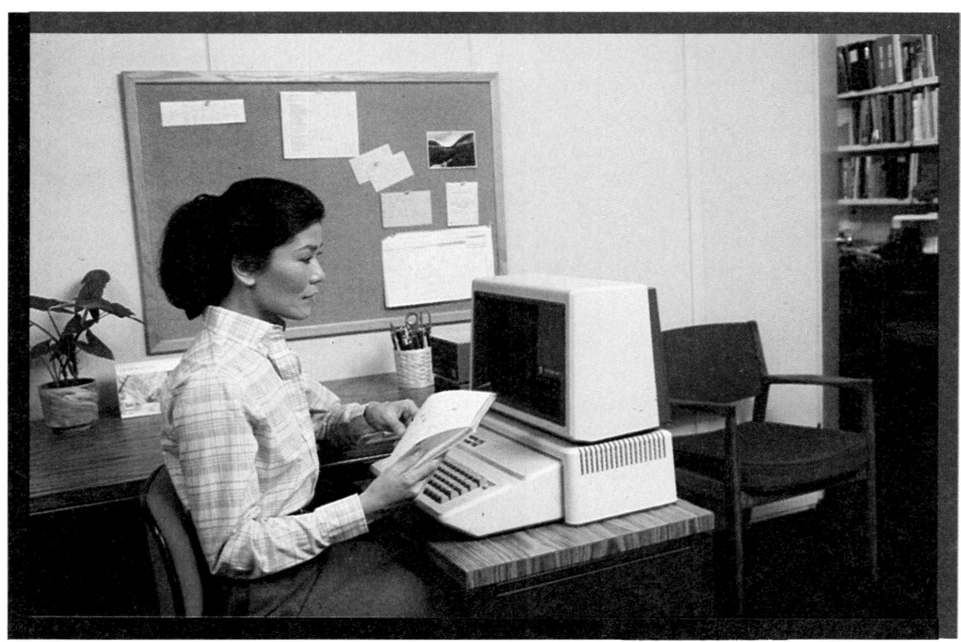

Microprocessors help improve transcription speed because errors caught in proofreading are corrected electronically.

ser

par

[183]

3

ter·mi·nal

ser

sound·proof

thought·ful

gov·ern·ment

par

[136]

4

ap

Wednes·day

de·scribed

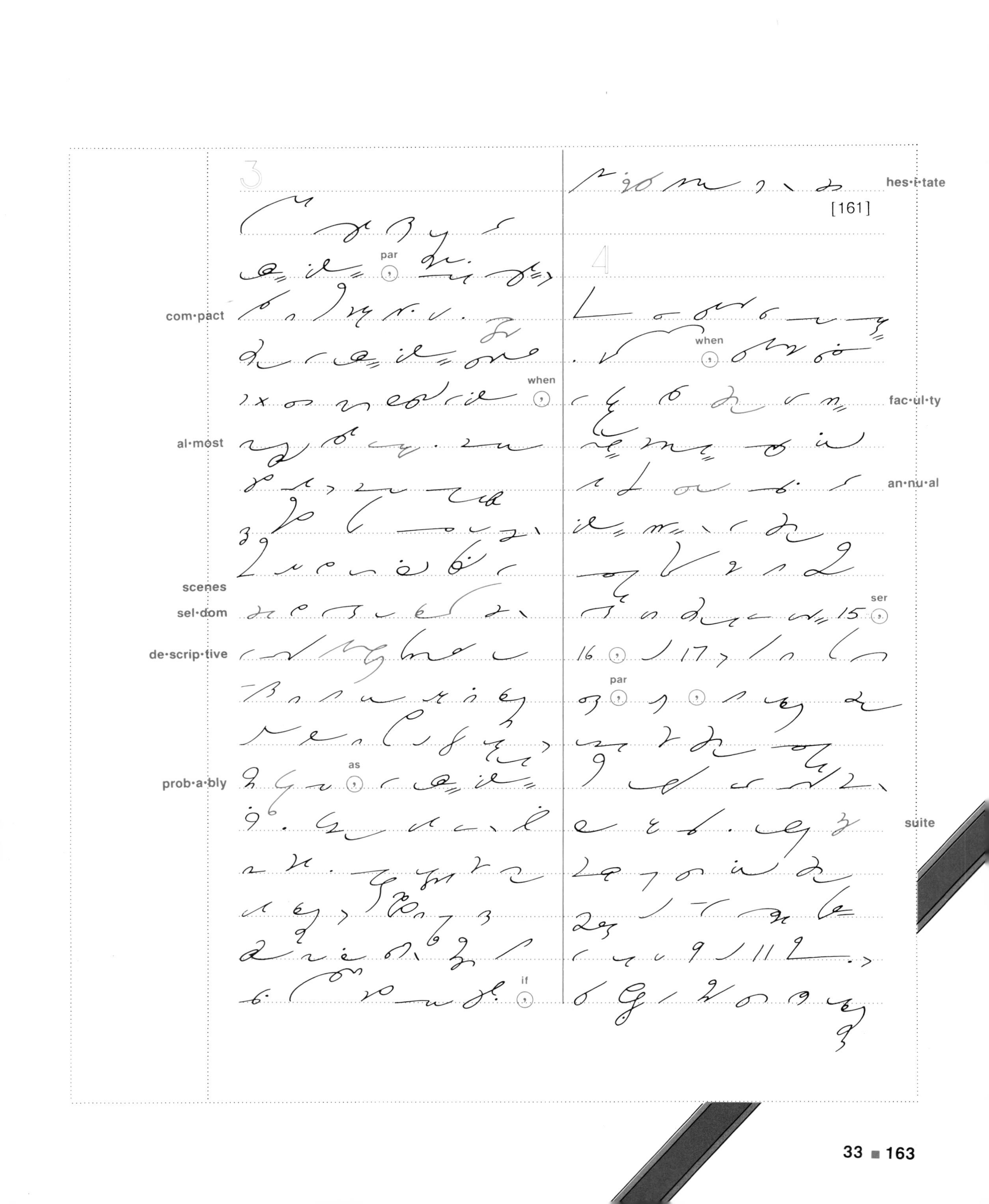

3

com·pact

par

when

al·most

scenes

sel·dom

de·scrip·tive

as

prob·a·bly

if

hes·i·tate

[161]

4

when

fac·ul·ty

an·nu·al

ser

15

16

17

par

suite

[161]

5

ra·di·a·tion

ef·fect

re·gard·ing

par

ser

suc·cess·ful

pro·gres·sive

ser

in·stalled

par

par

[97]

ser

ser

clean·li·ness

as·sure

par

in·ci·den·tal·ly

[220]

2

fi·del·i·ty

ser

sur·pris·ing·ly

ad·van·tage

par

when

re·ceive

ton·al

clar·i·ty

if

[189]

Principles

Word Beginnings Inter-, Intr-, Enter-, Entr-

These similar-sounding word beginnings (and the word *enter*) are represented by a disjoined *n.* These disjoined word beginnings, as well as other disjoined word beginnings that you will study in later lessons, are placed above the line of writing close to the remainder of the word.

Inter-

Spell: inter-s-t, interest

interest .... international .... interrupt ....

interview .... interval .... internal ....

Intr-

Spell: intro-d-oo-s, introduce

introduce .... intruder .... intricate ....

Enter-

Spell: enter-ing, entering

entering .... entertain .... enterprise ....

entered .... entertainment .... enterprising ....

Building Transcription Skills

Punctuation Practice ■ , when clause

A subordinate clause introduced by *when* and followed by the main clause is separated from the main clause by a comma.

When I have an opportunity, I will call him.
When you finish the assignment, raise your hand.

Each time a subordinate clause beginning with *when* occurs in the Reading and Writing Practice, it will be indicated thus in the shorthand: when (,)

Business Vocabulary Builder

individuality Personality; a quality distinguishing one from another.

tonal A quality relating to sound, as in music.

compact (adjective) Closely drawn together or joined.

Reading and Writing Practice

Brief-Form Review Letter

when (,)

lead

pleas·ant

ser (,)

in·de·pen·dent

in·di·vid·u·al·i·ty

ser (,)

(,)

Entr-

Spell: enter-n-s, entrance

entrance .... entrances .... entrant ....

Word Ending -ings

The word ending *-ings* is represented by a disjoined left *s.*

Spell: s-a-v-ings, savings

savings .... furnishings .... proceedings ....

openings .... earnings .... hearings ....

Omission of Words in Phrases

It is often possible to omit one or more unimportant words in a shorthand phrase. In the phrase *one of the,* for example, the word *of* is omitted; we write *one the.* When transcribing, the stenographer would insert *of,* as the phrase would make no sense without that word.

one of the .... some of the .... many of the ....

one of them .... up to date .... in the future ....

some of our .... in the world .... two or three ....

Building Transcription Skills

Similar-Words Drill ■ addition, edition

addition Anything added.

She will be a valuable *addition* to our staff.

edition All the copies of a book or periodical printed at one time.

It will appear in the next *edition* of our newspaper.

Principles

Word Ending -lity

The word ending *-lity* (and a preceding vowel) is represented by a disjoined *l.*

Spell: a-b-lity, ability

ability .... locality .... qualities ....

personality .... reliability .... responsibilities ....

Word Ending -lty

The word ending *-lty* (and a preceding vowel) is also represented by a disjoined *l.*

Spell: f-a-k-ulty, faculty

faculty .... loyalty .... penalty ....

Word Ending -self

The word ending *-self* is represented by *s.*

Spell: h-e-r-self, herself

herself .... itself .... myself ....

himself .... yourself .... oneself ....

Word Ending -selves

The word ending *-selves* is represented by *ses.*

Spell: them-selves, themselves

themselves .... ourselves .... yourselves ....

Business Vocabulary Builder

unduly Unnecessarily; too much.

interior The inside of something.

initiative A first step.

Reading and Writing Practice

Brief-Form Review Letter

cor·re·spond·ing

par

ser

de·light·ful

grasp

ad·di·tion

par

[149] in·ter·view

as

raise

de·duc·tions

ap·prox·i·mate

dis·abled

even·tu·al·ly

if

in·for·ma·tion

par

[193]

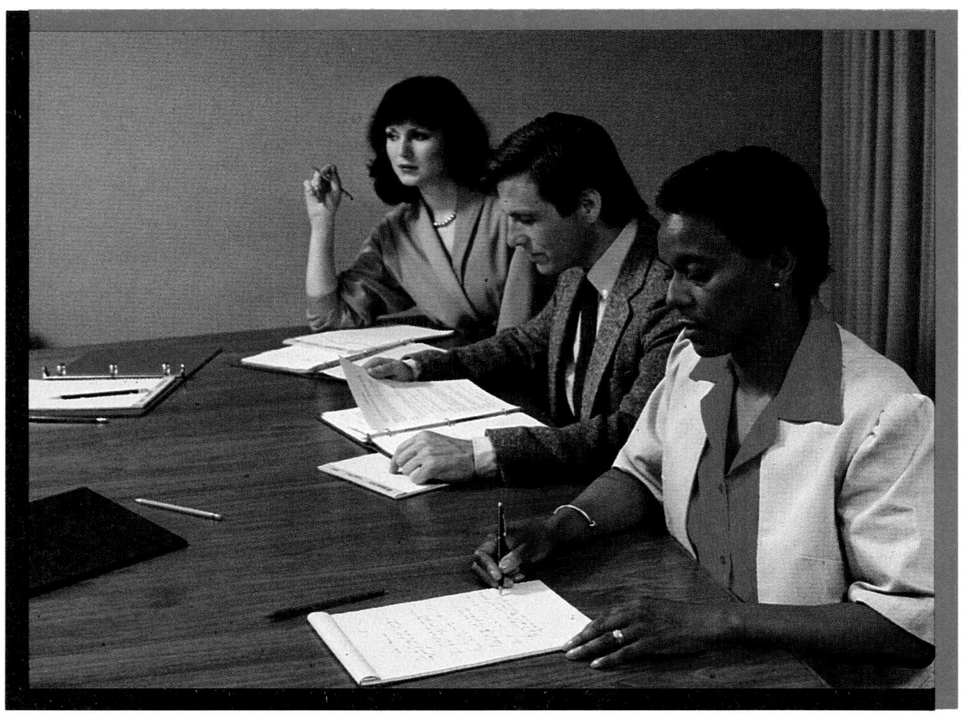

Executives who take shorthand notes during a meeting capture the main points being discussed and note any actions that must be taken afterwards.

ser

un·du·ly

de·layed

par

[128]

3

de·scrip·tion

ap

ap

edi·tion

par

ap·peals

ex·cept

com·plete

par

ac·tu·al·ly

[144]

4

in·teg·ri·ty

sign

ser

as

amaz·ing·ly

[164]

3

pleas·ant

ac·cept·ed

con·grat·u·late

em·bossed

par

as

ap

Chem·ist

pe·ri·od·i·cal

ser

au·thor·i·ties

ev·er·last·ing

[158]

4

if

ma·jor·i·ty

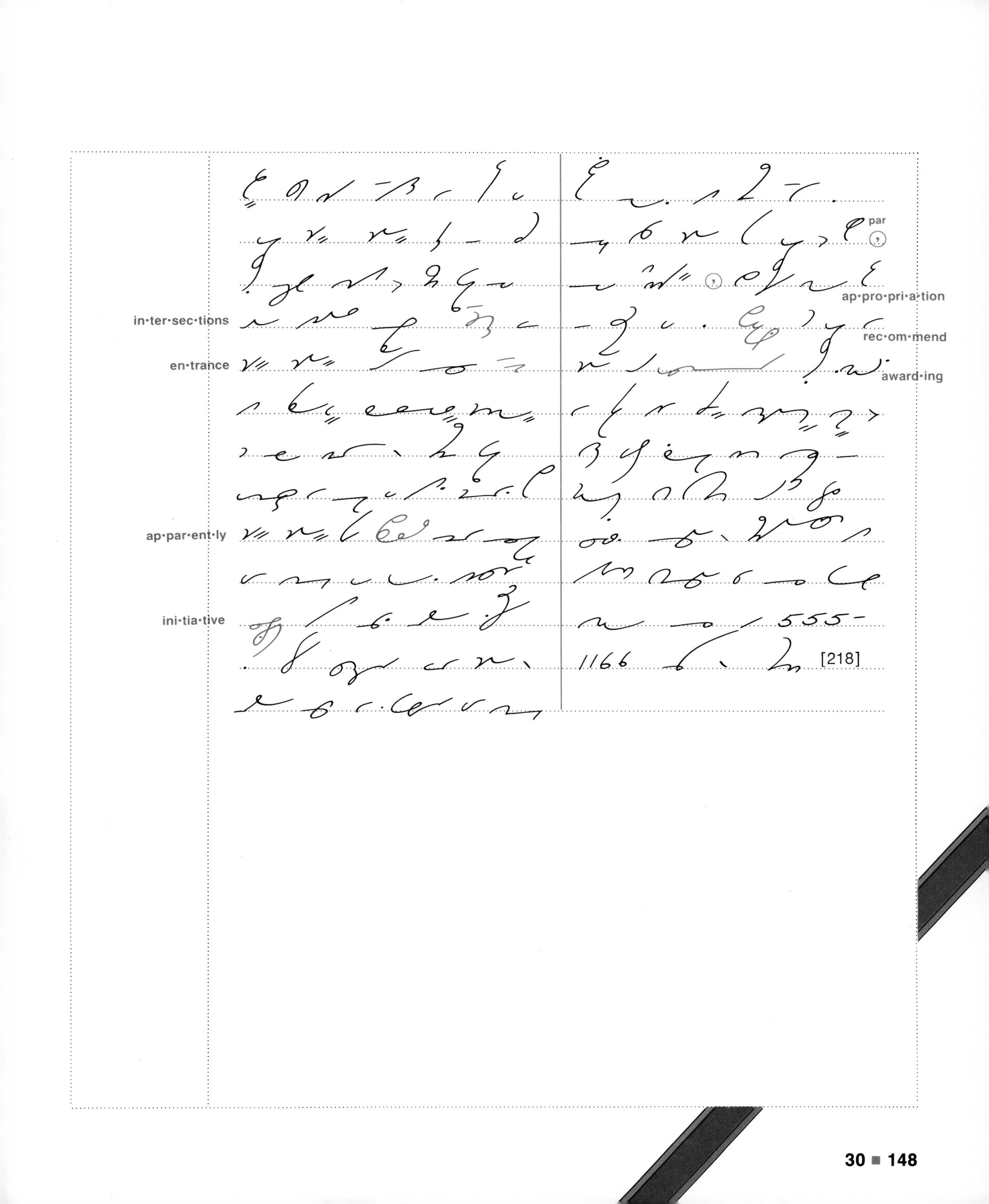

in·ter·sec·tions

en·trance

ap·par·ent·ly

ini·tia·tive

par

ap·pro·pri·a·tion

rec·om·mend

award·ing

555-1166

[218]

Reading and Writing Practice

Brief-Form Review Letter

in·tro·duc·to·ry

let·ter·head

Sub·ur·ban

as

ma·jor

quar·ter·ly

ser

[192]

al·most

im·pres·sive

ex·ec·u·tive

if

ser

Principles

Word Ending -ingly

The word ending *-ingly* is represented by a disjoined *e* circle.

Spell: n-o-ingly, knowingly

knowingly .... increasingly .... seemingly ....

accordingly .... surprisingly .... exceedingly ....

Word Beginning Im-

The word beginning *im-* is represented by *m.*

Spell: im-p-o-s, impose

impose .... import .... improvement ....

impossible .... impartial .... impression ....

Word Beginning Em-

The word beginning *em-* is also represented by *m.*

Spell: em-p-l-oi, employ

employ .... emphasis .... empire ....

employment .... emphasize .... embarrass ....

Word Ending -ulation

The word ending *-ulation* is represented by *oo-shun.*

Spell: r-e-gay-ulation, regulation

regulation .... population .... stipulations ....

accumulation .... insulation .... congratulations ....

Word Ending -rity

The word ending *-rity* (and a preceding vowel) is represented by a disjoined *r.*

Spell: chay-rity, charity

charity .... prosperity .... authorities ....

majority .... sincerity .... securities ....

maturity .... minority .... integrity ....

Building Transcription Skills

Punctuation Practice ■ , as clause

A subordinate clause introduced by *as* and followed by the main clause is separated from the main clause by a comma.

As you can see, most of the work is finished.
As you probably know, Ms. Jane Ortega was made president of the company.

Each time a subordinate clause beginning with *as* occurs in the Reading and Writing Practice, it will be indicated thus in the shorthand: as (,)

Business Vocabulary Builder

suburban Relating to the area on the outskirts of a city.

integrity Complete honesty.

everlasting Continuing indefinitely.

Im-, Em- Followed by a Vowel

When *im-, em-* are followed by a vowel, they are written in full.

immodest ...... immortal ...... emotional ......

Omission of Minor Vowel

When two vowel sounds come together, the minor vowel may be omitted.

serious ...... period ...... situate ......

obvious ...... ideal ...... situated ......

various ...... theory ...... situation ......

Building Transcription Skills

Punctuation Practice ■ , if clause

An error sometimes made by the beginning transcriber is failing to make a complete sentence. In many cases the incomplete sentence is a dependent or subordinate introductory clause starting with a word such as *if, when,* or *as.* The clause is deceiving because it would be a complete sentence if it were not introduced by one of these words. This type of clause requires another clause to complete the thought.

The dependent or subordinate introductory clause often signals the coming of the main clause by means of a subordinate conjunction. The commonest subordinating conjunctions are *if, as,* and *when.* Other subordinating conjunctions include *though, although, whether, unless, because, since, while, where, after, whenever, until,* and *before.*

In this lesson you will consider only those clauses introduced by *if.* A subordinate clause introduced by *if* and followed by a main clause is separated from the main clause by a comma.

If you complete the lesson, you may leave.

If you would like to have one of our representatives call you, please let us know.

Each time a subordinate clause beginning with *if* occurs in the Reading and Writing Practice, it will be indicated thus in the shorthand: if (,)

Business Vocabulary Builder

forceful Having drive; effective.

morale The mental and emotional condition of an individual or of a group.

employment agencies Companies that find jobs for people or find people to fill jobs.

Principles

Word Ending -ship

The word ending *-ship* is represented by a disjoined *ish.*

Spell: f-r-end-ship, friendship

friendship .... membership .... scholarships ....
hardship .... ownership .... relationships ....

Word Beginning Sub-

The word beginning *sub-* is represented by *s.*

Spell: sub-m-e-t, submit

submit .... subdivision .... suburban ....
subscribe .... substantiate .... sublease ....

Word Ending -ulate

The word ending *-ulate* is represented by a disjoined *oo* hook.

Spell: r-e-gay-ulate, regulate

regulate .... formulates .... calculate ....
congratulate .... speculated .... calculator ....

Reading and Writing Practice

Brief-Form Review Letter

em·bar·rassed

par

ap

dis·cov·ered

18

Des Moines

ser

15

if

in·for·ma·tion

[163]

ser

im·par·tial·ly

par

un·for·tu·nate·ly

ob·vi·ous·ly

par

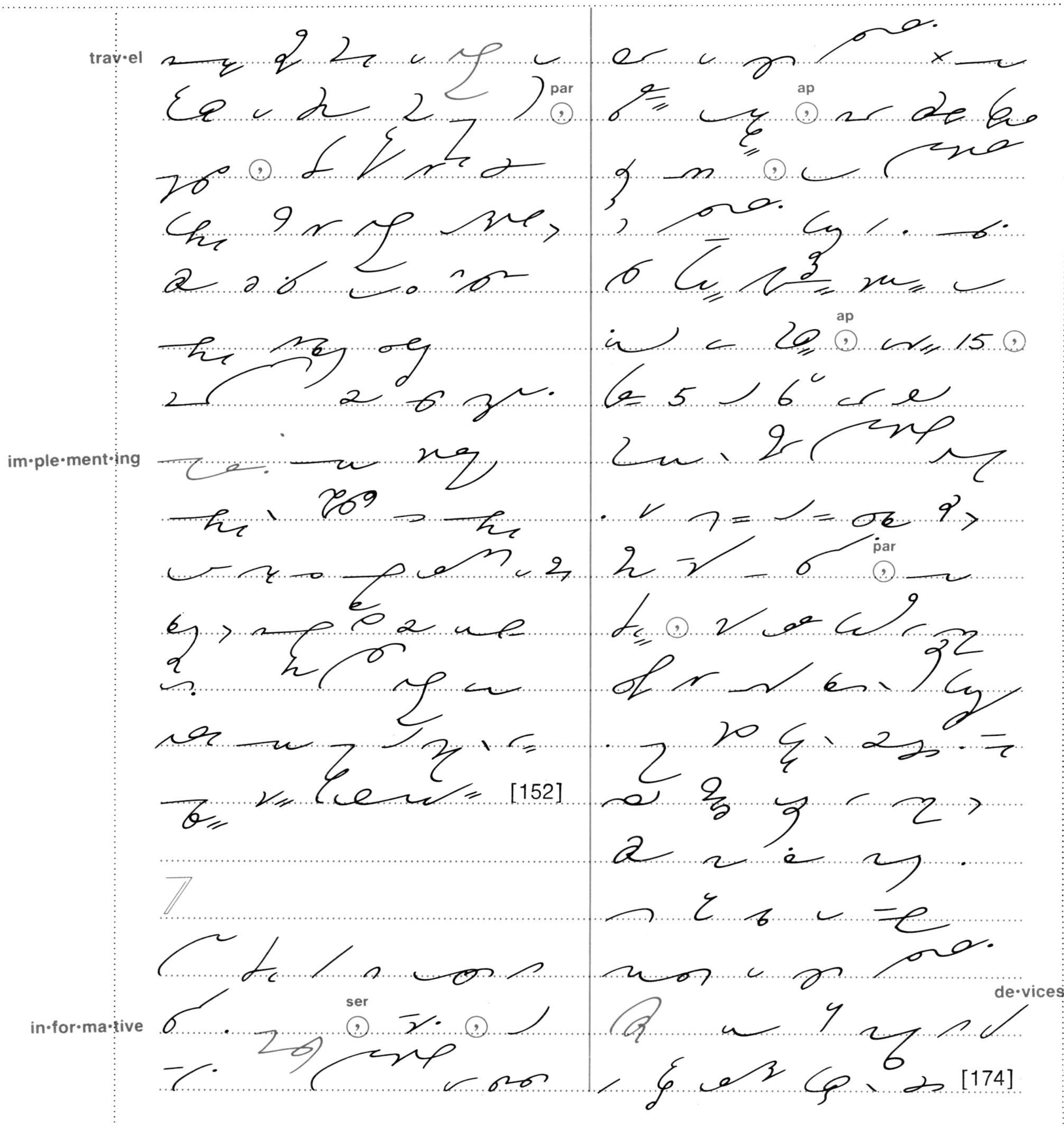

trav·el

par

im·ple·ment·ing

[152]

7

ser

in·for·ma·tive

ap

ap

par

de·vices

[174]

area

[162]

3

em·ployed

gov·ern·ment

clas·si·fied

per·son·nel

im·pact

ob·jec·tive

lead·ing

[171]

4

div·i·dends

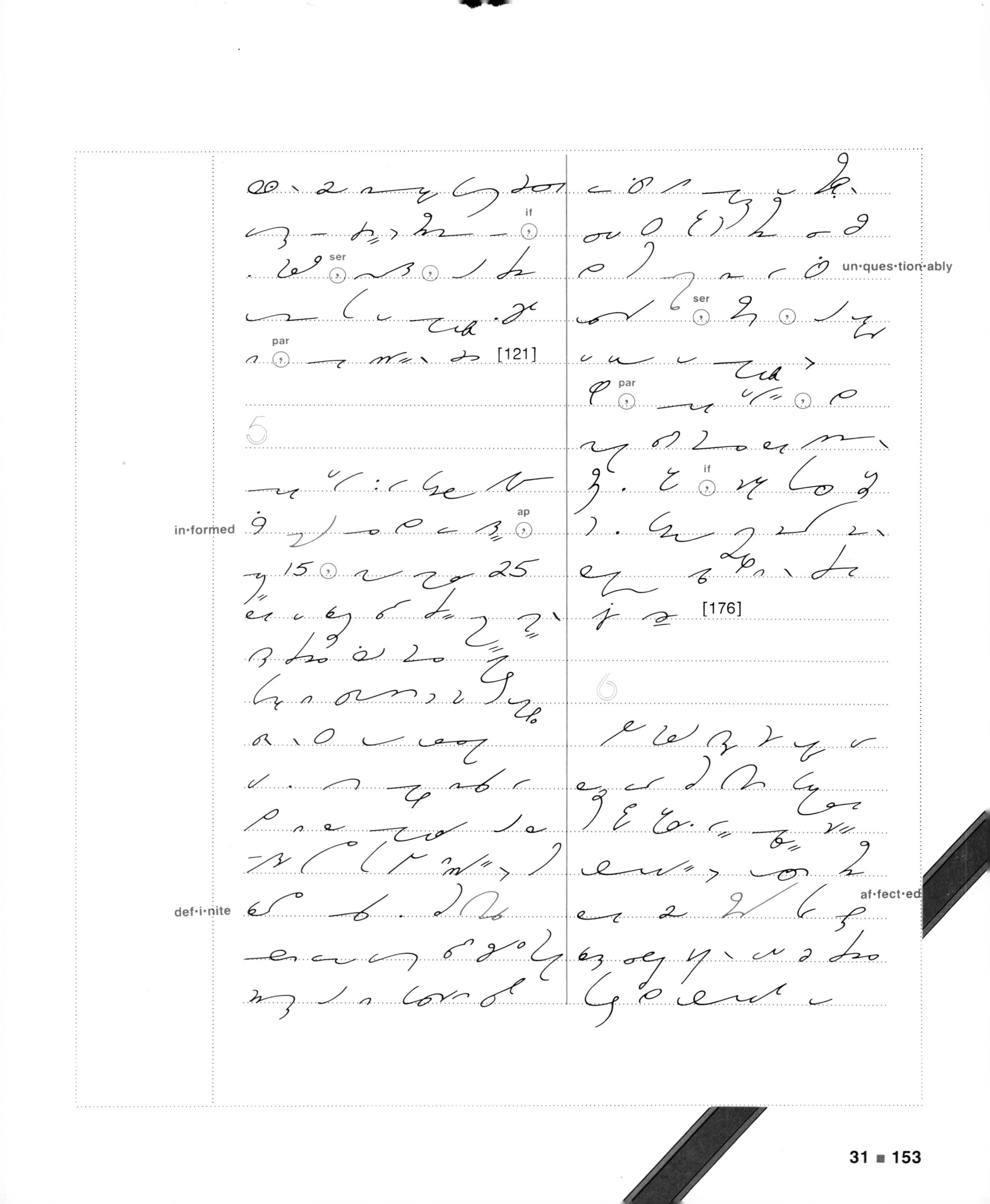

if

ser

par [121]

5

in·formed

ap

15 25

def·i·nite

un·ques·tion·ably

ser

par

if

[176]

6

af·fect·ed